Stolen Hours

"Anyone in recovery will recognize the ground covered in **Stolen Hours**. Addictions wind through dark and mysterious ways. John Prin's book provides much welcome light along this difficult journey. Everyone in recovery will benefit from this read."

Earnie Larsen, best-selling author of
Stage II Recovery and *From Anger to Forgiveness*

"As a recovering alcoholic for more than 20 years, I found **Stolen Hours** to be an impressive and important contribution to our nation's efforts to stem the epidemic of addiction in America. The secret is out about this fine book. John Prin delivers a powerful message about recovery and the new resources available to address the No. 1 public health problem facing our nation."

U.S. Congressman Jim Ramstad

"I found **Stolen Hours** to be a book I could not put down. John Prin's compelling story of his journey through various addictions and life challenges to a God-given wholeness will resonate with many readers. I especially appreciate Prin's demonstration of how the Secret Keeper's "guilt cycle" of excitement, pleasure, and delight can be transformed into the excitement of seeking God, the pleasure of sharing divine presence, and the delight of being loved and comforted."

David Paul Lenz, Pastor
Hope Presbyterian Church, Richfield, Minnesota

www.jc

Stolen Hours

JOHN HOWARD PRIN

Breaking Free From Secret Addictions

March 2004
Dear Terri,
Seek truth,
Learn honesty,
do good,
In Christ 'n love,
John

SYREN BOOK COMPANY
SAINT PAUL

Most Syren Book Company books are available at special quantity discounts for bulk purchases for sales promotions, premiums, fund-raising, and educational needs. For details, write Syren Book Company, Special Sales Department, 2402 University Avenue West, Suite 206, Saint Paul, Minnesota 55114.

Published by
Syren Book Company LLC
2402 University Avenue West
Saint Paul, Minnesota 55114

Printed in the United States of America on acid-free paper.

ISBN 0-929636-21-X

LCCN—2004100058

To order additional copies of this book see the order form at the back of the book or Amazon.com.

Dedicated to Mr. Everett Anderson,
my high school English teacher and mentor

Acknowledgments

A great many people contributed to the creation of this book. To express thanks to all of them would take its own book. Yet a blanket thank-you seems inadequate. So, for those of you who encouraged me or made a difference in some other way, please regard the following acknowledgment as a gesture of my heartfelt appreciation. I truly feel grateful for everything you've done and wish you many rich blessings.

Persons who have supported my writing
over the years or this project in particular:

Carrie Almaer, Roy Arnold, Bruce Barbour, Kathryn Bode, Rebecca Bryden, Tony Doyle, Jim and Ginny Dultz, Bob Elm, Sid Farrar, Kent Garborg, Katy Gurtner-Murphy, Sandra Krebs Hirsh, Dan Humiston, Fran Jackson, Rick Jakubowski, Marcia Jedd, Chris Jones, Pat and Laurie Judd, Jane Kise, Rick Killian, Lenore Knudson, Carol Krebs, Cindy Lamont, Don Leeper, Richard Leider, Doris Little, Jane MacCarter, Tim Mahoney, Rick Mattson, Ed Newman, Ron Olson, Tristine Rainer, Gary Rosch, Julie Saffrin, Pat Samples, Therese Samudio, Dave Schneider, Gary Tandberg, Paul Walker, Stan West, Betsy Williams, and Bob Wuornos. Special thanks to Tanya Dean for her help and encouragement in the early stages of writing.

There are also groups of folks: Marty Hesselroth and her book club pals; Jane Smalkoski, Steve Pipkin and the fabulous serving staff at the Original Pancake House; and Rick Sanders and the design staff at Allegra Print & Imaging.

Persons who have supported my
alcohol/drug recovery or professional development
as a clinical counselor over the years:

Carol Ackley, Dakota Baker, Peter Bell, Mark Brandow, Tom Berscheid, Don Caplinger, Steve Casey, John Driscoll, Russ Engle, Dave Hartford, Janie Hartnett, Jack Hungelmann, Bruce Larson, William Cope Moyers,

Craig Nakken, Peter Nordell, Tim Norheim, Terry Peach, Lois Porcelain, Jack Rowe, Jerome Schoenecker, David Schreiber, Saul Selby, Bev Sockwell, and Dar Trnka.

There is also my AA home group: Jeff H., Gene S., Gary S. and the remainder of the rowdy Boiler Room Gang.

Persons who have supported my
spiritual development over the years:

Al Bloch, Joanie Babcock, Mary Ellen Conners, Greg and Barb Cornell, Rev. Bob Dickson, John DeJong, Jack and Anna Kerr, Bruce and Donna Kirkpatrick, Fred Kopplin, Larry Lorence, Rosie Maykowski, Dennis and Ann Monikowski, Eric and Jeanne Ness, Mike and Susie Northrop, Rev. Lloyd Ogilvie, Dave Olson, Rev. Ralph Osborne, Rex and Pam Cooper, Bernie and Pat Johnson, Ted and Hildur Perkins, Cecil and Betty Selness, Gary Sprague, Joe Steward, Roger and Debbie Stoesz, Rev. Allan Talley, and Rob and Joan vonEdeskuty.

There are also many more friends from the vibrant communities of Hope Presbyterian Church in Minnesota and Hollywood Presbyterian Church in California.

No doubt, I've missed someone. Please forgive me, and thanks.

Finally, I want to thank my family, beginning with my wife of 34 years, Susie. As any reader of this book will discover, she is a huge part of the story of my transformation and healing. I also thank my brothers David and Tom, who lived through major parts of this story as well, and my daughter Emily and her cousins. Lastly, despite some very tough times, I wish to express my deep love and gratitude for Ellen and Toby Prin—when we reunite again in another place, Mom and Dad, I will run to hug and embrace you.

Table of Contents

Part 1

Stolen Hours
is written for:

- People who have secrets that make them unhealthy or unhappy.
- Practicing Secret Keepers who are looking for solutions to the suffering caused by the double-minded choices of their secret lives.
- Persons living with a Secret Keeper, frequently burdened or weary, who are seeking encouragement but don't know how to get it.
- Readers of inspirational books who are seeking practical and spiritual help via the experience of someone's trials and triumphs, defeats and victories.
- Professionals in the counseling, social work, and pastoral fields who deal with secret-keeping behaviors and who will use this book's ideas, theories, and practical advice to help their clients.

**Certain names have been changed
out of respect for the real persons' privacy.**

**The information in *Stolen Hours* should not
be regarded as a substitute for individualized
professional services or counseling.**

Confessions of a Liberated Secret Keeper

From age eleven to 51, I lived two parallel lives. Based solely on outward appearances, I looked normal, made a good impression, and was a high-functioning teenager as well as adult. The volcanic drama of my hidden addictive life, however, and the ways it gained control over me are another story altogether.

My decades as an active Secret Keeper certainly made me ill. Gradually the ways I kept secrets and the resulting pattern of living a double life of lies, cover-ups, and addictions (what I came to call "stealing hours") subverted any hope of living a fulfilling life. But I've discovered I was hardly alone. In time I learned the simple truth:

We are as sick as our secrets.

This inner story that I alone experienced—and how everybody was fooled—is only half of the story, though. The even bigger story is that my life mirrors the experience of millions of other people.

Stolen Hours is based on the premise that duality is at the root of everybody's life. To some extent, everyone hides certain secrets and battles duality. Double-mindedness can take root and compulsive patterns, at some time or to some degree, can develop. Secret Keepers are people whose secrets have power over them and cause them to become sick, to misbehave, or to violate others. Behind the masks of sincerity and friendly smiles lies a far darker side: the sordid, ugly, slippery domain of double-mindedness.

At the root of double-mindedness is addiction—the constant shifting back and forth between two opposing mindsets: "normal on the outside" and "abnormal on the inside." For me daily life became a burdensome struggle that led to a breakdown, then bottoming out. In *Stolen Hours*, you will see how my private life remained hidden by the façade that everyone around me observed. The forty years that I lived in two worlds, ricocheting between public respectability and private temptations, were years I would never choose to repeat, although they taught me invaluable lessons that eventually led to the joys of whole-mindedness. By my thirties, I was addicted to drugs, plagued by an ulcer, in bondage to philandering and pornography, and living a double life haunted by suicidal and homicidal urges. On a chilly, windswept November afternoon in 1977, my wayward life collapsed and I faced the gut-wrenching moment of nearly ending my life.

As time passed, however, I unearthed the many ways I kept secrets and became sick from this destructive habit. I also discovered that I was not alone, that numerous others led secret lives. In my current professional role as a counselor of addicted clients, I've heard numerous stories of secret-keeping from clients who tell of *their* double lives. Like all addicts, they are doing harm to themselves, others, or both. Where my clients differ, however, is that unlike addicts who practice their addictions openly, the clients I counsel often feel sabotaged by their hidden double lives and have ended up hating their split reality. They are among the more than 20,000,000 Americans who are secretly addicted yet still function in their jobs, in their homes, and with their families—and they walk among us every day.

My counseling work has centered on developing effective therapies to help clients who, like me, have "stolen hours" and struggled with the tensions of a secret life. My passion remains to assist as many as possible, to help them to identify and redeem *their* double lives. In short, my journey to wholeness has served to not only unlock the secrets that made me sick, but the secrets that have made others sick as well.

In the following pages, you will discover the myriad challenges one might face on the path to change. In my own case, at times I failed, at times I triumphed. Eventually I discovered the main underlying problem that had so disabled me for decades and prevented me from fulfilling my life's destiny: my habit of keeping secrets. Since then I have relied on divine help as a way out and devoted my waking efforts to assisting everyone I meet to renounce the detours, deceptions, and dead ends of secret-keeping, so they too can live the best lives they can live. *Stolen Hours* is meant to make this motivating knowledge available to millions more than I can serve personally. Think of it as an expanded case history more than as an autobiography or memoir.

Along the way, you will find shaded pages titled "MetaViews." The purpose of these instructional pages is to share valuable insights I have gained along my journey that I believe will help you. You may read them as they appear or skip over them to read later.

Turn the page and encounter the ways secrets overtook and overwhelmed me, then explore the eight mindsets of a Secret Keeper that characterize the one out of every fifteen people who actively live double lives. You will also explore how the categories of *simple secrets, silent secrets, secret-keeping,* and *crime* interrelate and can help you determine your personal level of secret-keeping. Most important, you will experience how God's mighty love transformed a fellow mortal's hurt and hate into a life of healing and wholeness—a love that can do the same for you and millions more.

The simple truth? We are as sick as our secrets . . . but there's hope!

John Howard Prin, BA, LADC
Licensed Alcohol & Drug Counselor

"If one is lucky, a solitary fantasy can totally transform one million realities."

Maya Angelou

⌯⌯⌯ Prologue

Stealing Thrills

Memories of my exhilarating runs in the woods kept calling to me, beckoning at a primal level. One hot summer evening when I was alone at home, I felt the scary thrill of leaving the house naked. I darted from the kitchen door to the woods, all of my clothes left behind. My run on the secluded trail felt jubilant and freeing.

The sensuality I experienced whenever I ran along the deer trail beside the lake spiked my emotions. My mind calculated the risks of getting caught, but I assured myself that I'd never been caught before, why should anyone catch me this time? Still, what if *this* time was different? Engulfed by acres of oak and birch trees, with a powder-blue sky above, I knew I could turn back and play it safe. But no, I felt the thrill of stealing hours to do something daring *and* not get caught.

As I jogged gleefully along the deer path—light-footed, fleet, free, unrestrained—the danger, the sheer risk-risk-risk exhilarated me. These escapades made up for everything awful at home. My pleasure soared, my misery plunged. Exhilarated, feeling giddy and reckless, I sensed again the now familiar *pleasure/excitement/delight* cycle.

The Secret Keeper in me was growing.

Forty-five minutes later when I returned home, I found, to my horror, Aunt Flora and Uncle Don's '56 Oldsmobile parked in the driveway. Ducking low, I saw their shadows moving in the living room. I crept to a corner of the house and crouched in the underbrush on the fringe of the lakeshore with no way to get inside except being seen. I felt so exposed.

Pangs of fear!

Waves of shame!

No way to explain my nudity!

Naked and exposed—truly!

Something told me there had to be a way inside. It was dusk and twilight lurked close on its heels. Could some combination of stealth and darkness rescue me? I circled through the tall underbrush toward the side of the house to evade detection, risking injury to my face and limbs from the twigs slapping against me. Peeking around the corner of the garage, risking discovery by the neighbors, I looked and saw that Aunt Flora and Uncle Don had let themselves in through the kitchen door—perhaps to help prepare for Dad's expected return from the hospital. Fortunately, they would not be aware of the back door, if I could only get there and open it quickly. I circled back the way I'd come and positioned myself as close to the back of the house as possible in order to make a sudden dash to the door. Looking in several directions, I detected some neighbors with their lights on, but nobody paying attention. I took a huge breath, then beelined in a crouched position to the back door.

I turned the doorknob—locked!

Totally exposed, I had no time to regroup. In a flash I bolted toward my bedroom, hoping wildly that I'd left the window open. Feeling foolish, I scurried past the lakeside birches we boys had uprooted and replanted. Speeding around the corner, I saw the window *was* open about eight inches. I duck-walked to it, staying low, then pulled myself up onto the sill with one hand and pushed the screen with the other. The aluminum frame refused to give. I shoved harder, and harder. At last the frame buckled. I was in luck. I quietly rammed it with my fist, breaking the hardware, enough for me to head-butt myself inside.

Panting madly from exertion, also bleeding from a nasty scratch to my thigh, I toweled myself off and felt indescribable relief. Jumping into my high-school gym shorts and T-shirt, I took deep breaths and worked to calm myself. Ecstatic gratitude, mixed with shame, coursed through me: the thought of defaming our family's name horrified me. Taking slow breaths, I headed down the hallway to greet my aunt and uncle, and—an academy award performance later—they believed my phony story about doing push-ups in my bedroom with Elvis on the radio and not being able to hear them at the other end of the house when they let themselves in. We chatted while they waited for Mom to come home from work and asked about Dad's illness.

Within me, I shouted thanks to some unnamed force for smiling down on me—and laughed to myself at their cluelessness.

Talk about feeling one way while acting another!

The lessons from this near calamity served me well in the months and years ahead. I pondered the implications of these new, brash secrets to keep. I vowed to never ever *ever* take such a wanton risk again. But, of course, my days as a Secret Keeper would have ended then and three-and-a-half decades still lay ahead.

Once the exhilaration faded, I realized I'd gone far past the boundaries of acceptability and proved dangerously fearless beyond my own limits, more than I ever believed possible. Doing so set the stage for stealing more hours and secret-keeping at new levels. Beyond secret solo romps in the woods or "getting lost" in other ways, lurking in the depths of my soul remained the deepest and darkest secret of all, the one I prevented acting out more than any other and spent future hours struggling to conquer.

"Just as the twig is bent, the tree's inclined."

Alexander Pope
Epistles

രඏ *Chapter One*

Tender Roots, Twisted

To look at our family's white colonial house on the cozy residential street in Minneapolis where I grew up, you would never guess that somebody inside would end up living a secret life.

We lived in a two-story house with flower gardens on three sides tended by my mom, a plant-lover, at Huntington Avenue and 37th Street. Dad parked his sea-green '49 Chevy coupe in the one-car garage near the crabapple tree. I loved that tree for its sweet-smelling pink blossoms in the spring and for its branches that cradled my tree fort. Our family lived in the "City of Lakes" and left the front door unlocked all year long. We boys played games outside on the lawn until after dark with neighbor kids; Kick-the-Can and Hide-and-Seek were our favorites. It was the late 1940s and video games like "Mortal Kombat" or "Grand Theft Auto" didn't exist yet.

The Midwest was a friendly, gentle place where it snowed so much in the winter that kids stayed home from school, threw snowballs, sledded down steep hills, and rolled balls of snow into snowmen. In those years, running in school and chewing gum in class were offenses that could send you to the principal's office, so I made sure to slow down and spit out my wad of Juicy Fruit on the way into school—because I was a good boy and never wanted to be a problem.

My greatest offense in terms of keeping secrets back then was stealing cookies, especially Mom's home-baked chocolate chip or peanut butter specialties. I'd climb up on a chair next to the kitchen counter, crawl quietly to the cookie jar, lift the lid ever so slowly, and swipe a handful—always listening carefully for her footsteps from the next room. Part of the thrill was knowing she could walk in on me at any second and catch me red-handed in a forbidden act.

In this way I learned early the first key principles of secret-keeping:

> ➔ the *excitement* of breaking rules,
> ➔ the *pleasure* of eating tasty treats, and
> ➔ the *delight* of not getting caught.

This triad of *excitement/pleasure/delight* became imbedded in the secret-keeping dynamic that was to grip me later on. Of course, stealing cookies is any child's "sin" and is not condemnable as genuine secret-keeping. It's part of many kids' upbringing and leads to nothing more serious. Stealing cookies can, however, start a secret-keeping pattern as it did for me, but for most kids it's as far as their double-mindedness ever goes (other than telling little white lies or breaking laws like driving over the speed limit).

In a unique way, another factor contributed to my split psyche. I led a double life as a twin. My genetically identical brother, David, and I were exact mirror look-alikes, born just four minutes apart—he first, I was last. Mom dressed us the same wherever we went. I recall when as toddlers we wore matching red snow suits in January and bibbed seersucker sun suits in July. Whenever people saw us together in public, they would marvel and exclaim, "How cute! How darling! Which one is which?"

By first grade, Dave and I got tired of it all and started asserting ourselves. We'd leave the house for school, turn the corner near the bus stop, and switch quickly into different shirts or pants that he and I had sneaked out of the house—giggling the whole time. That was how we Prin twins helped teachers and classmates tell us apart, and we had fun doing it. Again, more inoffensive secret-keeping training, this time paired with my twin brother: *excitement/pleasure/delight.*

At times when people showered attention on us, our brother Tommy stood by glaring. Three years older, he was the firstborn competing for attention against brothers who naively stole the spotlight, and he grew to treat us as rivals.

One afternoon in 1950, Tommy, Dave, and I arrived home from school and Mom swooped us up, hurrying us to the corner hardware store two blocks away. Excitedly she exclaimed, "Dad's going to be on television!" This news meant nothing to us because television was unheard of then. She urged us to move our little feet faster along the sidewalk to see something totally new and unknown.

When we arrived, a small crowd had gathered and everyone was ooh-ing and aahing. We looked through the plate-glass display window along with other onlookers standing on their tiptoes. Shivers of wonder raised goose bumps all over my body as I watched Dad's jolly, round, smiling face on the new seven-inch Motorola television set in front of us. How could he fit inside such a tiny space? Tingles of awe shot through me. It was Dad all right. The same dad we'd seen smoking cigars at home, now puffing away on one at the piano and playing a catchy tune.

In the months ahead, I came to understand my dad in an all-new light. Toby Prin, already revered as a local radio celebrity, became a pioneer who made the leap into the experimental medium of television. Dad's musical talent at the piano and his skill entertaining people won him a fresh place in people's hearts through this new apparatus with wire rabbit ears. A musical showman with a bald head and a big smile, known for his girth and 350 pounds, Dad came to be loved by thousands more Twin Cities fans who watched him on their black-and-white TVs. Wherever we went in public, he genially signed autographs and took fans' requests for tunes like "Has Anybody Seen My Gal?"

We boys rarely saw him at home, though. He'd shuffle in after midnight and return to the studio for his early morning music show the next day before we got up for breakfast. Dad's absences night and day, six days a week, fifty weeks a year, drove Mom to sulk or scream. She'd walk around muttering, "Why is he never home?" A day later when he wasn't at the table for supper, she'd holler, "He's late! And you boys are getting on my nerves!" It seemed to be her fate that she couldn't plan simple meals or social occasions like other housewives whose husbands arrived home at 5:00 or 6:00 P.M.

So we watched Mom become incredibly lonely.

Mother's volatile moods cast a shadow that we all had to live under. Ellen Prin was an attractive and ambitious lady, but privately edgy and anxious. She'd suffered from a nervous breakdown in 1949 and stayed in the hospital for six weeks. Having her gone from home was awkward and painful. One time while Dad was visiting her in her hospital room, we three waited for hours by ourselves in the hospital lounge and the receptionist kept scowling at us for being rowdy. When Dad finally appeared, looking pale and shaken, he whisked us away to the Chevy. On the way home, he broke the silence, "Sorry, boys, but your mother won't be coming home for another two or three weeks."

It was the closest I ever saw Dad come to crying.

When Mom at last returned home, she seemed dazed and moved like a robot. I overheard her sister Lucille, our aunt who'd taken care of us in Mom's absence, say that Mom had undergone electric shock treatments. I had no clue what that meant any more than what *nervous breakdown* meant. But it was obvious that things were very different. I noticed that Mom took pink pills to calm her nerves and yellow ones to help her sleep, then in the morning she took blue ones to "snap herself out of it." Her pill bottles soon filled a shelf in the medicine cabinet. Whenever she went to the doctor, it seemed another prescription bottle for tranquilizers appeared on her bedside table.

Unpredictable moods overwhelmed her at times. We'd walk through the door from school or play and it was anybody's guess what to expect—warm hugs or frigid silence. When eating dinner, she'd sometimes bang her silverware on the table and yell, "Stop chewing so loud! You're chewing in my ears!"

We learned to step lightly around Mom and to keep our distance on days when she gritted her teeth or slammed her hand on the kitchen counter for some mysterious reason. Whenever the phone rang, though, she would change in a split second to someone entirely pleasant and sweet, giving the caller the impression of being bubbly and amiable. Soon we boys learned to tell the difference between appearance and reality.

A prime essential of a double life—appearances first, reality second—got burned into my brain. And, once I learned that appearances counted more than reality, secrets became elevated above the truth. Along with Dave and Tommy, I kept her secrets without her ever asking, without ever thinking twice about it. It was automatic. I never dreamed of telling a teacher or anyone outside the family. Of course, some secrets are normal and present no harm; not everything needs to be disclosed.

Secrets, I discovered weeks later, could also be extremely beneficial whenever somebody got into trouble. Dave and I, the masters of mischief, roughhoused practically every day to burn off extra energy. One winter when temperatures fell to 30 below zero and the snowdrifts towered over our heads, Mom resisted our pleas to build a snow fort. "No playing outside today," Mom told us. "You'll freeze."

Hardly 15 minutes later, grumpy because we had to stay inside, I hit David on the nose because he wouldn't let go of my Hopalong Cassidy cap gun.

"Oooowwww! I'll get you back, Johnny!"

Just then blood as red as circus paint gushed from his nostrils. It spattered his face and splashed on the floor. My mouth flew open. "Holy cow!" I said. "Hold back your head. You're bleeding bad!"

Gripping his nose, then holding it tightly, I led Dave to the bathroom . . . carefully avoiding Mom in the kitchen. She was chopping up chicken for dinner and could easily have turned her head to see us. Each step toward the bathroom door, I feared he would blurt out and tattle on me, but he didn't even whimper, though tears were streaming down his cheeks. "Don't tell, please don't tell," I pleaded. Once inside, I pressed Kleenex firmly against his injury.

"I should," he said, blotting his nose. "But I won't. We're brothers, and brothers stick together."

Flabbergasted, I felt a wave of gratitude course through me. We managed to rinse the blood from his shirt and clean it off the floor. "Look," I said, "if you keep this a secret, next time you hit me, I won't tattle on you either."

"Deal," he said.

Dave's generosity of spirit boosted our bond of trust to new levels that day. From then on, I think Tommy noticed, and envied perhaps, our tighter bond. Tommy found ways to punish Dave and me for excluding him. One was to tease us by organizing football games in the backyard where he designated himself quarterback and us as blockers. He controlled the ball on every play and made us bang into each other, or he outran us, then pointed and laughed, "Look how slow you guys are!" We got tired of his sport and eventually quit altogether, satisfied to leave him to his own superior self.

Another secret Dave and I kept to ourselves was our mutual crush on a little blonde girl at school, Jane Meeker. It took awhile for us both to realize our mutual puppy love, but when we did, we laughed until our sides hurt. Oddly, we never competed for her. Our admiring remarks and glances drew us closer together, not further apart. One day in fourth grade during recess, I was the lucky one, not David, to kiss Jane behind the upright piano.

By fifth grade my chewing Butterfingers, Milky Ways, and Nut Goodies had become an unstoppable habit, so much so that Mom caught me stealing nickels and dimes from her purse to buy candy. Over the months, I had gained 80 pounds, mainly by stealing minutes away from playtime to indulge my sweet tooth. Classmates on the playground noticed and called me Fatso. I felt ashamed of my rolls of fat. I couldn't fit into my clothes. I bulged when I sat down. I waddled when I moved. I told myself I had to stop—had to, had to, *had to!* I tried chewing half of a Hershey chocolate bar but devoured it all. I hated the kids who weighed only what they should. I hated myself.

How could anything so good be so bad? I asked myself. Eating sweets was one compulsion I could never keep secret because the results showed.

My imagination became my refuge and I started to turn inward. I slipped into my own world of fantasy, especially after seeing B movies at the local theater like *Robin Hood and His Merry Men* or *The Lone Ranger*. Dad gave us each an allowance of 25 cents a week, and we boys piled in the Chevy on weekends and he dropped us off for the afternoon. For a dime (admission) and a nickel (popcorn), we watched cartoons and serials about pirate captains and knights in armor and Indian warriors in battle. I imagined myself as these action heroes and then, at home, made the sword and eye patch, the armor and lance, the war club and headdress to "become" these characters. "Making things," as I called it, became my passion, all without guidance or instruction from adults, with merely the materials I found at hand and my desire to change personalities.

In time I created a trunk full of artifacts, American Indian items especially: tempera-painted war shirts, tomahawks, moccasins, and feather headdresses. These endless hours became a way of life for me, a kind of private inner world, and the sheer involvement of working with my hands filled me with joy. I loved shaping, touching, smelling, and experimenting with the leather, wood, and glue, and thrilled at how each project opened doors to imaginary adventures.

Then came the day in fifth grade when Dave and I tried out for Little League. Dad came home on one of his rare days off from the television studio one bright April afternoon in 1953. He approached us, sounding enthused. "Come on, boys, hop in the car," he said, waving. "Let's get you two rascals baseball mitts, okay?"

"Okay!" we chimed in unison.

Off we went to the sporting goods store. Dave and I chattered about what kind of mitts we wanted. At the store we tried each kind and brand under Dad's watchful eye. Because Dave was right-handed, any mitt was available to him and he picked a heavily-padded catcher's glove. Because I was left-handed, the only kind available to me was a first-baseman's mitt.

Back home, Dad showed us how to form a pocket in our gloves by spitting in them and rubbing the saliva into the leather, then threw the baseball to us for a half hour. This was our first official game of catch with Dad, and we weren't trained or coordinated, so most balls sailed past us or bounced through our legs. "Okay," he announced, somewhat winded, "you guys play catch with each other and practice. Little League tryouts are Saturday morning."

With that, he was gone and we were on our own. Tommy joined us the next day, but his way of giving instructions made us feel stupid and clueless. Because of his three-year advantage on us, he showed off in every category and gloated about being speedier and more coordinated. This only made us avoid him more.

On Saturday Dad drove us to the Little League field. About 300 boys milled around batting, throwing, and running bases. All looked seasoned and well conditioned. Dave and I glanced at one another and gulped. Dad remained near the chain-link fence with the other fathers and gestured for us to walk to the coaches by home plate about 100 yards away. Because of his catcher's mitt, Dave was ordered by a large imposing stranger, "Go join that group of boys trying out for catcher." Another imposing stranger barked at me, "You! Go join that group of infielders." I was at a disadvantage because the baseball terms they used sounded foreign to me—I couldn't tell an infielder from an outfielder.

My discomfort turned to misery when the same imposing stranger instructed me to "hold your runner at first base" and other infielders threw balls at me. I had no idea what to do. I neither caught the balls nor held my foot against the base, like he bellowed at me to do. Seconds later he frowned, flung his hands in the air, and roared, "That's it! You're done! Go to the outfield!" I had no idea where the outfield was. He grabbed me by my arm, pointed to a crowd of boys by the chain-link fence, and shoved me in that direction.

Not ten minutes later, after I failed to catch fly balls batted high in the air to our group (which the experienced players caught easily), my Little League career ended. Another imposing stranger hollered, "You're cut, kid!" and swiped his outstretched fingers across his throat in the unmistakable gesture of termination.

The world stopped. The end had come so soon. Inside I choked up and felt the urge to pee. Dad, standing nearby, saw me cowering and stared at me, then hung his head. I felt rejected, humiliated, ashamed. With so little preparation, I'd failed to compete and show my stuff. The look in Dad's eyes pierced me like a laser. Hardly five minutes later, Dave walked up, shaking his head in humiliation too. We shuffled to Dad's Chevy and rode home in suffocating silence.

The secret of how deeply injured I felt got locked away in silence. When we arrived home and Mom asked how things went, I said nothing and sulked off to my room in sullen solitude, aching with self-doubts.

That summer Dave and I played with our BB guns and spent starry nights camping out in a pup tent pitched under the crabapple tree. My mood turned more upbeat, even mellow. Seldom do children realize their childhood bliss until it ends, and that's precisely the kind of summer I had, peacefully swimming and floating on a rubber inner tube in cool lakes. Playing Kick-the-Can with our neighbor pals Brian, Jimmy, and Byron. Visiting Grandma's house 200 miles "up north" on Minnesota's Iron Range. Trick-or-treating in masks as fearless pirates on Halloween.

Then, one evening when I was eleven, the bliss ended and my world spun upside down. Dave and I had just crawled under the covers and turned out the lights. Mom came into our room, sat quietly on the edge of the bed, and blindsided us.

"Boys, I have exciting news! We're moving to a big new house!"

"Huh?" Dave asked. "How come?"

"Daddy and I have been dreaming about it for a long time. Now, with a new variety show of his own on the air, we can finally afford it."

"But we like it here!" I cried.

"Now, now, you boys'll love it; you'll see. You can build a tree fort and play all day in the woods."

"Woods? But what about our friends?" Dave demanded.

"Do we have to?" I asked.

I looked at Dave and we both knew the answer. She made it sound like making new friends and going to a new school would be some kind of special adventure. I feared it meant having to put up with a new set of voices calling me Fatso.

"But why can't we stay here?" I protested.

She sat there talking on and on about her dream house, about how it would be nestled on a lovely lakeshore miles away from the city, a kind of country manor for all the world to see and admire. She whispered in an almost seductive, dreamy way, "The house will overlook the lake and you boys will have lots of room to run around, with big trees to climb and wide open spaces to shoot your BB guns . . ."

I looked at Dave. Not a chance. Now everything would be different and strange. Worst of all, I knew that he and I didn't have a vote—that what mattered to us counted for little. Cringing, I felt helpless to prevent what seemed like a tragic movie in the making, with us the victims and her the villain.

Days later on the first Saturday in November, 1955, we all piled into Dad's Chevy and visited the natural wild beauty of the lake property she'd talked about. The maple and oak and elm trees with their display of thousands of orange and yellow and brown leaves filled my view in every direction.

To our surprise, Mom ordered us to move a grove of birch trees 300 yards to the lakeshore, where she could enjoy viewing them someday through the then-imaginary picture window. We looked at Dad, who shrugged meekly, and our visit turned into a workday. At ten in the morning, our labor started. The sunny day became hot and we sweated in our T-shirts as we hauled the heavy, sloshing pails of lake water, uprooted dozens of young trees, put them in wheelbarrows, dug deep holes 300 yards away, and replanted them—all because "Mom said so." We lifted, we carried, we worked until dark.

Out of Mom's earshot, Tommy grumbled, "I'm sick of these stupid trees!"

Dave groaned, "She's so bossy! She must think we're her slaves!"

I growled, "Sweating till dark so she'll have a nice view? Bull!"

Mom acted hurt when she observed that we were miffed and finally called it quits. She displayed no consideration for us whatsoever, it seemed to me—I'd never seen her so intense. When we boys dropped into our beds at last back home, we gazed with sunken eyes at one another and nodded our heads. Our fears about the move had materialized: we were miserable.

Weeks later we moved from our beloved cozy white colonial home, and I stared out the rear window as we drove away in Dad's Buick, a fancy new model he'd just purchased that was more in keeping with our fancier new residence. I stared out the window long after the house disappeared, tears gushing down my hot cheeks.

From that day on, I felt less secure and my secret-keeping became a pattern—outwardly I showed respect for Mom, inwardly I seethed with smoldering anger toward her. I held this secret buried inside me and began doing what came to be a habit, feeling one way while acting another.

That day I became a confirmed Secret Keeper.

"Man is not truly one, but truly two."

Robert Louis Stevenson
Dr. Jekyll and Mr. Hyde

⚬⚬⚬ *Chapter Two*

Innocence Lost

When it came to stuffing feelings, I discovered I was an expert. The toxic power of keeping secrets and the painful splitting of myself into two opposing worlds had started. My insides no longer matched my outsides. At eleven years old, these two worlds sprang into being, and I was alone in them.

For the next two years, we Prins stood by helplessly and watched Dad's health deteriorate from his long hours of work on TV and his unceasing efforts to make Mom happy. The upheaval of building Mom's "palace by the pond" (my name for it) meant he had to drive twice as far to and from the television studio, still work the same hours, *and* oversee the builders working on the new house. By 1957, he was suffering from high blood sugar and high blood pressure.

One night he fell asleep at the steering wheel and drove the Buick off the road. The arresting police officer started writing a ticket for drunk driving, then smelled his breath and realized he was in a medical coma. The hospital admitted Dad and diagnosed severe diabetes. A parade of doctors' offices, erratic employment, more hospitalizations, and permanent disability followed. Two years later the surgeons at Mayo Clinic had to amputate his right leg. Altogether, he dropped more than 250 pounds and became a shell of his former self.

Mom became so disgusted at one point that she locked herself in a downstairs utility room for several months and invoked the silent treatment, only to come and go for her new job at a Twin Cities department store. It was clear the family finances required income, and she did the best she could by finding full-time employment, despite having to endure hour-long bus rides downtown because she'd never learned to drive. We boys realized she was "wacky again" and rotated the duty of sleeping beside Dad, in order to help him hobble to the bathroom in the middle of the night, to wrap the stump of his sawed-off leg with fresh bandages, and to fill glasses of water at his bedside for pain pills.

Did Mom's demands diminish? Not a bit. Except for her self-imposed exile to the basement, which we considered a vacation for us, her relentless decorating and landscaping projects continued, as did her treatment of us as slaves. Our free time for homework from school classes took a backseat to working for her: tiling floors, painting bedrooms, building shelves, planting flowerbeds. After school. Weekends. Holidays. Even meals hardly mattered anymore. We boys fixed our own while she pouted. As I saw it, she believed she was entitled to having us serve her, imposing her priorities over letting us have time for our own interests, and she sulked whenever we chafed at meeting her needs before our own.

As time passed, hatred kindled within me, deep hatred. Dad was either never around to protect us (prehospitalization) or never able to rescue us (postamputation) from her decrees. Although he understood she was tyrannical, he was too distracted or disabled to combat it.

A typical decorating project for Mom entailed working long hours, like the time we tiled the entire ground floor of the house. This task meant covering 1600 square feet—including a large rec room, a utility room, a furnace room, and a long hallway connecting them—with square one-foot plastic tiles. Apparently her idea was to save hundreds of dollars that would have been paid to professionals. We boys stared at the concrete floor and the boxes of vinyl floor tiles and a five-gallon bucket of black, sticky glue. We had no experience, but the end result we knew had to meet professional standards, that much was certain. Mom departed and left us to fend for ourselves. With no clue about how or where to start, I looked at Tommy and Dave.

Dave spoke first. "You're good at making things, Johnny. Any ideas?"

"Either we start at the edges of the rec room and go toward the center," I replied, "or we start at the center of the room and go toward the edges. I'm not sure."

Tommy sneered, "Screw, Mom." His cheeks turned red. "I'm not doing her dirty work anymore. You guys figure it out." He spun on his heel, walked up the stairs, and disappeared.

Dave shook his head and sighed. "There he goes again. So . . . let's lay out some tiles on the floor and see which way makes the most sense."

"I don't like Tommy not helping us," I said. "He can't just duck out of all this work, Dave."

"Let him go suck his thumb if he has to. Let's get busy, or it'll never get done."

Dave and I, forever a strong team, tried different ways and experimented by drawing a pencil line in the center of the rec room and gluing a single row of tiles along it. The tiles were brown with speckles going in one direction and Mom had made it clear that she wanted the tiles alternated. The result looked right to us and we laid another row, making sure to alternate them. Soon a rhythm developed between us. After three hours, both Dave and I were sweaty but pleased when we stood back and saw how professional the completed portion of the floor looked. Except for the edges, which needed tiles cut to size, we'd done the impossible.

Our joy lasted only minutes, though, because we discovered that heating the tiles was necessary in order to cut them to fit. That meant running up and down the stairs to the oven in the kitchen and making sure the tiles did not heat too long or they would melt. In all, the tiling took more than two weeks, without the benefit of knee pads or large scissors or Tommy's help or Mom's gratitude. Dad got up once a day from bed to inspect our labor. "You boys are doing a fine job," he'd say, then he'd point out some area needing improvement and stumble back upstairs on his crutches.

Life in that hideous house, in the upscale subdivision called Chippewa Hills, became warped and grossly distorted, our needs neglected in order to meet Mom's. School became a refuge, a safe place where the bells announced a sane, predictable schedule. Pleasant View Junior High was five miles away, five very long miles by foot on gravel roads if we missed the bus, but it was my sanctuary.

I loved everything about art class and enthusiastically studied drawing, painting, design, and color. I earned A's for my poster-sized pastel of a tooth and my clay sculpture of a shaggy buffalo. I also loved swimming class, in part because my athletic talents seemed better suited to the water and partly because seventh- and eighth-grade boys swam naked. Bashful at first about being nude, and especially about my fat, I gradually got past the embarrassment and came to revel in the fluidity of the water flowing freely over my skin. School was a haven where Dave and I faithfully kept the secrets of our home life to ourselves.

Shortly after Dave and I finished tiling the ground floor, Tommy followed Mom's example and locked himself away in his bedroom, invoking the silent treatment on everybody including Dave and me. So intense was his alienation that he did not talk, eat, or interact with the family for months. As Mom had done, he only came out to leave the house.

The main effect on me was his share of Mom's work got shifted to my shoulders, as well as his small share of Dad's caretaking duties. I resented him for chickening out, although inwardly I sympathized and shared his outrage. Ultimately, his self-imposed exile lasted three years.

The upside-down priorities and realities of those years overwhelmed my ability to cope and led to more escapist—secret-keeping—behaviors. I was a pubescent male of thirteen, dejected and hurt. Whenever Dave and I arrived home from school, we started playing a new game called Getting Lost. Evading Mom before she could trap us, we ran from the house and stayed out as long as possible, sometimes until dark. We knew we'd face her wrath when we got home, but what could she really do except holler at us? So we became numb to her shrill scoldings and kept "getting lost." Fortunately, she was now working more hours and this made evading her easier.

Another way I dealt with the distress was to spend time with our dog, a gentle-spirited Golden Retriever named Joy. She loved retrieving the ball, jumping in the lake, wagging her tail, and licking our faces. Having fun with her served as a pleasant diversion. In the winters, to help take my mind off tensions at home, I curled up with her on the floor and closed my eyes, petting her fur in long, smooth strokes while dreaming of peaceful places like Grandma's house up north and tranquil lakes on the Iron Range where I imagined swimming and canoeing.

Still another way of coping with the distress came from watching powerful movies and dramas on television. Being so isolated, five miles from the neighborhoods in town, I identified strongly with movies like *Rebel Without a Cause* starring James Dean and *Mr. Roberts* starring Henry Fonda. I also looked forward every week to top-notch shows on *Playhouse 90*. Dramas like "Requiem for a Heavyweight" or "Judgment at Nuremberg" stretched my view of humanity, stirred my sense of injustice, and opened my eyes to the ways tyranny hurts people.

The emotional impact of these masterpieces overwhelmed me as I realized the universality of suffering among humans. Because they portrayed the human condition so graphically, much as my own experiences felt at times, I sensed in my gut that my life's work would have something to do with exposing and eliminating the evils of abusive power.

Two of these programs especially bolstered the foundation of my secret-keeping tendencies: *I Led Three Lives* with Richard Carlson and *The Great Imposter* with Tony Curtis. Carlson's character, a spy in the Cold War, led a mundane domestic life while deceiving a wife and kids who never discovered he was *not* the corporate executive they believed he was.

Rather, he was a CIA operative fighting the Soviets. Curtis's character compulsively represented himself falsely, living an adventurous life pulling off daring deeds in exotic places. Both of these shows stirred me and demonstrated how someone clever could lead an exciting double life—by stealing hours from one in order to seek thrills in the other. Moreover, I'd already seen earlier tales about Robin Hood, the Lone Ranger, and Superman—all dashing heroes whose double identities aroused mystery and admiration.

During the summer before my freshman year of high school, I challenged myself to the kind of extreme self-discipline that heroes like these had modeled. I decided to stop eating for six weeks. I had tired of carrying the flab around my waist and staunchly determined to look normal (no more Fatso). I set a goal of losing sixty pounds. After a week, the hunger pangs faded and not eating slowly felt normal. I drank lots of water and chewed gum once a day to freshen my taste buds with some flavor. This process happened under Mom's and Dad's noses, but they were so distracted that they hardly noticed. Every week I looked in the mirror and marveled at the pounds slipping away and my trim physique emerging—I was handsome! I was slim again! My self-esteem soared.

"Getting Lost" took yet another form of stealing hours. Part of my initiation into puberty occurred while thumbing through *National Geographic* magazines, looking at naked tribal women. I also found *Playboy* magazines hidden in our older cousin's bedroom closet on summer visits to relatives in northern Minnesota.

My reaction to female nudity? A fireworks explosion of erotic pleasure!

One hot summer day while I was alone, escaping reality by playing Getting Lost in the woods, a flood of sensual thoughts aroused me and I removed my shorts and T-shirt. My swimming nude in gym class made the decision to strip off my briefs easier. Exhilarated, I ran barefoot along the wooded path fully naked—feeling giddy and reckless. This first experience was such a powerful high that I felt removed from the ugly reality at home and "floated" through the next few days until I could plan a similar escape again to repeat the now familiar *excitement/pleasure/delight* cycle.

The Secret Keeper in me was growing.

Back home, a series of events led to an even greater level of doublemindedness. I'd witnessed Tommy isolate himself by hiding in his room and refusing to talk. It was his way of reacting to the craziness of Mom's demands and Dad's demise, and in an odd way I envied him for it. That winter we all survived several subzero months with the heat level in the house set at 50 degrees or lower because Dad was out of work and the fuel bills were too high. We resorted to wearing winter coats and mittens indoors from December through March. We could see our breath, wispy white like tiny clouds.

Mom shut herself away again in the spare room in the basement and opted to work longer hours in the department store's housewares department in a new suburban mall. Dad did as many chores around the house as his meager health allowed, including errands like grocery shopping. Dave and I winced at the pathetic sight he made in the supermarket, staggering on crutches down the aisles, his right pants leg flopping, signaling his missing limb. He'd holler orders to Dave and me to pull the items on Mom's list and put them into the wire cart. At the cash register, he'd fumble in his wallet for the money to pay, causing me to stare down at the floor, mortified because dismayed shoppers looked on.

Little wonder that I felt intense, unbearable anger toward my bereft parents, Mom especially. This fury I harbored in my private world—and how I struggled to reconcile it with my genuine feelings of love for her. But in truth, I came to nurture thoughts of killing Mom.

Murderous thoughts sprang into my psyche one afternoon after school when I stepped off the bus and started walking home, reluctant to encounter Mom and resentful about having to play Getting Lost in order to avoid her. In a flash, the thought struck me: *Take a kitchen knife from the drawer and do her in.* I rejected the idea instantly, alarmed and appalled. But it stubbornly returned. My guts churned, my pulse raced, my breathing doubled. *What if. . . ? No, impossible!* I tried to rid myself of it, but it leaped back into mind. As I walked through the door and looked for Mom, I felt relieved to learn she was working that day and out of harm's way. For the moment.

I lay in bed that night when Mom came home, petrified of having these homicidal thoughts and fearful of acting on them. I needed some escape, some outlet. One outlet for my hostility that I came to depend on was my fantasy life alternative, the sensuality I experienced whenever I ran naked in the woods.

Each time I walked along the deer trail beside the lake, my heart jumped to my throat. My mind calculated the risks, but I left the house the next day regardless and kept telling myself I'd never been caught before, why should anyone catch me this time? Still, what if *this* time was different? What *if*? Engulfed by acres of oak and birch trees, I knew I could turn back and play it safe. But no, I hadn't come this far to play it safe; I was there for the thrill of doing something daring *and* not getting caught.

I loosened my shirt and tossed it on a nearby shrub. I stepped out of my jeans and felt a soft breeze on my bare thighs, then pulled down my underwear—with a carefree gesture I flung them away. Facing the gallery of nature *au natural,* I jogged gleefully along the deer path . . . light-footed, fleet, free, unrestrained.

The danger, the sheer risk excited me. These escapades made up for everything else. My pleasure soared, my misery plunged. Each time I went running, stealing hours in sensual solitude, the ritual became bolder and more daring.

Imagine the stark contrast I presented to the pastor of the local Lutheran church who taught confirmation classes. Reverend Rolf Johansson had no idea whatsoever that one of his junior-high students was leading an active secret life stealing hours in the nearby woods running naked. I sometimes giggled to myself at the thought. As one of 35 restless confirmands, I sat through his long-winded, well-intentioned, two-hour lessons about church history and doctrine every Tuesday evening.

My brother Dave, who also knew nothing of my *au natural* escapades, and I studied Bible passages and sang venerable hymns and with our buddies eyed all the cute girls. I thought of Jane Meeker who'd been left behind and who was no more. Not to fret, there were others, I told myself. Reverend Johansson comprehended our supercharged hormones and let us horseplay twice a night on 15-minute breaks. Setting aside my own devilish dual nature, it seemed a gross hypocrisy to attend a church that was ignored by Mom and Dad while studying a religion not practiced at home where no prayers were said and God's last name was "Dammit."

On August 19, 1958, a hot bright sunny day, Dave and I awoke to our fourteenth birthday. We'd invited five of our friends to our party, a festivity that meant going to a movie downtown in the afternoon and opening gifts back at home with birthday cake and candles. By noon the heat was above 95 degrees and still rising. Dad had promised to drive us downtown, but he appeared unexpectedly with a grim look on his face before anybody arrived.

"Boys, I have tough news. Your mother just called from the store and says the highway department is ripping apart Lyndale Avenue. New road construction. She says the paving stones are being thrown away, and today is the only day they can be claimed."

"So?" I asked.

"What about it?" said Dave.

Dad looked away. "You know she wants a patio by the rock garden in the back yard. She thinks the stones are perfect. And they're free. So she asked if you boys would take a couple of hours to bring home enough paving stones."

"What!" I cried. "Our party's starting in a couple of hours."

"Really, Dad?" David added. "It's our birthday."

He nodded. "Of course, I'm aware of that." He looked down and cleared his throat. "I called a gas station where we can rent a trailer. We can pick it up on the way and hook it up to the Buick."

David and I bristled. We shook our heads. We gazed down at the ground. My throat tightened. "You mean we have to tell our friends this late that the party's off?" I said.

Dad shrugged. "How about leaving a note asking 'em to wait here if we're a bit late coming back?"

"Dad!" David exclaimed. "You can't be serious!"

But serious he was. We left a note on the door telling our guests we'd return as soon as possible and to please stick around for the party. Then Dave and I accompanied Dad to the gas station seven miles away, hitched up the trailer, arrived at Lyndale Avenue, and faced the dirtiest, noisiest, dustiest, hottest construction site this side of the Mojave Desert. Without gloves, Dave and I lifted heavy concrete paving stones discarded by the road crew into the trailer. These were two-foot hexagonal slabs weighing about 50 to 60 pounds each. The heat baked our faces and made our bodies dripping wet. All the while, Dad gave orders, pointing out with his crutch the next stone to haul. David and I cursed under our breath each time we lifted another back-busting stone.

In the end we arrived home four hours later and only two friends were still waiting, Joe and Billy Daly. We thanked them for their patience and pleaded with each to have some cake.

But Dad announced, "Sorry, boys, but the trailer has to be returned before 6:00 P.M. And the stones have to be unloaded first." We groaned, cried foul, then pleaded with Joe and Billy to go home. They refused, perhaps because David and I looked so dirty, sweaty, and furious. For the next hour, we four teenagers finished the task and Dad drove off to return the trailer. We thanked our friends profusely, offered them cake, but they begged off and went home.

Dave and I stormed into the house, ripped off our clothes, and took long, cool showers. When Mom came home, she made a big show of saying, "Happy Birthday," and cutting the cake—but we wouldn't touch it, then turned our backs and left her staring at us. We "got lost" and I cried for almost an hour while watching the sunset and swatting mosquitoes.

Days later, I came home from school with my registration card for ninth-grade classes filled out. It required a parental signature. When Mom came home from the department store, I showed it to her. Dad had since been hospitalized to undergo more tests; otherwise I would've asked him to sign it. I made sure to avoid stepping on her precious white carpet in the living room, knowing she would blow a gasket if any of us broke her rule about "keeping the carpet clean for when company comes over" (never mind that in all those wasted Chippewa Hills years, company never came over).

She read the card and scowled. "Math and social science, fine, but why art?"

"It's the class I like the most."

"Why not a foreign language?"

"Because I want to take art, and I'm getting A's in it ."

"You can never make a living as an artist, Johnny. You'll have to make money someday. It's better if you learn French or German."

"Aw, Mom. You've seen my artwork."

"Yes, it's good. Very good. You're a natural and you have lots of talent. Right now, though, it's best if you learn another language. You can take art classes in college."

I stared at her in disbelief as she took a pen and scratched out *art* and wrote in the margin *foreign language*. Signing it, she handed it back to me.

Dumbfounded, I felt my face burning. The venom in me surged like a volcano. I stifled a murderous urge, but it came roaring back. Everything she did seemed to prevent me from being happy! She was squelching my fondest desire and putting my artistic growth into hibernation! She hated me and *I* hated *her!*

I ran out the door and staggered down the curving driveway to Joe and Billy Daly's house. As I approached the side door, I slowed down and caught my breath. I walked up to the screen door and looked inside, poised to call their names, as was our custom, when something I saw made my breathing stop. Through the open screen, I observed their mom, Mrs. Daly, walking topless, chatting with Joe and his brothers in the kitchen. She had on shorts and absolutely nothing above her waist. She made no attempt to cover her large breasts, but was opening the refrigerator and pouring juice, conversing about something routine.

My finger fumbled to find the doorbell . . . it rang. The boys' heads turned and they looked, startled, seeing me at the door. Mrs. Daly screamed, crossed her arms over her chest, and vanished.

Joe came running, stammering as he came to a stop and tried to talk: "I . . . ah . . . what the . . . ? Look, um . . . just pretend you never saw . . . you know. Get what I mean?"

"I just came over to talk, Joe. I didn't mean to . . ."

"Look, it's not a very good time right now. Okay?"

"Sure. Um, why don't you come over whenever." He nodded nervously and I left.

Nothing like what I'd just seen had ever happened to me, and I couldn't fathom it. Had I really seen her topless? Could my eyes have been playing tricks on me? But then, why would Joe have stammered? And not come outside to talk? For the next hour, I felt a jumble of mixed-up emotions.

I concluded that what I'd seen was real, very bizarre, and at an instinctual level, some kind of secret-keeping behavior. That their mother was parading herself in front of them, as she did apparently at other times, added layers upon layers of complexity to my growing worldview of secrecy. Evidently others carried out private rituals too!

The "Mrs. Daly incident" haunted me. I never talked about it with Joe or his brothers, ever, and they never with me. I began feeling more secret-keeping urges, though, but dared not act on them. I could be found out as easily as Mrs. Daly.

So I slipped into my fantasy world and reverted to the joy of making things as I'd done when younger and happier on Huntington Avenue. I imagined myself a Sioux brave or Chippewa warrior. But now the projects became far more sophisticated and intricate, like creating a full suit of buckskin leggings, a shirt, and moccasins. I created an authentic hunting knife with a fully beaded sheath and spent two months fashioning a 13-foot canoe from young saplings found in the woods surrounding our house. I lashed the saplings together with leather strips, covered the framework in canvas and tar pitch, then hand-carved two wooden paddles. The day when I excitedly launched the canoe proved successful—it floated—and useful, as I paddled it far away from home, stealing away more hours from that sick place where Mom ruled.

But memories of my exhilarating runs in the woods kept calling to me, beckoning at a primal level. One hot summer evening when I was alone at home, I felt the scary thrill of leaving the house naked. Thus began the episode already told in this book's prologue, of running on the trail jubilantly free of clothes and returning home to find, to my horror, my aunt and uncle there; of my desperate break-in through my bedroom window; of my fear about defaming the family name mixed with my ecstatic gratitude that my aunt and uncle bought my phony story about doing push-ups in my bedroom with Elvis on the radio; and of my vow to never ever *ever* take such wanton risks again.

But, in truth, the stage was set for stealing more hours and secret-keeping at new levels. Beyond these secret romps in the woods or "getting lost" in other ways, lurking in the depths of my soul remained the deepest and darkest secret of all, the one I spent future hours struggling to prevent acting out more than any other: fantasies of killing Mom.

MetaViews to Muse #1

The thoughts and ideas on these shaded pages are intended to help you recognize and confront secret-keeping tendencies and habits. I'm calling them MetaViews, based on the ancient Greek definition of *meta* meaning "above, higher, transcending," and *view* meaning, of course, "to behold from a vantage point." The vantage point in this case is that of hindsight, the wonderful 20/20 insight we gain from experience, wisdom, and hard knocks—or, if you like, the potholes, pitfalls, and pratfalls of life!

From my perspective as a professional counselor and recovering Secret Keeper, I hope these reflections on what you've read till now will encourage you to consider your own life's challenges and choices.

✳ The triad of secret-keeping emotions below traps one in a guilt cycle:
> ✦ the *excitement* of breaking rules,
> ✦ the *pleasure* of indulging in what's forbidden, and
> ✦ the *delight* of not getting caught.

✳ Secret-keeping can start as innocently as eating too much candy. A secret life can start long before becoming addicted to mood-altering chemicals. Of course, some secrets are normal and present no harm—not everything about a person needs to be shared.

Think of the kinds of secrets you keep. Are yours normal? Do they present no harm? Or are they addictive in nature? Would they cause shame if brought into the light?

✳ Dual-mindedness turns toxic when events betray one's childhood perspective on life and the individual smothers heavy feelings. In my case, secrets became elevated above the truth. I never dreamed of telling anyone outside the family what was going on. In this way a split mindset of secret-keeping—*placing appearances first, reality second*—became second nature.

Ask yourself if and when you practice putting appearances first, reality second.

* Skewed priorities imposed on children set up the conditions for a secret life to fester and grow—painful daily reality urged me to escape the source of shame/pain. And shame in one's environment "requires" keeping secret in public what goes on privately. Escaping from the source of shame/pain took the form, in my case, of stealing hours away by geographically isolating myself ("getting lost"). By stealing hours, a universal characteristic of secret-keeping, I escaped "real" life and discovered a risky, self-defeating life of thrill-seeking.

Examine your own upbringing for these tendencies. Were real-life shameful/painful things going on at home that you wanted to keep secret and at the same time escape from?

* Movies, television, and literature present dashing heroes whose double identities arouse mystery and admiration for children seeking role models. I watched tall tales about Robin Hood, Superman, Batman, and the Lone Ranger. Think of their counterparts today! Far less tame!

Who are your heroes? Do you try to emulate them? In what way do you do this?

* Eventually, painful feelings are harbored internally, while at the same time, the Secret Keeper feels compelled to make things look normal on the outside. The individual's outsides no longer match his or her insides. I became an expert at this split mindset of secret-keeping: *acting one way while feeling another.*

Reflect on ways your life may demonstrate this dynamic.

* **The following are two of the eight splintered mindsets of a Secret Keeper:**
    + Placing appearances first, reality second.
    + Acting one way while feeling another.

> "Life is a battleground. It always has been, and always will be; and if it were not so, existence would come to an end."
>
> *Carl Jung*

∽ *Chapter Three*

Sanity Regained

In April, 1959, good news came at last: Mom and Dad sold the Chippewa Hills house because they couldn't afford it. A new lease on sanity began. Our move to a smaller, less expensive house in the same suburb closer to the center of town helped us boys feel more connected socially, both in the new neighborhood as well as at school.

For Tommy, now seventeen and freshly graduated from high school, this meant working at Walgreen's as a clerk and buying a beat-up '50 Ford sedan. For Dave it meant varsity football and lettering in sports. For me it meant flirting with pretty girls and working part-time as a dishwasher. Because Dave and I now lived just six blocks from school, we met friends after classes and played touch football and got together for poker games or movies on weekends.

Tommy came out of his three-year deepfreeze and joined the living. Dave and I attributed his upbeat mood to living in a regular neighborhood again, having a car and having easier access to his chums. We three acted more like brothers and invented silly games, loving the expressive outlet cooperation created. We became closer than ever and humor returned to our lives.

For Mom, however, nothing was ever funny. The move from Chippewa Hills meant the painful demise of her dream. No sooner had we moved into the new house on Parkside Circle than she insisted on renovating the rooms and grounds. Determined to resurrect the glory of her Chippewa Hills projects, I suppose, her expectations and bossiness reached horrendous levels. Sick and tired of the slavery, we mutinied.

"Mom, I'm dishwashing at Garrety's now, remember?" I replied to one of her demands to build a storage closet.

Her face went stern and scrunched up at hearing my denial. It was spoken as a taunt, I admit. But it was based on fact—I'd been hired for $.75 an hour at a popular coffee shop a mile away and would show up late if I didn't hop on my bike to get there.

"You're the only one handy enough who can help me, Johnny," she whined. "No one else is ever around."

I chuckled to myself hearing this. Of course no one else was ever around. Tommy had his job, his car, his college friends. Dave had football practices most afternoons and on weekends. I was the only son around to do her bidding, so she thought. "Sorry, Mom. I gotta leave now before I'm late for work."

"But you're my favorite, Johnny. Nobody has your gift with tools or can make things the way you do."

She was hoping flattery would get me to promise some of my free time to her. I felt a major tug to "show my stuff," but I knew she was being manipulative. In junior high, my straight A's in art had been two years running, and everyone acknowledged that making things was my forte. But I'd decided to stop permitting myself to be used and abused.

"Like I said, Mom, I gotta go. See ya." With that, I left her standing at the door alone, with only her invalid husband lying sick in the bedroom to depend on.

She trumped us, however. Dad had just come home from the hospital after receiving a new artificial leg, and she'd managed to get him to paint the exterior siding of the house shortly afterwards. Dave and I couldn't stand to see him wobble and struggle, so we picked up paint brushes and began slapping on paint, insisting that he sit down and rest. Dave murmured, "She's making us all miserable like she did in the last house!" Tommy relied on his former strategy and isolated himself in his room for several days.

My own hatred of Mom reignited. I couldn't grasp why she was repeating the same destructive behavior we'd just escaped from in Chippewa Hills. But she clearly couldn't, or wouldn't, let herself see the damage her relentless fix-up projects were causing, so I seethed with spite and hostility. Once I even envisioned bashing in her head with a hammer, but I was always careful to keep these feelings a secret.

At high school, my good fortune skyrocketed during my sophomore year when the biology teacher changed our seating assignments. I lucked out and got to sit next to the prettiest cheerleader in school, Bonnie Witten. My weight loss of 60 pounds really paid off now. Bonnie noticed me and smiled, sending me into orbit. I took this as a favorable sign and made a joke that she found funny. From that moment on, we bonded and exchanged quips freely.

Bonnie's beauty affected me profoundly. There are young women who enter a room and all heads turn. They carry themselves with grace and ease, entirely comfortable in their bodies and satisfied with their appearance. That was Bonnie. Her dark, long hair framed her flawless face, and her tight-fitting blue-and-white cheerleading uniform showed off her perfectly curved body and legs. Her teeth sparkled when she smiled, and her chocolate-brown eyes radiated mystery.

Every school day after lunch, I looked forward to fourth hour when Bonnie and I would share 50 minutes of bliss together. It felt to me like we were dating, even though I was a year younger and not a letterman, and in some ways it may have seemed that way to her. She'd glance at me dozens of times and pass paper notes or whisper silly one-liners. I came to believe in myself. My confidence soared. I could now hold the attention of the prettiest, and surely one of the most popular, girls in my universe.

In a reverie, daydreaming about Bonnie, I heard through a mental fog my boss at Garrety's Drug holler, "Time for a break, John!" I shut off the hot water filling the stainless-steel rinse basin that was piled with soapy dishes and looked up. There stood Otis Hansen, my supervisor and chief fast-order cook at Garrety's, a thin man in a loose apron with a perpetual cigarette hanging from his mouth. "The dinner rush'll start soon and you'll need to be back on duty."

I untied my apron, walked to the customer side of the serving counter, sat on a chrome stool, and wiped the sweat from my brow. A pretty waitress named Janice walked up, winked at me, and asked for my order. Janice was one of the six or seven cute high-school gals who earned spending money at Garrety's Drug, like I did.

"I'll have a cheeseburger, fries, and a cherry Coke," I said, winking back.

Janice raised her eyebrows. "Coming right up, sir!"

In that self-esteem-boosting manner, I sailed through my sophomore year, enjoying classes and girls and playing B-squad ice hockey as a goalie. What captivated my imagination that summer was Alfred Hitchcock's *Rear Window*. I marveled at Jimmy Stewart's powers of observation as he spied on residents in his New York City apartment complex with his telephoto lens. He spent hours invading the privacy of ordinary folks living their ordinary lives. Something about his voyeurism hooked me, made me spellbound. His prying served a noble purpose, that of helping solve a murder, and it seemed harmless. But my growing dual nature and inclination toward escapism hit a new low early in the fall of my junior year when I imitated Stewart and acted out a new secret behavior: window-peeping.

I was sitting in the bleachers of the high-school gym watching six gorgeous cheerleaders lead a pep rally for our football team. Next to Bonnie, a senior, was a sophomore girl new to the squad, Cindy Foster. After Bonnie, Cindy was the prettiest and the peppiest of the bunch. She had the smile of Debbie Reynolds and the energy of Lucy on *I Love Lucy*. Her every jump and shimmy and "Go team!" excited me. Secretly, I was already thinking about seeing her again later that night—through her window. She lived only two blocks away. But first I needed to get through classes and my chores at home, including cooking dinner and washing the dishes, then put in a couple of hours on my U.S. history and algebra homework. *Then* I would slip out after dark.

That night, obeying the irresistible urge to satisfy my curiosity, I crept up to the windows of Cindy's house, staying in the shadows, and peered inside. Through a crack in the bathroom curtains, I saw the silhouette of a young woman undressing. But she was blurry and out of focus—like an impressionist's painting of a nude. My heart pounded madly. Catching glimpses of her excited me greatly. So risky, so reckless! In an instant Cindy stepped into the bathtub and disappeared from view altogether. I couldn't risk waiting for her to finish bathing, so I ducked away on silent cat's feet and merged with the shrubbery, disappearing into the shadows with my heart pounding madly.

Like my running naked in the woods, the profound rush of this new thrill led me into another variation of my double life, a new habit that proved difficult to break. The subconscious payoff of numbing my persistent heavy feelings was mighty. In the same way that I experienced the secret-keeping triad of *excitement/pleasure/delight* early in life, it now became even more deeply ingrained:

the *excitement* of breaking rules,

the *pleasure* of spying on Cindy, and

the *delight* of getting away with it.

As the seasons passed, I timed my visits to Cindy's house days or even weeks apart in order not to arouse suspicion. These escapades added adventure to the routine of school classes, dishwashing at Garrety's, evading Mom's projects, and watching Dad's health worsen.

There remained at school, though, one endeavor I still wished to develop—acting. Notice of tryouts for the class play that year, "The Mousetrap" by Agatha Christie, caught my eye. Within me beat the heart of an actor who enjoyed changing personalities. I put my all into the part, responding to the student opposite me reading her lines, trying not to stumble on the playwright's elevated dialogue. The director, an English teacher I didn't know, asked another student to take my place. I sat quietly, trying to guess who might get the part, then the tryouts finished and the director said, "The cast list will be posted in two days." The suspense lasted for 48 hours until I excitedly scanned the posted sheet of names. But my name wasn't on it. My aspirations to act ebbed away like one of Ms. Christie's murder victims bleeding to death.

I contented myself with raking leaves for neighbors to earn extra spending money, using the exercise to vent my frustrations. Doing so got me out of the house and away from Mom, as did mowing neighbors' grass in the summer and shoveling snow from their driveways in the winter. In school, my favorite class was U.S. history, taught by Mr. Matlan. He had a ready wit and loved a good laugh and wrote in my yearbook, "To the top student of second hour, best of luck!" Also high on my list was my German teacher, Mr./Herr Szendry, an older European man fluent in four languages, whom I appreciated for his World War II experiences. He wrote in my yearbook: "To my fine student, John Prin. Keep up your intellectual curiosity all the time."

As before, solace also came from the hours of vicarious escape I enjoyed in darkened movie theaters, watching great films like *Ben Hur, Psycho, The Hunchback of Notre Dame, Days of Wine and Roses,* and *To Kill a Mockingbird.* Films like these transported me, often mirroring my own life's drama by showing me heroes overcoming injustice.

By late October 1960, my all-consuming passion as a junior became trying out for varsity ice hockey. Chuck Bennett was the first-string varsity goalie, an all-around good athlete who starred as quarterback on the football team and as catcher on the varsity baseball team. On all three teams, he was elected captain. I envisioned myself wearing a Grizzly varsity uniform and getting a white G letter to wear on a new blue letter jacket (G stood for *Grayton,* the name of our community and school) and earning the privilege of going to the Minnesota State Hockey Tournament.

Secretly, I wanted to win approval, so I could become popular. I felt desperate to prove myself. Oddly, Chuck and I became buddies in social studies class and often clowned around when bored or when the teacher wasn't looking. His nickname for me was "Prinsky" and mine for him was "Beaner." My secret wish? That he might get sick or injured, so I could step into his place and become the team's starting goalie—hopefully, *starring* goalie. To succeed in the eyes of others publicly was my goal.

For years Grayton's hockey team had proved to be a contender for the annual statewide hockey tournament, a highly spirited event in icy Minnesota. Our coach, Homer "Buzz" Mack, a no-nonsense hockey legend who went on to win the most games ever as a coach in high-school hockey, burned that year with determination to "go to State."

The season began with weeks of strenuous skating drills and practice scrimmages; we won the first seven games easily. My role as backup goalie meant that I sat on the bench the entire game and went in to play only if Beaner got hurt. During blow-out games, I kept looking at Coach Buzz for the nod to play late in the game. He just ignored me. I became a benchwarmer, discouraged about my value to the team, especially when the scores became lopsided.

In the eighth game, we led 7–0, but I still didn't get Coach Mack's nod. With five minutes remaining, it only made sense that any coach would put in his second-string goalie, if merely to give him game experience—at bare minimum to prepare him should the first-stringer ever get injured. I'd played my heart out during practices, missed none, and stopped my share of shots. So doubt hounded my psyche. *What is wrong with me? Why is this happening to me?*

Like any boy in his midteens hoping to make his mark in the eyes of peers, I had to excel in one of three ways: academically, artistically, or athletically. These were the three avenues of achievement open to me. Academically I was a B student, artistically a former A student. Athletically, I'd played little more than B-squad hockey and intramural volleyball. The unspoken truth? Boys who starred in sports were idolized, boys who got A's were thought of as eggheads or student council geeks, and boys who excelled in art or theatre were considered sissies or queer.

Sitting there on the bench, holding my oversized goalie stick and observing the lopsided game, I felt at a gut level that hockey could, even *should*, be my salvation. I'd worked hard and deserved it. I recalled the day in fifth grade when I'd tried out for Little League—the humiliation, the shame. Being hollered at. The sad look on Dad's face. I wanted to make up for that aborted opportunity and excel at something athletic. I turned my head and looked for Dad in the stands. His faithful attendance at many of my games humbled me. As always, he hobbled to a seat in the bleachers on his artificial leg with his face looking sunken from hundreds of pounds' weight loss, ever the loyal father supporting his second-string son. Sure enough, there he was, sitting near the top row.

"Prin!" Coach Buzz's voice hollered. "Prin, get in goal!"

My heart leaped to my throat. I came out of my reverie. Beaner skated toward the bench and Coach Mack waved at me to take his place on the ice. I heard cheers from Bonnie and Cindy. I stood up and made my way on wobbly legs past the players to the ice.

"Go get 'em, Prinsky!" Beaner whispered.

I skated to the empty net and warmed up, taking a dozen practice shots from our players. Then the referee's whistle blew and the game resumed. A whirl of jerseys and sticks. Cheers from the crowd. I moved with the action but felt cold. Being in the game felt awkward. Play moved to the opponents' end and I took deep breaths, looking in the stands for Dad; he seemed to have disappeared and everything was a blur. I felt unsteady, unsure. My catching glove felt stiff and inflexible, so I spit in it and tried to flex it more.

Now the opposing players attacked with fury and my teammates got out-maneuvered. A pass came to an open opponent just ten feet in front of me. He fired a high shot to my glove side. I reached for it but the puck sailed past my glove—*bzzzzzz!* I heard the awful noise all goalies detest, the buzzer signaling a goal.

The opposing crowd roared and jumped to their feet.

My teammates kicked their sticks and stared at the ice.

Our cheerleaders stood mute and hunched their shoulders.

I tried to find Dad in the stands and imagined the hangdog look on his face. With just two minutes of game time to go, I'd failed to compete and "show my stuff"—a non-athlete in a varsity uniform. A fake. A sham. A worthless joke of an athlete. An ugly replay of being rejected, humiliated, and ashamed years ago.

I looked at Coach Mack and saw him shaking his head. Inwardly, I wanted to die. I was just a body in front of a net. Inside me raging took place, self-hatred mounted. The referee whistled the game to continue, dropped the puck, and the final two minutes presented me with routine, yet redemptive, saves.

In the remaining dozen games that season, I played once more, a nonconference game with a private school where I played the entire final twenty minutes of the game. In that contest I stopped all the shots, thirteen total, including a lone break. This time the cheerleaders shouted *my* name: "*Prin . . . Prin . . . he's our man, if he can't do it, nobody can!*" greatly boosting my spirits. The bonus came when Dad, standing on his artificial leg in the bleachers, whooped and hollered along with the rest of the crowd. For that moment he was no longer hard to find or blurry, and the pride and love in his eyes shined. Later, he pounded me on the back and praised my play.

A loss in the regional final on a disputed goal ended our hockey season abruptly. My hopes of a trip to State evaporated. I consoled myself with the knowledge that I'd soon be wearing a blue letter jacket with a large white G. Also, there was the cherished memory of stopping the thirteen shots in the nonconference game and the echo of my name being cheered by fans and the likes of Bonnie and Cindy. And Dad's pounding me on the back.

By springtime I returned to my old secret-keeping habits and now timed my nocturnal visits to Cindy's to be days or even weeks apart in order not to get caught. Eventually, I became less diligent about safeguarding my presence, and after two close calls, a bright floodlight over Cindy's back door flicked on. In the next instant, her dad flung open the door and shouted at me, "Who the hell are you? What the hell are you doing here?"

Stunned, I couldn't reply at first. Luckily I was closer to the back fence than the house itself, about 30 feet from the door, and somehow I had the presence of mind to wave hello instead of run. "It's just me cutting through your yard; sorry!" I kept walking nonchalantly, looking for an opening to duck through, but then Cindy appeared at the back door and identified me. The look on her face was ghastly.

"Oh, my God! John! It's John Prin!"

My heart flip-flopped, then sank. I could hear her tell her dad and mom about me.

I waved again, like everything was normal, and kept walking. I couldn't tell from their expressions whether they were sure my story was true or not. I cringed, waiting for the dreaded "Wait! . . . come back here!" but thankfully, it never came.

When I arrived home, I fretted that the phone would ring, or the doorbell would ring—that my world would cave in and I'd be exposed as a pervert. Nothing happened.

In school the next day, Cindy acted shocked and angry, staying hurt and distrustful of me thereafter, justifiably. It was a steep price to pay for my stolen hours at her windows. Exactly why I was spared punishment by Cindy's parents, who never called the police or alerted Mom and Dad, I'll never know. But I felt spared for some reason.

My shame and the aftermath of getting caught motivated me to stop peeping. In time I learned that if one's external motivation is strong enough, then one's internal motivation can be curbed. I've never window-peeped since.

Balance and sanity returned to my life. School remained my haven, home my hell. But I knew deep down that stealing hours could no longer be an option. Never, ever again.

> **"Each moment in time we have it all,
> even when we think we don't."**
>
> *Melody Beattie*

⌒∞⌒ Chapter Four

Secrets Shared

With the prom coming up, I had to ditch the idea of asking Cindy. Instead I asked a more anonymous girl whom I'd flirted with on and off: Brenda. She accepted my invitation, and the rest of that May, the student body focused on getting our yearbooks signed and cutting classes. Other than the hoopla surrounding the prom, the major event—as my junior year wound down at Grayton High—was the all-school pep rally where varsity athletes received G letters for the year.

This was the grand moment I'd waited for, the recompense for our hockey team not going to the state tournament. Finally, I would be awarded the personal reward of my loyal efforts and could strut down the halls wearing my blue letter jacket adorned with the coveted G. My hard work and the dozens of freezing-cold practices were now fading memories, but my days of basking in glory and name recognition, of fame and acclaim, lay ahead.

On the day of the pep rally, 1400 sophomores, juniors, and seniors filled the gym. The cheerleaders yelled cheers and the band blared school songs. My gut rumbled from two opposing feelings: elation and dread. Elation, because my time for recognition and popularity had come; dread, because nobody had told me to sit at floor-level with my teammates on the folding chairs. Instead, a teacher holding a clipboard of athletes' names directed me to file into the spectator stands.

My heart pounded in confusion. *Surely my name will be called! Surely there's been a mistake!*

I saw the various teams sitting in designated sections, among them David sitting with the football players, as well as my hockey teammates jostling one another self-consciously, acting like the festivities were no big deal. Then the principal stepped up to the microphone and announced the start of the rally. I had no choice other than to sit anxiously in the bleachers and gaze at my 14 teammates joking and elbowing one another. Even the student trainer kidded with them and sat next to Coach Mack.

The long drawn-out minutes became more painful as the football team received awards. The coach announced Dave's name among the many others over the loudspeaker. I cheered eagerly as my twin shook hands with the coach and received his letter and framed parchment certificate. At least one of us had hit the mark! Then came the basketball and swim teams. At long last, the hockey team.

Coach Mack stepped up and cleared his throat. He spoke awkwardly and, for a few seconds, I pitied him. During the season, rather than inspiring locker-room speeches, he would hammer the mechanics of hockey into his players, seldom if ever motivating their souls or spirits. His ineptness stood out again in today's public forum, but he was mercifully brief. One by one he called the players' names, and I half-believed mine would be coming. My mind raced, thinking of the photo printed in the sports section of the yearbook showing me with my teammates, part of the six-page hockey spread. How could I be a recognized team member in print and not here? The last name he called was the student trainer's. Then he sat down.

My heart plunged, my breathing stopped, my mind flip-flopped. Suddenly I was a nonperson. I'd suited up for every game and more than fifty practices and scrimmages. But I was disregarded, discarded, disowned. Everybody knew Chuck Bennett would still play first-string goalie next season.

My one and only chance for a letter . . . *dashed!* I'd earned my day in the spotlight . . . *but NO!*

Dave walked home with me, commiserating on the way. Everything he said rattled in my ears like hollow clichés. He meant well and felt especially bad about earning his own letter.

"Don't, Dave. You worked hard for it and deserve it fair and square," I told him.

"But you got reamed! It's impossible Mack could've forgotten you!"

"Impossible, maybe. But it happened just the same."

"What could have been going through his mind? What?"

"I wonder if it was a mistake or on purpose." The injustice of it made me want to wring Mack's neck. Hatred boiled up within me. Dave could tell I felt the same rage toward the coach that I did toward Mom and insisted I go back and talk to him.

"Dave, I'll have to corner him some other time and ask why, but it hurts too much right now," I answered. Secretly, I wanted Coach Mack to suffer horribly and writhe in torment. He was a worthless joke of a coach. A murderous, vengeful grudge kindled within me. I started to throb with urges to retaliate, to inflict harm.

The split in my personality grew. I had more appalling thoughts to keep to myself now, to stuff and bury. Another reason to act one way while feeling another, to keep up appearances. Phooey on appearances! I punched the door of my bedroom closet, pounding my fist into it savagely, leaving an ugly dent in the wood. My hand ached for hours and the knuckles took a week to heal.

It bugged me that Dave's mild manner seemed so much healthier than mine. He never hit the extremes the way I did. His easygoing demeanor made me wonder how he did it. How could he let irksome things roll off so easily? Then it struck me that he hadn't faced the same kinds of injustices. He had his letter. He hadn't been a benchwarmer. He felt pressured less often by Mom to satisfy her demands. He was right-handed in a right-handed world. He hadn't been called Fatso. He'd gone window-peeping with me at night once or twice, but never got into the habit the way I had. I doubted he'd ever run naked in the woods. In all likelihood, he wasn't carrying the emotional baggage, wasn't juggling as many secrets, as his identical, but not-so-identical, twin.

One thing Dave and I both felt deeply sad about was standing by and witnessing Dad's continued weight loss, reduced to 150 pounds by now. His hospital stays became more frequent and seemed longer and more financially draining. Mom backed off on her decorating and landscaping demands for a while because she came home exhausted most nights from her decorating job at the department store. She'd been promoted from receptionist in the interior decorating studio to assistant interior decorator, a position she loved because it channeled her creative talents and offered the prestige she craved.

As for Tommy, he spent most days at the University of Minnesota campus far across town attending pharmacy classes, and he worked part-time hours at Walgreen's, so we seldom saw him at home or his Ford parked outside. Our darling dog, Joy, began limping, then eating less food, and eventually vomited up piles of smelly gunk. We took her to the vet, who gave her pills with the advice that we love and comfort her as much as possible in what could be her final months. As always, she wagged her tail and licked our faces whenever we arrived home or petted her.

During finals week at school, I hatched a plan to confront Coach Mack. He did hall monitor duty every day. One morning I approached him, but he saw me coming and pretended not to notice. My heart jumped to my throat. Steely determined, I walked up and uttered my rehearsed opening line: "Coach, I played all season on your team. Can you tell me why I didn't get a letter?"

Silence.

"I'm asking why I didn't get a letter. I deserved one."

He still looked away, then cleared his throat. "Not enough minutes. You didn't have enough game minutes."

"Game minutes? I . . . I made every practice and suited up for every game," I stammered, in shock. "My picture is in the yearbook. I . . . I . . ."

He turned vaguely in my direction. "Backup goalies don't get letters. That's policy. You need a certain number of game minutes. There's nothing more to it."

"Nobody ever said anything about that. *Now* you tell me?"

I stood staring. Game minutes were under his control, not mine. How could he fault *me?* He refused to look me in the eye, then turned his back on me, and cleared his throat again—even louder. I got the hint. Not only had a mistake *not* been made, he'd intentionally denied me. He was a worse monster than I'd imagined! I felt more shaken and bewildered than at the pep rally. *Why was I being punished?*

He remained tight-lipped. I sulked away.

That summer I wrestled with the meaning of this nasty encounter. Beyond disappointment or failure, it felt like a betrayal, a crushing defeat. As the days of vacation passed, I washed dishes at Garrety's 40 hours a week plus some overtime hours. During the monotony of scraping dirty dishes and cleaning the grease trap of smelly sludge, an idea hatched that would not leave my mind. It became another of my secrets that nurtured itself stubbornly in my solitary moments.

My hatred for Coach Mack spawned a profound resolve to get even. I committed to practice my goalie skills and improve them every available waking minute during the summer until tryouts the next fall, then surpass Beaner when it came time for making first string. I would beat out Chuck Bennett and convince the very coach who'd snubbed me of my superiority.

To accomplish such a feat, I spent my paycheck on ice skating time at the local all-year arena, where a group of college players with their own practice needs scrimmaged after midnights and on weekends. That was the easy part. The hard part was not having any goalie pads. I asked to borrow the school's, and an office worker told me they were packed away in storage until fall. I tried to find a used pair in sporting goods stores but found just one new pair for $100—not a chance. So my talent for making things reawakened, and I plunged into a two-week, hell-bent frenzy to sew by hand the bulky leather leg-protectors from scratch.

The project was on the scale of making my canoe. Envy of Chuck Bennett spurred me on and so did visions of winning a trophy at the state tournament. I measured my legs and drew full-size patterns, bought a hide of leather and sheets of industrial felt padding, then sewed for hours each day, prompting remarks of amazement from my parents and brothers—even they had never seen such an ambitious undertaking completed in a span of only two weeks.

Loading the dishwasher and working long hours at Garrety's gave me time to reflect. I envisioned Dad's shrinking physique lying frail on yet another hospital bed. I made a sincere effort to think of Mom in a better light based on her diligence working at a fulltime job, in an era when women generally didn't earn wages outside the home.

I pondered where my life was headed and how the difficulties and disappointments so far were affecting me and complicating my progress. I dreamed of dating some curvaceous girl who desired me and making out with her passionately. It helped that the cute waitresses at Garrety's like Janice flirted and made coy, suggestive remarks, helping mold my appreciation for feminine companionship.

It also occurred to me one day that my paychecks from Garrety's did not include the extra hours I usually stayed after closing time to clean up. The store closed at 10:00 P.M. and my wage was now $.90 an hour. Most nights I stayed an extra half hour doing chores like scrubbing the grill, emptying the grease trap, or mopping the floor. I mentioned the lack of pay to Otis Hansen, my supervisor who signed my time cards. He shrugged: "Sorry, John, but you'll have to bring up a matter like that with Mr. Nash." With a frown, he added, "You have my sympathy."

Every employee knew the store's general manager, Harlan Nash. He was stern and cross, not to be tangled with, never one to greet you or say a kind word. With the same assertiveness as when I'd approached Coach Mack, I generated a strategy and picked a time that would maximize my chances. I wore a clean apron at the start of my shift and walked up to Mr. Nash's office behind the pharmacy counter, took a deep breath, then knocked on his door.

"Yes, what is it?" he grumbled from inside.

I stepped into the small room and recited my rehearsed opening line, "Good afternoon, Mr. Nash. I think there's a problem with my time card. I'd like to ask why I'm not getting paid for the hours I've worked after ten o'clock cleaning up."

I saw for the first time, now standing just feet from him, that he really did look like Ebenezer Scrooge, as many rumors had claimed.

"When the store closes," he growled, "you're supposed to be done with your work. Can't you see I'm busy?"

"But we have customers who sit at the counter until then, sir. And Mr. Hansen always asks me to stay. The customers' dishes need to be washed and dried before I leave."

"Hardly my problem." He looked down at his papers, ignoring me.

"But if I work till 10:30, shouldn't I get paid for it?"

"You little—" he sneered, cutting himself off. Sitting up, he looked straight at me. "Are you questioning store policy?"

"What I'm questioning is why I don't get paid for the time I actually work. It's only a few cents. If you want me to leave at ten, why not close the grill at 9:30?"

He turned red and looked like he might explode. "*You* presume to tell *me* how to run *my* store?" He took a huge breath. "Get out! Get out right now! And count yourself lucky you're not fired!"

I stared at him, amazed, then turned and left his pathetic, foul lair. "I still don't think it's fair."

My chest heaved. My cheeks burned. I stomped to the kitchen and resumed my duties. Like a robot on remote control, indignation ignited in me and I loaded dirty dishes into the dishwasher, furiously flipping the "on" switch. Tears suddenly came. The spray of water filling the dishwasher masked the whimpering sound of my wet sobs. I pounded my fist on the empty metal racks beside me. *How could he be so petty? How could a few cents mean so much? He's as mean-hearted as Mom!"* I resolved then and there to find another job. No pig-headed boss was going to squelch my legitimate request for an honest day's pay.

Within a week, I'd interviewed at another pharmacy two miles away in a strip mall, Haugen Brothers' Drug. I accepted owner Ron Haugen's offer to start as a clerk at $1.50 an hour and rejoiced in my good fortune. My first career victory included a whopping raise! My duties consisted of restocking shelves, operating the cash register, and using my fountain skills gained at Garrety's to serve the customers ice cream floats, sundaes, and cones—all for better pay.

When I reported this news to Otis Hansen, he turned sad-faced and lit another of his perpetual cigarettes. "Well, John, you certainly deserve better, and I take my hat off to you. But it's gonna be one hard act to replace you. You're a hard worker and never call in sick." He shook his head, looked toward Mr. Nash's office, and grumbled, "The fool! He's a numbers man and just doesn't understand the first thing about people. Nothing but a Scrooge!"

My sympathy went out to Otis. "I've always liked working for you, Mr. Hansen. I'm actually sorry about leaving, sorry we won't be working together anymore." It was no secret between us, this information, and disclosing it didn't hurt.

He looked at me directly, his eyes clear. "You've got tons of potential, John. I'm happy you've found something better. You're the kind of kid who's going to go a long way." He snubbed out his cigarette and we shook hands.

Days later I hung up my apron for the last time and wished him well, then walked out the back door past the dumpster. He shouted after me, "I'm sorry things around here didn't work out. Don't be a stranger, young man! Come back for a free hamburger anytime!"

A highlight of the summer of 1961 before my senior year was getting Tommy's old '50 Ford. Dave and I shared the hand-me-down, of course. Tommy had sunk his money into a spiffy used '56 Buick convertible from his Walgreens wages—bright pink, which he christened "Big Mamoo"—so Dave and I finally had our own transportation. With Tommy joyriding in "Big Mamoo," we could now drive back and forth to work, to hockey practice, and on dates.

The first thing you'd notice about that run-down Ford was that it was a total wreck on four wheels. The dark blue paint had been rubbed away, only patches here and there on bare metal. The radiator leaked, so we kept gallon jugs of water in the backseat to replenish the fluid levels whenever we parked longer than 15 minutes. The crowning blow was its rusted-out floor, both driver's and passenger's sides. The rotted-away metal showed the street pavement visible through one's feet, which got splashed from puddles in rain or snow—prompting loads of laughs.

My hockey practices that summer fortunately occurred after midnight three nights a week, so making arrangements with Dave to use the car was easy. At the hockey scrimmages, my handmade goalie pads proved priceless. The anger and hurt I felt about Mack's refusal to give me a letter fueled my creative intensity during the weeks I'd spent making them, and when I strapped the pads on at the ice arena, they looked so professional that the other skaters didn't notice they weren't.

On the ice I played my heart out, constantly striving to speed up my reflexes and skills. Some of the best players in the Twin Cites skated during these wee-hour sessions, mainly to keep up their off-season conditioning. My conditioning improved too, but mainly I worked to improve my goaltending. These practices helped boost my confidence by making up for the years while isolated in Chippewa Hills from 5th to 9th grades when I had not played Bantam hockey like my varsity teammates. And improve I did. One night I stopped over fifty shots. Facing college level players, I began playing at their level, their speed, their caliber. I told myself I could beat out Beaner and would certainly surprise Coach Mack during tryouts come October.

My clerking job at Haugen Brothers' Drug got off to a solid start. By Labor Day and the beginning of school classes, I was adept at greeting customers, using the cash register, making hot fudge sundaes at the fountain, and delivering prescriptions to customers' homes while driving Ron Haugen's station wagon. With each customer interaction, I discovered I had a natural gift for helping people. I enjoyed seeing folks leave the store satisfied. New skills I hadn't known about developed, and all at $.60 more an hour than dishwashing.

My development as a Secret Keeper grew at Haugen Brothers too.

One day on Ron's day off, a middle-aged man walked up to the main counter and asked for a *Playboy* magazine. I had no idea that the store carried them. He said he'd just come from the pharmacy counter where he'd tried to find Ron's brother Fred, Ron's business partner and co-pharmacist. "Fred's nowhere around and I'm in a hurry, young man. Can you help me?"

I nodded, scurried to the pharmacy area—an elevated platform set apart from the main store by a swinging door—and looked among the shelves under the counter where the man said *Playboys* were hidden away. Of all the people you'd never want to run afoul of, Fred was it. Unlike easygoing Ron, he was brittle, rigid, ornery, and lacked smiling muscles (like "Ebenezer" Nash!). I looked for Fred, but he was nowhere in sight. The customer hurriedly whispered instructions to me, and I knelt down low, looking where he told me to. Sure enough, a stack of *Playboys* sat piled behind a pharmaceutical box. I grabbed a copy and handed it to him. He thanked me and quickly paid for it, then folded it, making it inconspicuous, and left the store.

Seconds later Fred returned and bellowed, "What in blazes are *you* doing back here?" I explained, but he looked at me suspiciously, his brow wrinkled in sour folds like Mr. Nash's frown. "Get back to work," he commanded. His Scrooge-like look gave me the willies, but it also made me giggle to myself—*What's the matter with these sourpuss bosses? Are they members of the same club?*

So it came to pass that *Playboy* became a gateway to new secret-keeping endeavors and more stolen hours. I became part of a much larger camaraderie in society: males only, "Ssshhh, don't tell," wink, wink. I was not alone. Others kept secrets too. In the days ahead, I sneaked back occasionally to ogle the latest centerfold, experiencing once more the *excitement/pleasure/delight* cycle in solitary stolen moments.

This new exposure to a grander network of men breaking rules and not getting caught (or not caring if they did), gripped me strongly. Secret-keeping became more than solitary stolen hours, now it could be communal, a delicious conspiracy spurred by a contraband magazine. Besides the fabulously sexy photos in *Playboy,* a well-thought-out rationale called the "Playboy Philosophy" supported this communal network. We men now had a defense, a reasoned argument, to fend off women's criticism and their claims of us being perverts. I cherished this new source of shared intrigue and the underground nature accompanying it.

Another shared delight marked the start of my senior year at Grayton High. A real girlfriend entered my life—with a bang. Sheryl Simmons, a perky and attractive A student with a zest for fun, literally banged into my open locker door the first week of school. "Sorry!" she exclaimed. "I'm . . . I'm new here and wasn't looking where I was going."

"No problem. It's okay." I looked more closely and liked the person I saw. She smiled (nice teeth) and had sparkly eyes (nice personality).

"I . . . ah . . ." she cleared her throat, "I just moved here from St. Louis a few weeks ago. My dad manages Sears stores and got transferred here. By the way, I'm Sheryl. Sheryl Simmons."

We exchanged names and the human connection I so needed—not through a window or a magazine, but a real girl—filled my empty spaces for a whole year. My dream of dating a curvaceous girl who desired me became reality. High-school life from that moment on became a wild ride.

Sheryl and I did everything together: walking to classes, meeting after school, holding hands, talking on the phone for hours. A dreamy daze enveloped us, two seniors who'd found each other and were going steady within a month. In my eyes, Sheryl delivered on everything Cindy could have except that Sheryl was approachable. We soon explored the boundaries of kissing and petting. My libido soared from our direct, skin-to-skin contact, and she told me hers soared too: "John, I love how you touch me!" We spent hours making out, mutually delirious in the darkened rec room of her basement.

"I love you, John!" she whispered.

"I love you too, Sheryl!" I echoed. Our hands roamed all over each other as we smooched on the couch with the phonograph playing the Everly Brothers and Chubby Checker.

My senior classes started off on a high note. In sixth-hour English, the new students including myself assembled in our seats the first day before the bell rang and checked one another out: who was the cutest? smartest? most popular? The bell rang, but the teacher was absent. This caused a buzz, as teachers were forever at their desks making seating assignments or telling us which book titles to study. An entire minute went by. We started buzzing, making jokes: "Hey, acing this class is going to be a breeze!"

Just then, the door swung open—whoosh!—and a tiny man with a booming voice dashed in reciting poetry in Old English. We sat dumbfounded. When he stopped, he clapped his hands and announced, "That was *Beowulf*, the ancient epic poem. I'm Mr. Anderson. Welcome to senior English. Take out your pens, please. You're going to start writing your own epic poem."

Within five minutes, Mr. Anderson asked us to name our heroes—"John Kennedy, Eleanor Roosevelt, Mickey Mantle, Amelia Earhart"—then declared that "epic poems told tales about heroes doing heroic deeds motivated by noble virtues." In minutes our pens were moving, without the barriers of grammar or rhyme schemes to hinder us. I titled my poem "Tom Evans, King of Archers," about a Renaissance man confronting an unjust magistrate and winning the heart of the lovely Lady Rowena. Mr. Anderson encouraged us to recite our work orally, according to the epic tradition. I borrowed a friend's guitar and put my lines to music, then accompanied myself like a troubadour of ancient times in front of the class—a very scary but ultimately successful artistic "stretch."

Oh Tom Evans, king of archers,
hit the target true,
Oh Tom Evans, king of archers,
this today you must do . . .

With this refrain, I sang to my classmates. Their applause resounded like triumphant music in my ears.

We students also plunged ahead on assignments of writing sonnets, short stories, essays, limericks, haiku, and free verse. Mr. Anderson, so tiny and intense and daring, stood one day on a student's desk to invoke the passion of Mercutio's soliloquy from *Romeo and Juliet*. Other days he roamed the aisles, leaning near students' faces and peering into their eyes at random, exclaiming, "The eyes are the windows of the soul!" I thrilled to his every word and gesture. He pushed limits and boundaries, opening up the world of literature for me, awakening the power of words. He relegated the nitpicky rules of grammar and spelling into their proper, secondary place—after theme, character, and dramatic action.

Decades later, I saw Robin Williams in the movie *Dead Poet's Society* and thought fondly of Mr. Anderson. Without question, his class was the Mount Everest of my 12 years of academic life. Thanks to Mr. Anderson, I became eager to attend college, to major in English, and to explore the enchantments of advanced learning. Studying under him set me free.

Another spectacular high note during my senior year was the bunch of great guys I hung out with, a group of senior boys formed into an indivisible corps of buddies. By some mysterious beneficent force, we instinctively bonded like superglue: Mike Gibbs, Bobby Harris, Dave Rydel, Rick Killdare, Forrest Morelin, Jay Wilson, and the Prin twins. After school we'd gather to play touch football, and on Friday nights we'd pile into one car together and hit the biggest aftergame party. As part of this group of guys, I felt empowered and special, and an exciting social life evolved. Over time other high-school buddies joined us, guys like Sheryl's younger brother Clark and his pal Mark Brandow, both hilarious pranksters of the first order.

My evolution as a Secret Keeper grew another giant step when we guys picked X-rated movies to sneak off to. In those days, X-rated films were tame. Only two theatres in the seediest part of town, the Avalon and Rialto on Lake Street, played "girlie films." We had to lie about our age at the box office to get in. Then we'd bust a gut laughing once we got inside because the ticket seller always was an elderly spinster who, we realized, had "innocently" played along with our scam. She sold the outrageously priced tickets of five dollars regardless—all while pretending to believe our fibs.

Once, at Rick Killdare's suggestion (he was the acknowledged leader when it came to far-out fun), our squad of guys climbed the stairs to the balcony of the Avalon and sat shoulder to shoulder in the front row. Below us, we noticed male-only patrons sitting several seats apart dotted throughout the auditorium. The main problem with X-rated films in those early days was that the "juicy parts" lasted sixty seconds or less, and then you had to sit through long, boring stretches of inane plot developments before the next brief exposure of flesh. Privately, I found myself experiencing the *excitement/pleasure/delight* cycle at these parts with the bonus that I was officially one of the larger network of men breaking rules and not getting caught (or not caring if we did)—that males-only, "Ssshhh-don't-tell," wink-wink conspiracy. Like discovering *Playboy*, I cherished this new kind of communal secrecy and reveled in its underground nature. We guys were in this together. Basically, we stole hours collectively and felt secure in our immunity from criticism or protests by our mothers or girl friends.

During one of the movie's long, boring plot sections, Rick got restless and whispered, "Hey, guys, as soon as the next juicy part comes along, let's all dump our popcorn over the railing and then peel out of here before they kick us out." We all nodded.

Moments later the actress on screen started undressing, and on cue, we all emptied our popcorn boxes over the railing onto the heads of patrons seated on the main floor. Loud protests erupted. The thunder of a dozen adolescent feet tramping down the stairs and out the door reverberated. We ran to the parking lot where we belly-laughed in hysterics, then jammed into the '50 Ford and made a fast getaway like Al Capone's mobsters evading Elliott Ness's untouchable commandos.

Later, Sheryl heard about our antics and laughed heartily. "Do you think my going to 'adult' movies is wicked or wrong?" I asked.

"Hardly," she replied. "I think it's normal and nothing to fret about."

⁂

Late in the fall when oak and maple leaves floated to the ground, the day of hockey tryouts arrived. Three goalies were on the tryout list for the two goaltending positions. Besides Chuck Bennett, my competition was an up-and-coming sophomore. I strapped on my homemade pads and made an impressive showing, stopping dozens of shots with greater ease and speed than Coach Mack or Beaner had ever seen. The surprised looks in their eyes said so. Then came the sophomore, who did well but appeared nervous. Then came Beaner, who put in a more-than-perfunctory showing as if he really *was* competing for the top spot.

In the locker room later, Coach Mack scratched my name off the list. Apparently his mind had already been made up. I surmised he needed the younger sophomore in order to groom him to take Chuck's place the next season. As was Buzz's stoic style, he said nothing to me.

Beaner told me later while we were showering, "Hey, Prinsky! You really made me work for it. Nice going. You're miles better than last year. Sorry to see you go. You're one great guy."

Walking home in the frigid dusk air, I hung my head and bit my lip for having gambled so much and lost so hard. My ego felt as dull gray as the overcast sky. My disappointment stung like the harsh wind. At home, I told David about the discouraging tryout and we talked for hours. We ended by both of us deciding to play on local park board teams that winter, comprised of the vast pool of nonvarsity hockey players who abounded in the suburban areas.

"Johnny," he concluded, "it's time for hockey to be fun for you again."

I nodded. "At least we'll play every game and not warm the bench." And with that, my days as a varsity athlete withered quietly into the shadows.

Still one other tryout remained. Yet another gamble at recognition. If my ego couldn't be salvaged athletically, maybe it could be salvaged artistically. I put my name on the tryout list for the class play, "The Reluctant Debutante." This time I wasn't going to read unprepared. I asked for a copy of the script and rehearsed lines on my own until they felt natural. Sheryl helped me by reading dialogue and cheerleading my efforts.

The day of auditions arrived. Again, I put my all into the reading, showing confidence on the outside but nervous inside about my getting the role. Later that week, I again scanned the posted sheet of selected actors, but my name did not appear.

What does it take? Will I ever find my place in the world?

The director's no-feedback rule rankled me. I wanted to knock on his door and ask him what he didn't like about my acting. In order to improve, I needed to know. But I felt too defeated to try. It seemed that whenever I'd confronted other authority figures like Coach Buzz or Harlan Nash, they'd already made up their minds and my attempts were bluntly dismissed. My efforts seemed useless in changing the hoped-for outcomes. So the mold was set for years to come; the absence of feedback from an authority figure to me, an aspiring underling, would keep me dumb and in my place until I managed to find out what I needed some other way.

The minute Sheryl heard about my hockey and acting defeats, she commiserated with my low feelings and gave me handmade sympathy cards. She did everything in her power to change my mood, and her loving empathy lifted me out of the doldrums. I wrote her a love letter and handed it to her while we were chatting on the couch in her basement late one night.

"You are so loveable, John!" she cooed, reading the letter. "I love you, love you, love you!"

"Sheryl," I echoed, "I love you, love you, love you too!"

Totally smitten, we shared hours of soul-searching conversations and eye contact. Our necking and petting with the lights low in the privacy of her rec-room led us to discover a deeper connection sensually in what we thought was a healthy, open way. We stopped short of going "all the way," however. Sheryl's mother frequently puttered upstairs in the kitchen, but she never once invaded our privacy, never once walked down the stairs and confronted us.

"Do you think your mom has any idea what we're doing down here?" I asked Sheryl, as our hands caressed each other's bare skin.

"I think she has some idea, but not how far we've gone. She trusts me."

"I guess so! Because I sure like what we're doing!"

"Actually, I heard her say she trusts *you* too."

"Oh?" A rush of amazement surged through me, making me blush. "That's neat to hear."

Sheryl and I *shared* the secrecy of making out in her basement; we crossed intimate boundaries *together*. By keeping to ourselves, we formed an unspoken pact. Sheryl gave so much of herself that the only term to describe it is loving generosity. For those awesome months, the grip of the addictive cycle on me steadily loosened and freed me from its grasp. I did the honest, true, wholesome thing with another person's full consent and blessing.

Highlights of the remainder of that unforgettable year included a coed ski trip with sixty giddy classmates, the '50 Ford's bald tires on slick ice in winter that forced us to get out and push it everywhere, and a terrific prom and all-night graduation party. On weekends, Sheryl and I went to the movies, and I became even more of a huge movie fan, especially of classics like *Anatomy of a Murder, The Apartment, Some Like It Hot,* and *Spartacus*. In pristine ways, we had loads of fun without drinking or smoking cigarettes, thanks in part to the times—the pre-drugs-and-protest era of the 1960s.

Our reverie lasted until the fall of 1962 when Sheryl and I went off to separate colleges. I will always remember Sheryl's fabulous giving of herself to me. With her I learned that I was not a cad who spent stolen hours in solitary indulgence but was just a regular guy who, at times, got caught in a bind between my honor and my hormones—and one who could share wholeheartedly two-way love with a real woman.

Sharing love with Sheryl was no secret, no secret at all.

MetaViews to Muse   #2

The thoughts and ideas on these shaded pages, called MetaViews (see MetaView #1 after Chapter 2), are intended to help you recognize and confront secret-keeping tendencies and habits. From my perspective as a professional counselor and recovering Secret-Keeper, I hope these reflections on what you've read in the past several pages will encourage you to consider your own life's challenges and choices.

✳ Secret lives center on substances, objects, or events—not people with whom we are meant to connect. Window-peeping offered me thrills and the subconscious payoff of numbing persistent heavy feelings.

In what ways might you have secretly withdrawn or disconnected from family, friends, work associates, or the larger community?

✳ Secret-keeping can become more than solitary stolen hours, it can also be communal. In my case, a "males only" camaraderie developed around *Playboy* magazines and X-rated movies. This opened the way to shared intrigue, which fed the underground nature of my activities.

Are you part of a similar kind of group that provides safety in numbers?

✳ Other forms of stealing hours may involve fantasy—removing oneself psychologically from the source of shame/pain, such as indulging in sensual pleasure and intensity. When my outside world turned hostile, I hid my pain by putting on a happy face in public while lusting after cheerleaders or ogling magazine photos of naked women in private.

What role might such fantasies play in your life?

✳ Secret Keepers keep their private thoughts locked away in mental solitary confinement. I held my angry, vengeful thoughts about Coach Mack and "Ebenezer" Nash deep in my innermost self, which elevated my physical and emotional stress.

Any of this sound familiar to you? If so, can you identify the emotions that you have locked inside? How does this affect you physically and emotionally?

✳ A secret life demands high levels of calculation and hair-splitting between two worlds—yet another source of stress. Whenever I had to explain myself, I came up with alibis or made excuses, which really were just lies.

Are you walking a tightrope between two opposing worlds like I did? If so, what toll are your lies taking on your personal integrity or your relationships with loved ones?

✳ **The following are two of the eight splintered mindsets of a Secret Keeper:**
   ➤ Stealing hours doing what is required to feel better.
   ➤ Walking a tightrope between two opposing worlds.

"Death cancels everything but truth."

William Hazlitt
The Spirit of the Age

꽈 *Chapter Five*

Death's Door

Dad's declining health dominated our lives for the next two years. Seeing Dad in a hospital bed sickened me. Every time I visited him, a jumble of twisted emotions agitated me. From a robust 350 pounds when I was little, he'd dropped more than 250 pounds in the intervening years to 100. Besides diabetes—which impaired blood circulation to his hands and feet so that they stayed cold, clammy, and blue—his kidneys started failing, his heart became enlarged, and he could only sit up for an hour or two a day. Gone completely were the glory days when his jolly, round, smiling face lit up the television sets of happy fans in Minnesota and Wisconsin.

The stress on Mom due to his relentless decline became unbearable at times. She worked five days a week at the department store by now and had progressed to full-time interior decorator. She actually thrived on the client contact and creativity of the job. This was both a blessing and a curse: her mind focused for hours on something other than her husband's ailments, a blessing; but she carried home with her the tensions of the added job responsibilities, a curse.

Almost daily, I listened to her complain about the late fabric shipments, undelivered furniture orders promised by the factory, or how she had to explain to her customers the shipping problems and delays that were beyond her control. I offered my suggestions, but nothing ever changed. I eventually burned out listening to her repetitive, seemingly insoluble dilemmas that the store's upper management never addressed or resolved.

Financially, the huge drain on our household accounts beleaguered

Mom. Dad's staggering hospital and medical bills had exhausted our insurance. Her wages, along with those that we boys earned from part-time jobs, literally kept us fed and the lights on. You could see how the mounting financial burden weighed on her. Her eye sockets became sunken and her posture stooped. Her moods turned all the more short-tempered whenever a free evening came along, because it meant driving to the hospital for yet another visit to see Dad. I learned on one of those drives that Dad had cashed out all his savings and life insurance policies to pay medical bills, altogether $80,000 (about $300,000 in today's dollars).

The ugly reality she faced of her decorating and landscaping projects at home having fallen by the wayside added more stress on Mom. Her irritable outbursts increased and the prescription pill bottles on her bedside table multiplied. In my eyes, Mom *resigned* herself to not completing these endless projects, but she never *accepted* that they wouldn't get done—a big difference. Her resignation meant that she still wanted things to go her way and she pouted because conditions didn't permit it, rather than accepting that things couldn't go her way and willingly letting go of the self-imposed necessity that they get done. Too bad, I thought. How much easier life would've been for us and her.

Once again my secret homicidal urges stirred murderous impulses that threatened to surface.

In all, Mom stayed the course and kept putting one foot in front of the other, doggedly getting through the numerous challenges one day at a time. Her stamina and sheer grit earned her grudging credit in my eyes, as did her loyalty to Dad. At times she even softened and became the mother I remembered as a little boy, saying simple things like, "Let's have some ice cream and watch a TV special," as a way to relax and bond.

Death's first visit during those years came when our dog, Joy, now 14, could no longer hold down her food. Despite our loving and comforting efforts, it came time to end her misery. It fell on Dave and me to decide to take her to the vet one last time. We petted Joy as we carried her anemic body from the '50 Ford and watched her stagger a final time on her wobbly legs into the vet's office. In just three or four minutes, he returned and said, "She's at peace now." Dave and I looked at one another and shared the grief, holding back tears from streaking down our cheeks.

As we'd learned during the stressful days of Chippewa Hills, we still kept the secrets of our home life to ourselves. We wanted to appear normal and not stand out. To survive, I blocked from my mind Dad's hospital stays and Mom's pill-induced conduct—more practice at acting one way while feeling another. I generally acted strong and confident while feeling defective and abnormal. Occasionally, school buddies noticed our family's difficulties and asked if they could help in some way. Bobby Harris, continually cheerful and chipper, asked me one day, "Geez, I never quite realized all you guys are going through, Johnny. What's it like having your dad in the hospital all the time?"

"Horrible. It really stinks."

"Anything I can do?"

"Just be Bobby. Stay 'up' and keep making your goofy jokes."

"That's it? Nothing like bringing you meals? I can't imagine my dad being sick all the time and never being around."

"You get used to it. Sort of. We're managing, I guess. Like I said, the best thing is to keep 'up' and be funny . . . make us laugh, Bobby. Having fun is really important."

And we guys did keep having fun, the kind of silly outings like dumping our popcorn over the railing at the X-rated Avalon movie theatre. Other times we traveled to Wisconsin for a weekend of downhill skiing and we'd nearly drive into a ditch laughing so hard at dirty jokes. But times like these became fewer and fewer due to college plans that sent our gang off in separate directions: Bobby went to St. Cloud State, 100 miles north of the Twin Cites, known as a party school; Mike Gibbs traveled to Columbia University in New York City, known for its scholarship; and so on. We'd all gather together for Thanksgiving or Christmas holidays and have more fun times, but the high-school loyalties dissolved unavoidably as each of us flew from the nest in different directions.

My own flight took me to Duluth, 175 miles north on the shore of Lake Superior. David and I, along with our pal Jay Wilson, stayed in an off-campus boarding house for students the first quarter of classes at the regional campus of the University of Minnesota. Freshmen tuition was only $102 per quarter at UM-Duluth for state residents. Besides math and biology, I took English and art classes, enjoyed both immensely, and made progress learning how to creatively express myself in words and paint. Dave and Jay drank and partied more often than I did, and beer became essential to their having fun. I joined them at times, but never plunged into the drinking scene as deeply as they did.

On visits home, reminders of how good it felt to be away from the daily stress of Mom's moods and the grind of Dad's medical care jumped out at me. Dad looked more like a skeleton with skin on than ever. That Christmas, Sheryl returned from Kansas University. I'd anticipated our reunion with great enthusiasm. In weekly letters, we'd promised to send loving thoughts to each other, but her letter-writing had dropped off to once a month. Lovesick, I ran to meet her, rang her doorbell, and waited for her smiling face to appear. The door opened. Her face was not smiling. The minute we hugged, I knew something had changed. She was cold, rigid, distant.

"Sheryl, what's wrong?"

"John, I . . . I no longer care for you the same way."

"Huh? What's changed?"

"I'm not sure I can really say. I don't really know. Going to a different school and meeting different people . . . I'm not sure . . . ," her voice trailed off.

My throat went dry and my breathing sped up. "Is there another guy?"

She sighed, letting her shoulders slump. "Um, not really but, well . . . I don't know why, John. All I know is we can't keep seeing each other."

I stared into her empty eyes. "Can't?"

"It's over," she added.

My heart pounded madly. *Over?* I asked her to explain, but she couldn't, or wouldn't—stalemate.

For the next two weeks, I came unglued. Christmas was anything but merry and New Years anything but happy. I couldn't comprehend what had changed. I just wanted Sheryl back. Betrayed, downcast, I opened the mail the day after New Years 1963 and my report card from UM-Duluth for fall quarter contained two A's, two Bs, and a C. The two A's, for English and art, made my spirits soar, as did the GPA of 3.3.

Later that afternoon, Dave opened his report card containing one B, two Cs, and two Ds. He told me that Jay had earned similar grades, even an F, and that they'd already decided something. Something big.

All ears, I asked, "What?"

"We're sick of studying. Jay and I are signing up for the National Guard."

I looked at him incredulously. "You guys are crazy! The army?"

"Yep, you're probably right. It means six months of active duty and army boot camp. Crazy? I hope not, but that's how it is."

"The military? No, don't be ridiculous!"

"Ridiculous or not," he nodded, "we're going through with it sometime later this month. They told us we'd go through basic together and advance training too. They also promised we'd be assigned to the same unit back home afterwards."

Dave urged me to join them, but I refused. "My grades are too good, Dave. I can't see interrupting such a good thing."

He understood my point, shrugged, and made one more attempt to persuade me before letting it go.

Two weeks later, Dave and I stood at the train station and parted for the first time in our lives. Saying good-bye felt about as bad as seeing Joy led away by the vet and knowing Dad would die young, before his time. Jay shook my hand, and off they went to boot camp at Fort Leonardwood in Missouri.

My return to college in Duluth started minus two pals and a girlfriend. I experienced loneliness and heartache the same way one experiences the loss of limbs. I began writing a letter to Sheryl one evening when a sudden revelation occurred to me. While writing about my pain, it seemed to transfer to the page. The more I wrote, the less it hurt. After several pages, I transferred from stationery to a spiral notebook and wrote down how we met, all the things we'd said, the puppy-love things we'd done together, the petting and the parties, and our breaking up at Christmas. Seeing the events and feelings unfold on paper night after night as I wrote excited me. In the course of two wintry, below-zero months, I had penned 315 pages. Proudly I claimed authorship of my first manuscript, what amounted to a book. From my pain, something positive had emerged. Something my English teacher Mr. Anderson would have affirmed, I thought.

My use of art to deal with the depths of my heavy emotions—doubt, disappointment, discouragement—felt similar to the surge of energy from hand-making the goalie pads, crafting the canoe, and setting my "Tom Evans" poem to music. Like the outlet those creative efforts provided, my upset emotions found another safe outlet in my letter-turned-book. Often I'd gone to extremes, at times overreacting. But now my tendency to overreact seemed to have become an ingrained habit, even when constructive rather than destructive.

Later I came to learn, overreacting is typical for Secret Keepers. Overreaction generates intensity. Intensity goes with keeping secrets and burying feelings, leading the individual to mistake intensity for intimacy. When something negative or hurtful happens, the person with secret-keeping tendencies responds more intensely than what the event requires. The intensity of feeling gets confused with the desire for connection, which isn't there. (In my case, rejections by Coach Mack, Harlan Nash, and Sheryl were *dis*connections that were out of my control, that prompted my intense need to take control over *something*).

To maintain emotional equilibrium, the Secret Keeper stuffs negative feelings and acts one way while feeling another. Here, in this 315-page manuscript, was my revenge against a meaningless breakup. Sheryl would see it and change her mind about us. It said all I couldn't say in person. It would patch up our relationship. It had already helped heal my pain. Would it help heal us?

It took months, until that summer, before I worked up the courage to show my "letter" to her. In that time, David had returned from boot camp as a PFC, private first class, assigned to a local medical unit that held National Guard meetings one weekend a month in the armory downtown. *He* had changed and become more intense too. Sternly, he warned me about an upcoming military conflict in a strange place overseas called Vietnam.

"There's a war brewing in that God-forsaken place, Johnny. We heard about it all the time. Believe me, you'll pay big time if you don't enlist for six months before the draft gets you. It's the only way to keep from being drafted, because you won't get a deferment once you graduate. Mark my words."

In that mindset, I showed Sheryl my "letter" and asked her to read it. She gasped, amazed at its length. I said its abundance of pages indicated the vast love I still felt for her. She looked at me rather pathetically, then promised to read it and call me before returning that fall to Kansas University. Whether she sensed the contradiction of my healthy love and not-so-healthy intensity, or whether she wasn't moved by my wishful thinking or the melodrama in the book, the fact is she never called.

By late August, I reluctantly took Dave's advice and signed up, as he and Jay had done, for six months active/six years inactive duty. I rode the train to Fort Leonardwood in Missouri, and reluctantly put on a U.S. Army uniform.

The next year and a half became a harrowing blur. The 12 weeks of basic toughened me and, in the end, demonstrated my mettle. Specifically I learned that harsh conditioning physically and mentally could in fact make me stronger and wiser. One sadistic drill instructor reminded me of Mom and behaved especially cruelly.

My transfer to Fort Sam Houston in San Antonio, Texas followed. There I studied to become a medic, having chosen this course for my advanced training on the premise that preserving life while wearing a uniform was superior to destroying life as a uniformed killing machine.

I also started smoking cigarettes. Smoke breaks occurred several times a day, and my bunk-mates heckled me into trying a Camel one afternoon, insisting that I inhale it deeply. The next thing I knew, I was falling backwards and landed on the rocky ground where I hit my head.

Nearly passed out, my brain swooned inside from the nicotine and my skull swelled outside from the fall. They picked me up, laughing their heads off, then made certain I smoked the rest of it, much the same as when you fall off a horse and get back on the saddle right away.

While earning top honors in my class of 65 trainees, a most awful national tragedy desecrated our country's history: President John F. Kennedy died from an assassin's bullet. November 22, 1963, became a day of infamy. Our entire army base spent the next week on high alert while the nation grieved and asked *why?*

The main negative of my army active-duty days turned out to be my sense of injury, of becoming more of a victim. Drill sergeants' cruelty, exhausting 18-hour schedules of duty, a closed system where enlisted men routinely faced demeaning tasks and name-calling. Together, they assaulted my well-being and threatened to mold me into a mere cog in the military's chauvinistic chain of command.

But these forces molded me on the outside only. Comply, yes. Obey willingly, never. The army became another colossal-sized indoctrination into acting one way while feeling another and keeping up appearances. The army's absolute authority over enlisted men made me feel vulnerable and insecure. Its powerful might-versus-right rules really did make an individual soldier feel like a miserable puny pawn. Things happened *to* you in the army; *you* didn't make things happen. It ran you, you didn't run it. And whatever they dished out, you either swallowed or faced harsh discipline.

So much like Mom in so many ways.

I didn't realize this victimhood cognitively at the time, but I sure felt it in my gut. Subconsciously, I walked around expecting life to dump on me. It had hurt me so many times already. From this free-floating sense of injury, came anger. And from anger, rage. If threatened, I'd strike back. RAGE! If I saw something unjust, I'd lash out. RAGE!

Intensity? You bet, more than ever.

The main positive of my active-duty days came after my return home when I met the sister of one of my army buddies. Rosie Kowalsek lived in St. Paul, a short drive across the Mississippi River from Minneapolis, and we dated regularly during the summer of 1964, at a time when Dad rotated between weeklong stays in the hospital and home. Rosie was Bonnie Witten and Sheryl Simmons rolled into one. Tall and graceful, Rosie sported Bonnie's knockout body and Sheryl's wide-open vulnerability. A practicing Catholic from a family of six kids—one of whom was a nun, her older sister whom she idolized—Rosie opened my eyes to the wonders of the Spirit. She downplayed her physical advantages and strove to direct my attention to her spiritual blessings.

Late one night while we were making out on her porch with the fan blowing in the stifling summer heat, she leaned back and said, "God wants you to know He loves you, John."

I leaned back, mildly dumbfounded. "God wants me to know *what?*"

"He said He loves you, John."

"You heard Him? Actually heard Him? He . . . He talked to you, Rosie?"

"He does often, but not every day. He wants you to know He loves you very much."

"Well, how about that? Who'd ever know? I can't say as I *feel* He loves me. So . . . so when did He talk to you and say that?"

"Just now."

"While we were making out? Just like that?"

She chuckled. "Uh-huh, just like that! Why do you find it strange that God talks to people?"

Now I chuckled. "Why!" I stared at her and she appeared to still be her normal, earthly, beautiful self. "Saying you hear Him is one thing. People 'hear' all kinds of things. Saying He said He loves *me* is a whole other bag."

I explained about my shaky history regarding spiritual matters, the tedious confirmation classes, being dropped off at the Lutheran church, our home life where no prayers were said. She told of her home life, exactly the opposite, and of how happily she'd grown up believing in God. We talked for several minutes in this vein, still holding and caressing one another.

Late nights like these made attending college classes the next morning much tougher. By spring of 1965, Dave and I both commuted five days a week to the main Minneapolis campus of the 35,000-student University of Minnesota, an hour's drive through city streets and dozens of traffic lights. UM-Duluth was no longer practical and had become too costly. In the afternoons, we worked a few hours at our part-time jobs—his, at an auto-parts distributor, delivering orders to repair-shop customers; and mine, at a J.C. Penney's store, serving shoppers in the men's department. Then we made evening visits to see Dad in the hospital.

Tommy took classes as a music major at a local private arts college, having abandoned pharmacy and dentistry as an underclassman. He successfully followed in Dad's footsteps at the piano, having taken lessons from Dad for years at the Baldwin piano in our living room, whenever Dad's health allowed a few minutes of freedom from his sick bed. Tommy then became engaged to another music student, Carolyn Williams, and one of Dad's last pleasures in life was attending their wedding that summer in July.

Dad's final trip to the hospital lasted five weeks. One evening I walked into his room and saw a large plastic oxygen tent placed over his body. Having been unconscious in a coma for days, his breathing labored, he held on to life aided now by a constant supply of oxygen. Somehow he sputtered and kept hanging on. My feelings of utter powerlessness overwhelmed me.

In those quiet moments when I stared at his shrunken body, now down to 90 pounds, I thought for the first time of how he'd brought on his own premature demise: overworking, overeating, too little exercise, and never enough sleep. I also reflected on his unrequited love for Mom. No matter how much or how often he had tried to please her, she withheld approval and demanded more. At 59, he'd finally given out.

"Dad, it's Johnny," I whispered. "Can you hear me?"

No response. Although the plastic tent between us hampered my voice, it was his coma that really held him captive and mute. Mom and I asked the doctor for the oxygen tent to be removed a few days later because it wasn't helping him. We wanted to spare Dad further life preservation measures and let nature take its course. The doctor nodded in agreement and gave us his best wishes.

So it came to pass on a dismal rainy Sunday—November 14, 1965—nothing stood between Dad and death. To us it was just another visiting day like the hundreds before it. Mom rode with me to Methodist Hospital in my used '58 Chevy tan sedan and sat in a corner of Dad's room, sewing quietly on her needlework. Tommy and his wife Carolyn had departed earlier for Wisconsin where their teaching jobs awaited them the next morning. Dave and his new girlfriend were expected to arrive soon. I stood at Dad's bedside humming his favorite song from his boyhood years, "A Simple Melody." He'd played and sung it many times, and I hoped it soothed him now. Lately I hadn't seen so much as his eyes blink, and I waited minute by minute for his final breath.

You can imagine my surprise when his head arched upward and his eyes opened wide. A smile even cracked his face as he looked straight up at something invisible—invisible to me but clearly not to him. I reared back, speechless, witnessing what seemed a miracle. In complete silence, his eyes shined with a supernatural radiance and his smile broadened. It was as though he had made contact with a divine, unseen presence, one that apparently nurtured and welcomed him right at that moment.

I leaned closer, less than two feet away, and observed his eyes close in complete peace. His last breath came with a slow sigh.

The message that seared into my psyche was:

> *Johnny, I've gone to a place of peace, rest, and comfort—*
> *have no fear, no doubt, no worry. Tell others.*

Mom looked up from her needlework because neither she nor I heard his breathing anymore. My eyes went to hers and, by eye contact alone, *we knew.* "It's over, Mom," I said aloud. She dropped her needlework and came over to his bed, glanced at his face, touched his hand, then burst into tears.

"Toby! No, Toby! Don't leave us! Toby, come back!" she sobbed.

I burst into my own fiery blast of emotions, feeling a raging inferno inside, but cold as a glacier outside. Anger, grief, pity, despair coursed through my veins. My blood pressure shot sky high, my heart plunged deep into sorrow.

Dad, I never knew you! Does this have to be the end? DAD, I NEVER KNEW YOU!

An orderly in a white uniform entered the room, and I stood back as he hailed a nurse. Why was I the family member who received the gift of seeing Dad's earthly farewell from inches away? Why was I there to see this wondrous moment? Whatever it was, I sensed it was my privilege to witness the peace that finally covered his gaunt, anguished face. Somebody had to be a witness, I surmised, and somehow I was chosen.

At the funeral, a massive sense of loss weighed on us all. At some metaphysical level, a seething volcano erupted in me. So much that needed to be said had never been said. Dad was a man of very, very few words. Seldom had we spent time together as father and son: once attending a pro baseball game together, once fishing for lake trout, once horseback riding on vacation—that was about it in twenty years. He'd been there for my hockey games, yes, but I never *knew* him! And he never knew *me!* Now it was too late. Something inside me cracked and I held back fiery tears of resentment. While Mom greeted the dozens of close friends and television fans who paid their respects, I observed her as if through a haze. She had done so much to strain his health and, I believed, prematurely end his life.

I still hated her. As much as ever. Murderous hate.

On a snowy Wednesday, we all stood at his graveside and listened to a minister dedicate Dad's remains to God. The high-sounding eulogy seemed like a huge sham because our family had never attended church a day in our lives. Fine for Rosie that she believed in God, but at that moment, I sure didn't. Dave's and my high-school pals Bobby Harris, Jay Wilson, Rick Killdare, and Dave Rydel stood beside us. Moments later, Mom put a rose on Dad's casket and it was lowered into the grave. The ceremony ended. We trudged away, wounded, exhausted, downtrodden.

Death wasn't finished yet with the Prins, however. Not quite. My secret murderous urges toward Mom kept boiling hotter and hotter. I seethed at any little thing she said or did in the weeks after Dad's departure. She adjusted to becoming a widow, and I found her loyal efforts at her full-time job commendable; but medical and funeral bills meant we owed more than $25,000. The sole major asset remaining was the Parkside Circle house. So the day came all too soon when she sold our cherished home and we moved down to a smaller, more affordable, rundown bungalow on a deceptively nice-sounding street named Maple Ridge Avenue. With Tommy married and living in Wisconsin, Dave and I again, as always, shared a bedroom.

Once again Dave and I tolerated another round of Mom's fix-up and redecorating projects, on top of hauling carloads of "carryables" (anything besides the heaviest furniture and appliances) in order to cut down on paying professional movers. Four months after New Years 1966, my murderous rage finally boiled over when Mom got spring fever and insisted that I ignore my college homework so that I could build shelves for her geraniums.

"Mom!" I protested. "I just finished wallpapering your bedroom a week ago. I deserve a break, okay?"

"Johnny, drop everything and come down here!"

But no, I would not. It was time for a standoff. She came to our bedroom where I was studying and demanded that I listen to her plans. I'd tolerated her inflated sense of entitlement, so evident in her bossy orders, and despised her thinking of me as her fix-it boy more than ever. She hadn't softened a bit, hadn't learned a thing since Dad's passing.

"Johnny, come downstairs *now!* Don't make me say it again!"

Enough was enough. "I'll hear what you have to say," I bargained, "but I'll get to it some other time."

"Okay," she replied. "Come and take a look."

I followed her downstairs to a damp corner of the basement where she rattled off instructions. I felt sick of acting one way (agreeable) while feeling another (antagonistic), of appearing cooperative when really feeling combative, so this time my emotions erupted out of control and I lost it, no longer able to contain my pent-up homicidal fury. While her back was turned, I reached for a nearby folding chair and lifted it to use as a weapon. I meant to club her with it until she lost life and died. My mind instantly flooded with scenes from the awful days when we moved the birch trees, from the days of tiling the rec-room floor, from our 14th birthday hauling those god-awful paving stones from Lyndale Avenue, from . . .

Death's door opened and I saw Mom in her casket!

Suddenly, *my* future flashed before me, and I grasped the idea that *by destroying her I would be destroying myself*. By killing her, I would be ruining my future and putting to death my hopes for a happier life. Before she turned around, I lowered the chair and charged up the stairs for the door.

"Where are you going, Johnny?" she demanded. "I'm not done talking to you!"

"Oh yes, you are! I hate your guts, Mom, and I'm not coming back! I'm leaving!"

I never saw her stunned reaction, because the door slammed behind me on my way out. I drove away and came back a day later when I knew she was working, then cleared out all my clothes and books and did not return to that bungalow again.

But the murderous fury I'd kept secret was on the loose—no longer a secret—and fiercer than ever.

Part 2

> **"It is only those who know neither an inner call nor an outer doctrine whose plight truly is desperate."**
>
> *Joseph Campbell*
> *The Hero with a Thousand Faces*

∽ *Chapter Six*

Breaking Free Away from Home

The whiskey flowed from the brown bottle and tumbled over the ice cubes in my glass, making a cheerful *clug-clug-clug* sound. I lifted the glass to my lips and swallowed the amber fluid, swirling it over my tongue and savoring its musky flavor. A blast of fire descended down my throat, followed by a pleasant tingle in my face and scalp that felt like a healing tonic to my jagged nerves. I took another drink and the numbing tingle occurred again. I looked out the window of my one-room attic flat at the small wedge of Kansas City skyline visible to my view.

I was alone. I was edgy. I was drunk. Again.

My slide into addiction didn't feel like secret-keeping at first, nor did it even seem addicting. Drinking alone didn't require that I keep it a secret because nobody was present to observe or disapprove of it and it wasn't a compulsive ritual—yet. I was 24, it was August 1968, and I'd recently graduated from the University of Minnesota with a bachelor's degree in English and Theatre Arts, then hitchhiked 500 miles south to start my new film career in Missouri. I'd gone from drinking beer in college and in the army to hard liquor, because the numbing effects of straight booze worked faster and stronger than beer.

In the past two months, I'd been hired as a 16mm film editor at Gorden Film Labs in Kansas City for $72 a week. A large Midwestern production company, Gorden Labs specialized in industrial films for clients like Caterpillar, Eli Lilly, and John Deere corporations. At the time I had no car, so after my interview I'd taken the local bus to a residential neighborhood about three miles away. I then walked the streets carrying my suitcase until I found a "Room for Rent" sign. The elderly widow who lived on the main floor of the large, three-story home welcomed me when I rang her doorbell. We climbed up three flights of stairs and she showed me the tiny but furnished space. Clean and quiet, it contained three slanted sections with an easy chair and lamp, a sink and refrigerator, and a bed.

"Where's the bathroom?" I inquired.

Mrs. Russell, the kindly widow, informed me, "You'll need to share the bathroom on the second floor with my two other tenants, both spinster ladies."

This seemed awkward, but acceptable. "How much is the rent?"

"Ten dollars a week," Mrs. Russell answered.

I agreed and we shook hands. I paid her the first week's rent, then went to the corner liquor store where I bought a quart of Jim Beam whisky to celebrate my good fortune. The racially mixed community surrounding Mrs. Russell's house provided a Laundromat, a reasonably priced supermarket, a drugstore, and the nearby bus line.

My appreciation of the pain-numbing effects of alcohol and the ritual of drinking alone became rooted that day. My pain no longer centered mainly around Mom, whom I'd avoided over the past two years while finishing college, but from the haunting loss of Dad, the recent breakup with my fiancée, and the nagging sense that I was defective and ill-equipped for life's journey.

On long evenings by myself, a pattern developed: I rode the bus home from Gorden Labs, stopped at the corner liquor store for a bottle of whisky, went to my attic refuge, and drank. And smoked Old Gold cigarettes. And looked out the window. And repeated the process the next evening, and the next—sometimes knocking down more than half a quart and passing out before bedtime.

Chief among the pains that jangled my nerves was the sad demise of my just-ended, year-long love affair with Karen Iverson, an attractive, outgoing 22-year-old nurse. I absolutely adored her looks and vivacious personality and felt pleased that we made a handsome-looking couple. She cared little for academic subjects, but we got along great in the backseat of my '58 Chevy sedan. Our stolen hours of mutual delight offered the exact counterpoint I needed to my college schedule; we petted heavily and really struggled to keep from "going all the way" for fear of pregnancy. This temptation dampened our relationship often, but we stayed true to our vow to wait until marriage. Love and respect grew into full-blown wedding plans.

Our engagement split up, though, because the closer the wedding date approached, the more I felt pressured to get married too soon—too soon after Dad's death, too soon after getting my bachelor's degree, too soon after tasting independence for the first time in my life. I ached from profound sadness over the breakup, because I cared for Karen so deeply. In her arms, I experienced the same wide-open acceptance as from Sheryl and the same blissful connection as from Rosie. But Karen just couldn't tolerate waiting another year before I found my wings professionally and financially.

"All my life I've marched to somebody else's drumbeat," I told her the final time we talked. My grief stabbed at me and I couldn't hold back showing it.

"But, Johnny, we've told everybody we're getting married this summer!"

"Yes, but I've got to be free for a while, Karen, don't you see? I just can't jump from sixteen years of school *and* working full time *and* all those ugly years when Dad was dying *and* having to attend National Guard meetings straight into marriage."

"But we can't back out now! We've told everybody!" Her natural blond hair obscured her pretty face and the tears streaming down her cheeks. "We can't put it off till next year!"

"I love you, Karen, but *now* is not the time—and time is all I'm asking for. Instead of settling down, I need some room. Some time to breathe. Some space to find out who I am. A few months not to feel so crowded."

"I'm not waiting, Johnny. We're already committed. It's now or never . . ."

With those stern words, we parted ways. She turned hysterical and wouldn't let me touch her. She splurged on a month-long spree of redoing her hair, buying new clothes, drinking heavily, and staying incommunicado.

When Mom heard the news about our breakup, she cursed and called me a fool: "You'll regret this stupid decision, Johnny. A girl as nice as Karen doesn't come along every day." David was far more sympathetic; Tommy hardly muttered a word. By June 1968, four months later, Karen had moved to Colorado and started living with her sister where, I'd heard since, she was dating a new beau.

Now in my attic lair, I felt intensely lonely for Karen and drank more.

Pain also came in different shapes and sizes, including the months of depressing geographic separation from Dave. Our familiar "we twins" bond felt stretched and broken. Since his marriage the year before to the sole girlfriend he'd ever dated and the birth of their son, Andrew, I realized we'd already separated psychologically—two inseparable souls traveling divergent paths.

Feeling lonely for him also, I drank more.

Ruminating about these rueful events, staring out my attic window, inhaling Old Golds, and drinking Jim Beam, I experienced a wave of euphoria from the alcohol that anesthetized these unwelcome emotions. The whiskey offered an escape from the edgy uneasiness for a few hours. Besides mistaking intensity for intimacy, I was also being initiated into the lie of addiction: that something *outside* me could fix what was wrong *inside* me. Greedily, I guzzled more to hide from the clash of memories. While I was happy and excited to be independent and living on my own in a new town, especially to break free from Mom, I questioned my ability to guide myself through the uncertainties ahead. The drinking helped numb my anxious qualms.

On the job at my editing desk after a night of heavy drinking, my head would throb and my mouth would taste as though it was stuffed with cotton balls. During the first month after starting at Gorden, I'd fended off boredom while waiting for my boss to assign me a project. Why boredom? I'd trained with each of the eight editors in the department and was ready, willing, and able to plunge ahead on real film-editing tasks. But my boss, Henry Mayes, a milquetoast of a supervisor in a starched white shirt who was nearing retirement, didn't agree. Straight-laced Henry still hadn't accepted me, due, it appeared, to my having been interviewed and hired by an executive whom everybody, particularly Henry, despised. Confirmation of this came to me late one morning from Sam Keissel, a well-respected senior editor in his early thirties, who whispered the rumor into my ear and urged me to take bold action.

"Take a hint, John," Sam said. "Stand up for yourself. Walk into Henry's office after lunch and demand a project."

"Really?"

"Really."

All during lunch I worked up my courage, determined to overcome office politics, grumbling to myself about such petty obstacles. I recalled the "night of divine calling," a midnight incident in Rosie Kowalsek's living room after Dad's death when the inspiration for my life's purpose as a filmmaker surfaced. Rosie and I had been talking about God after everyone in her family had gone to bed, and she asked me, "So what do you think God wants you to do with your life, John?"

I stammered, then replied, "My college theatre classes challenged me and were more exciting than English classes. Getting to direct and act in student plays pumped me up more than reading classics or writing essays." I told her how the outlet for my delayed dramatic talents had finally appeared and how audiences' applause and professors' straight A's confirmed what I'd known in my gut all along. I babbled enthusiastically to her about making movies, like the many memorable ones I'd seen.

"I've always loved movies and television, Rosie, even more than theatre. So, as a movie fan, I think the possibilities for my life and a career in film are very exciting."

Exactly at that moment, a supernatural "spell" came over me. It paralyzed my body—literally—for the next twenty minutes. Unable to talk or move, I stared at Rosie, who grasped what was happening and waited patiently. I felt a flood of warm, benevolent feelings, as if from a divine force. *As if God was talking to me!* The flood of feelings overflowed like ever-mounting ocean waves that seemed to lift me, leaving me limp and serene.

When the paralysis faded, I thanked Rosie for her understanding and for nurturing me spiritually. "You must be God's guardian angel for me."

"He loves you, John, remember? And He wants only the best for you."

Now back at Gorden Labs, I felt supercharged about persuading Henry Mayes and walked straight into his office. "Henry, I want a project," I declared. "It's time."

Henry looked up, taken aback. He glanced at me skeptically. "I'm not sure you're ready, John."

"I *am* ready, Henry. Just give me a chance to prove it, please."

He looked down, apparently wishing for me to go away. Bolstered by Sam's hint and the reminder of my "divine calling," I stepped closer. "Give me *one* chance to prove it, Mr. Mayes. If I goof up, you can fire me. Or I'll resign."

Henry paused. Then, before he could respond, another voice interrupted us: "I've got just the project for John that'll fit the bill, Henry."

Henry and I both turned. There in the doorway stood Sam Keissel.

Henry asked, "Is it something he can manage on his own, Sam?"

"Yes, if you just give the word. It's challenging, but not too difficult."

Henry cleared his throat. "Well, then . . . possibly. But only if you watch him like a hawk, Sam, and don't do any of the work yourself."

"Fine by me," Sam affirmed.

Henry's eyes penetrated mine. "Are you happy now?"

"Yes!" I exclaimed. "I'll get on it right away!"

Ten minutes later I was cutting, splicing, and matching film-edge numbers at Sam's editing desk. My work on his Caterpillar training film developed a rhythm of its own, and soon I was sailing along, making decisions without asking for Sam's input. Much like the years before when I enjoyed making things, my hands and fingers moved with their own logic and wisdom, maneuvering the film and feeding it through the splicer, every movement smooth and fluent. I kept whispering to Sam my thanks and appreciation that he'd come to my aid, but he merely shrugged and kept his attention on the task.

"Do this one right, John," he whispered, "and Henry'll get off your back for good."

In this manner I finished up Sam's training film the next day to Henry's beady-eyed satisfaction. Henry reluctantly gave me another film assignment, and I delivered another quality job, a solo effort without anyone's supervision. By the next week, I'd earned a starting position on Henry's roster, and the remaining editors, following Sam's and Henry's lead, accepted me on their team. They even invited me out for drinks after work one evening and congratulated me for toughing it out.

"We knew Henry hadn't hired y'all, and that was a big strike against you," admitted the chief perpetrator, Dixie Lee Cartwell, a large-boned woman in her late twenties with artificially blond hair and a southern accent. "Y'all came in 'pre-approved' by a bigwig and we had no say-so," she explained, apologizing for their lack of friendliness.

I challenged her. "That's it? Nothing about me personally?"

"Oh, we thought you were some uppity northerner at first," she sniffed, "but we gradually changed our minds."

"That's comforting. I didn't know I was a Yankee who'd invaded the Confederacy!"

We laughed and dropped our grudges that night, and my star rose quickly at Gorden from then on. Rounds of drinks paid for by the team made up for their rude snobbery. When I spotted Sam later at the bar and asked him why he had helped me, he said, "Henry was just being an old fuddy-duddy. I could see you had more talent than any three of us put together. Simple as that."

What nobody knew when we said good night was that my drinking did not end there. Back in my attic flat, I poured myself a stiff whisky-and-seven to celebrate. Regardless of how high or low I felt emotionally, I found drinking in private enhanced the highs and deadened the lows—at least for the hour or so when the alcohol actively circulated in my blood stream. Essentially, drinking in secret medicated the conflicts rumbling in my soul and numbed the distress of my self-doubt.

I pondered why Dave never developed these characteristics. Perhaps it was because he accepted reality more readily and detached from it

The underlying dynamics of addiction gradually gained ground over me, but I had no conscious knowledge of it then. Looking back, the dynamics stand out clearly:

✳ First, *resentments*—reliving past hurts in the present—hounded me. I nursed grudges toward Mom and still grieved over Dad, as well as stung from old hurts by Sheryl and authority figures like Coach Mack, Harlan Nash, and army drill instructors. Later, while attending Alcoholics Anonymous meetings, I would discover that resentments are the number-one destroyers of people who drink. More than anything else, resentments generate powerful negative emotions such as anger. Another thirty years would pass before these resentments lost their power.

Are you reliving past hurts in the present? If so, can you identify *why* you are angry?

✳ Second, I was *isolating.* My drinking intensified whenever I spent hours alone. I loved the wonderful freedom of making my own decisions, the independence; and I had never enjoyed the kind of privacy I had now. Such quiet hours became a pleasant diversion, and boozing became a pleasant way to fill the quiet time. Secretly, I was also taking advantage of the low visibility of indulging in a vice.

Are you isolating yourself in similar ways? Are you avoiding particular people or circumstances, then taking advantage of the low visibility to indulge in some secret activity?

✳ Third, *my histrionic and hysterical reactions* ruled me. Partly learned from Mom's open displays of temper, partly as an exaggerated way of responding to life itself, drama and crisis were ways I'd learned to express myself. Internally I'd become accustomed to the peaks and plunges of emotion I felt daily, even hourly—all magnified by more alcohol.

Do you find that your reactions to things are exaggerated and greater than the situations warrant? Are these emotions magnified by alcohol or drugs?

✳ Fourth, *delusional thinking* had formed a set of irrational beliefs. I believed the Lie of Addiction, that "something outside me could fix what was wrong or missing inside me." After being convinced of my calling to a film career, I'd already hatched a larger dream to make movies in Hollywood and—why stop there?—to win an Oscar. Excessive boozing inflated my unrealistic expectations and helped convince me that I could reverse ugly reality and salve my hurts by achieving sensational goals. I was setting myself up for failed expectations.

without external crutches or compulsive activities to alter his moods
or thinking. His earlier episodes of heavy drinking and occasional
gambling at card games had tapered off entirely. What made identical
twins behave so similarly on many things, but differ so strongly on others? He'd never touched a cigarette and only drank nowadays when the
occasion called for it. He'd tried marijuana once and never smoked it
again. His response to Mom in Chippewa Hills had been closer to stoic
irritation than rabid hatred, as evidenced by his shock when he learned
of my homicidal urges, although he felt sympathetic.

Perhaps it had something to do with his being right-handed (that is
left-brained; more logical, factual, sequential) and my being left-handed
(that is *right-brained;* more impulsive, fanciful, random). Whatever his
circumstances, he seemed impervious to resentments, histrionic reactions, exaggerated emotions, and delusional thinking. He was grounded
and steady. I envied him.

My continuing duty in the National Guard required a transfer to Fort
Riley, Kansas, where I served wounded Vietnam veterans in a hospital
ward one weekend a month and two weeks during the summer. The
soldiers arrived with amputated arms or legs, often suffering from severe
burns and Asian diseases. Theirs was the ugly reality of war inflicted on
their bodies and souls.

As an orderly, I offered bedside care: changing bandages, emptying
bedpans, pouring drinking water, delivering mail, adjusting TV sets.
Many times I felt justifiably disliked because I was whole, healthy, good-
humored, and the patients were not. They had served and suffered; I had
lucked out and kept clear of harm's way. My wholeness was a reminder
of their sacrifice. Selfishly speaking, I felt somewhat haunted that I'd
taken a coward's way out patriotically. I smoldered inside about the war's

devastation on our young men, our country, our morals. Maddened, I watched earnestly the protest marches and demonstrations on TV that mirrored my own indignation.

Back on the job, a new relationship at Gorden Labs changed the direction of my life. A new hire from Chicago, a long-haired hippie, arrived at the editing table next to mine to replace an editor who had taken maternity leave. Jim Harwell and I recognized each other as kindred spirits from the first handshake. This pleased Henry, who'd taken a chance on hiring him. Our ready acceptance of each other somehow helped thaw the departmental deepfreeze even further, and Henry positively glowed at seeing the department's more buoyant morale.

A few days later Jim asked me, "Have you got space for a roommate, John?"

I felt protective of my long-sought, short-lived privacy, and suggested a week-long trial run. I also sensed something vaguely precarious about saying yes, but went ahead anyway. Jim camped out on the floor of my flat in his sleeping bag for three nights. Nothing precarious occurred until, near bedtime the third night, he introduced me to a new phenomenon on the national scene—marijuana. "Go ahead, John, try it."

I stared at the hand-rolled joint he'd licked with his tongue and now offered to me.

"Uh, this is my place, Jim, and I don't like the idea of anybody smelling it up. We could get arrested and go to jail."

He chuckled. "Hardly. But I respect your hesitation. I can leave if you want and find somewhere else to smoke it. Don't feel you have to. That's cool."

I held up my hand, gesturing for him to stay put. Jim turned out to love grass and taught me to smoke my first joint—adding to my growing list of addictions. Its hallucinatory and time-warping effects made me feel silly and I giggled a lot, the kind of mood swing I came to delight in. Turned on by my first puffs of weed, I craved it from the first. Because of Jim, a new counterculture lifestyle also opened up to me. We visited hippie pads where his college friends lived at a nearby university. We wore bell bottoms and beads, "got loaded" and "crashed." Because of Jim's influence, I grew my hair long to shoulder-length, reveled in rebellion, flaunted fashion customs, and thumbed my nose at the Establishment. In just two months, I became a confirmed pot-smoker *and* drinker.

Burning to advance my calling, I asked Jim to help me shoot my first film. He agreed and suggested that I scale down my grandiose plans of filming in several locations to one simple day in a neighborhood park.

We borrowed a 16mm silent camera from Gorden and spent a Saturday in late autumn filming a five-minute fantasy, which I later titled *Hitchhiker*. Casting myself in the role of a luckless young man hitching rides, I walked by a playground and paused to remedy the character's frustrations by playing like a six-year-old on the swing, slide, and teeter-totter. A kind of stop-and-smell-the-roses message.

Jim and I worked well together, collaborating on camera setups and in other creative ways that confirmed we *were* true kindred spirits. Back at my editing table, I stole numerous hours after work and on weekends cutting the show. Meanwhile word spread that "John is making a movie." I went to Henry and reassured him that I was not shirking clients' projects, and he actually took pride in the fact that one of his charges was sprouting wings as a filmmaker. He even made it possible for me to record a sound track of children's songs in Gorden's sound department. The screening of the finished work turned out to be a success, applauded by Henry Mayes himself, as well as the gang of editors that took Jim and me out afterwards for drinks to celebrate.

"John, you did it!" they all toasted.

We showed the film numerous times at smoke-filled film societies and on a local television talk show. My first venture into filmmaking earned me new respect and stature. The film was a smash. I was in heaven. I felt convinced that my career was headed in the right direction and my calling was assured.

Was it just beginner's luck? The first sign of a divinely inspired career? I chose to think God had a hand in it and felt waves of overwhelming gratitude. For days I dreamed about new projects. Maybe Rosie was right about God after all.

One icy, cold March day, eight months after starting at Gorden Labs, another new relationship changed the direction of my life. Henry assigned me to edit a film for a visiting client from New York City, Maggie Claudel. By now Henry's confidence in me had multiplied because my work never came back from the printer. I was now one of Henry's aces, along with Sam and Dixie Lee.

Spunky and single, Maggie was intelligent, genteel, and hot for sex. Jim had agreed to crash at a hippie college friend's so she and I could be alone, and in the span of 48 hours, we'd edited her documentary show, gone out to dinner, and coupled in my humble bed—a sort of free love, overnight sexual spree. The aftertaste in my emotions about the loss of my virginity amounted to the effects of mild intoxication with the thought, "So *this* is what everybody's talked about all these years."

As Maggie rushed off to her plane, bombarding me with kisses, she promised to call and made me promise to as well. "I'll be back next month, John. We have to repeat this hundreds of times!" Dazed, I waved good-bye and realized that I'd just met someone more histrionic/exaggerated/delusional than myself.

It all happened so fast, I hardly had time to zip up my pants.

Shortly afterwards, another young lady crossed my path and changed—really, *really* changed—the direction of my life. On a camera shoot in Gorden's studios one Saturday, a pixylike crew member of the Kansas City Ballet, our client, commanded my attention. As the assistant director, my duties involved walking from set to set, supervising the placement of scenery and props. Sitting on the floor of a modern set, draping black fabric over the wheels of an aluminum scaffolding, sat the cheeriest person I'd seen all morning. She was cute and attractive. Infatuated, I observed her, amused and enchanted by her whimsical energy. Abruptly, she looked up at me.

Startled, I blurted the only words that came to mind: "Haven't I seen you somewhere before?"

Laughing, she said no.

My cheeks turned rosy red at hearing myself say the oldest pickup line ever. "Ahhh ..." I stammered, "are you sure? You look familiar."

Laughing even louder, she replied, "Sorry. But nice try anyway." She smiled, returned to her chore, and that seemed to be the end of it. Later in the afternoon, during the shooting of the modern dance segment when dancers performed like gymnasts on the scaffolding, I chatted with her again between takes. "So what do you do when you're not volunteering for the ballet?"

"I work at the Natural History Museum."

I drew back, surprised. "As a secretary or office assistant?" I said, but wished instantly that I'd kept this thought to myself.

She appeared beset and sighed. "I'm the curator of anthropology."

My eyes widened. She looked at me for a few seconds, her eyes twinkling now, evidently aware of the impact of her statement. I couldn't hide that it had hooked me.

When the camera crew "wrapped" at the end of the day, I summoned my courage, walked up to her, and asked for a date.

"Sorry, I'm already busy tomorrow night," came her reply.

One tough lady, I said to myself. Spinning on my heel, slightly miffed, I started to leave when she cleared her throat and added, "But how about some time *earlier?*"

I spun back around. "Hey, sure!"

"Say tomorrow afternoon around two?"

"Ahh . . . you bet. How about the Nelson Art Gallery? There's a Picasso show going on there." In seconds we'd arranged our first date for 2:00 P.M. the next day at Kansas City's premier art institution. I learned her name, Susan Troeller, and said good-bye, then skipped away with a lighter step in my shoes, humming to myself the familiar refrain of the then-popular number-one national hit tune, "Kansas City":[1]

I'm going to Kansas City,
Kansas City here I come,
they've got some pretty little women there
and I'm gonna get me one.

Susan's and my date went off without a hitch: a tour of the gallery, easy conversation, a light snack in the gardens. The message? We seemed compatible. Thanks also to Dixie Lee's gracious offer to lend me her aging Corvair, I drove to pick up Susan and made a good first impression. Within a week Susan and I were seeing each other regularly. She enjoyed hearing about my work at Gorden, and I learned more about her job at the Natural History Museum.

Soon we went on dates in her '68 Chevy Nova, and I heard about her growing-up years in New Jersey as well as her recent breaking off an engagement with her fiancé; and she learned about my growing-up years in Minnesota as well as the recent breaking off of Karen's and my engagement. We took long walks together, ate and drank in restaurants and bars, but my pot-smoking I kept a carefully held secret. Within a month, we were spending evenings at her apartment two miles from mine, and one night she visited my pad to meet Jim Harwell.

That night Jim rolled a joint and the secret was out. He politely offered it to her and she politely refused; then minutes later, she gave it a try and seemed to enjoy it. The next evening as we were necking on the couch in her apartment, I declared, "I love you." She cooed back, "I love you too, John." We kissed deeply and made love for the first time.

With Maggie calling me every few days, however, things got complicated. One weekend Maggie flew to Kansas City for a surprise visit, and Susan found out about the "other woman." Seeing the handwriting on the wall, Susan put her feelings to me bluntly: "It's up to you, John. It's either she or I, but you can't have both. If she's the one, just say so. I'll blend back into the woodwork."

"No, no," I replied. "Don't do that!"

"Well, your seeing both of us isn't fair. So decide one way or the other. Call me when you've made up your mind. Meanwhile, I've got some thinking to do."

My two-timing dating pattern had finally caught up with me. Susan's protest of my dishonest dating behavior posed the first major threat to our relationship, a direct consequence of my secret-keeping patterns. It was true that I'd carried on with Maggie while dating Susan, dividing my time (and psyche) between both, and keeping each unaware of the other. I'd talk "bedroom babble" on the phone long distance with Maggie, then hang up and ask Susan to spend the night together in bed. During the months I'd gone steady with Sheryl, Rosie, and Karen, I had been faithful, but I'd never made a you're-the-one-and-only pact with other girls I'd casually dated.

The summer before meeting Karen, for instance, I'd three-timed Barb, Sandy, and Diane, never spilling the beans to any of them about the other two. I reasoned, "Who needs to know?" A sort of *Playboy* mentality guided me. To me casual dating implied variety, not fidelity; romantic experimentation, not sexual exclusivity. It appealed to my lower nature, that invisible place where pride/envy/lust/ego reside. I tried to outwardly live up to the opposite, my higher nature, by working hard at part-time jobs, studying diligently, doing homework, making things as I'd done as a kid, graduating from college with a 3.2 GPA, then following my calling to make films and staying faithful to Sheryl, Rosie, and Karen.

I felt torn having to walk a tightrope between two worlds—jumping back and forth between risky adventures and close calls in one domain versus hard-won grades and bona fide professional achievements in the other. Switching back and forth made me feel a measure of security though, because of always having an out. My survival at that time depended on having a safe place to hide, a safe place to "get lost." Whenever the world's harsh forces bore down on me, my emotions spun out of control and I sought comfort and escape in the secret reality of my double life.

Now came the test. Susan had demanded that I decide. Her ultimatum challenged my two-timing tendencies. As I'd done by renouncing window-peeping and running naked in the woods, never returning to them again, I resolved that it must be time to renounce my two-timing dating behavior and stay true to one person only. Susan was worth the sacrifice, I decided—although it felt more like losing than choosing, making it quite the sacrifice.

"Maggie's just a fling," I told Susan. "You're the real thing."

Maggie's spitfire sexuality amounted to a superficial fling, I explained, compared to Susan's more inviting and long-term romantic attractions. With Maggie I'd only given away my body, not my heart. I declared my loyalty to Susan and promised to inform Maggie, which I did in a letter. Susan accepted all this and set aside her qualms. In the process, I came nose to nose with my duplicity and believed it was all finally behind me—because I had said so. Back then I thought that by saying something was tamed, it meant that it *was* tamed.

Four months of courtship followed. On October 18, 1969, Susan and I were married in her hometown church in New Jersey, a white-steepled structure from the Revolutionary-War period. Her quiet ways were so unlike Mom's, something I admired. Susan meekly asked for what she wanted instead of insisting that others should be obligated to fulfill her whims. Her demeanor, a reflection of her upbringing and East-Coast etiquette, evinced more formality and propriety than mine, although by no means did she come off as straight-laced or lacking in charm.

Her parents made a lackluster impression on me, due largely to their stiff provincial pride in being sophisticates from the East Coast, as well as their ingrained drinking habits, which I saw hints of then, but learned later they'd curbed because of the importance of the wedding. Bill Troeller, a chemist at a global oil corporation, clearly idolized his only child and put her on a pedestal. Martha Troeller, a behind-the-scenes homemaker, quietly endured her husband's temperamental moods and put Susan's needs first. In time I discovered their being on good behavior masked a rat's nest of secrets and wreckage from stolen hours they'd spent a lifetime living out and which belied their respectable facade.

The new Mr. and Mrs. Prin relocated to Minneapolis. Mom, whom I'd barely been on speaking terms with since slamming the door behind me three years earlier, hosted a grand reception for us. Susan adjusted quickly to the new environs and fit right in with our family. She told me stories of her parents and upbringing that turned out to be similar to our kind of craziness. We worked hard at our new jobs, she as a curator at the art museum in St. Paul and I as a film editor at a production company across the river in Minneapolis. We drove to Kansas City to move back what few furnishings we had, said tearful good-byes to friends, then relocated to a tiny old house in residential Minneapolis that rented for $175 a month. Then a belated wedding present arrived in the mail, a welcome surprise from the National Guard, my honorable discharge.

In time, pot-smoking became the norm for both of us (compulsive for me) and prompted an "us versus them" family dynamic; no one ac-cepted this behavior and it developed into a double-life that Susan and I both carried on. Mom kept bugging me about the length of my hair and criticized Susan's miniskirts; and Mom's sharp tongue castigated our "hippie clothes that smell so awful" (from marijuana or hashish smoke). But it didn't matter because being husband and wife meant Susan and I answered to ourselves first and could shrug off Mom's bossy authority.

In a smoky-hazed state of satisfaction, I pondered my good fortune. My days of isolation had ended now that matrimony bound us together, my resentments remained at rest, my delusional thinking had retreated to the shadows, my grief over Dad no longer upset me, my two-timing dating pattern remained in check, my job presented gratifying artistic challenges, my calling accorded some measure of assurance, my emerg-ing addictions still served emotional needs without consequences piling up, my "twin time" with David existed again, my emotional distance from Mom stayed firmly established, and there existed—just maybe—a God who busied Himself setting things right after all.

By the dawn of the '70s, my double-mindedness lingered dormant and my secret-keeping seemed firmly behind me. I was acting the same way I was feeling, and reality came first, appearances second.

I stood on the edge of the future, poised to soar.

> **"Turn your face to the Great West and there build up your home and fortune."**
>
> *Horace Greeley*
> *New Yorker weekly column*

〜 *Chapter Seven*

Hollywood or Bust

The sweet aroma of expensive hashish wafted up our noses. The Beatles' *Sergeant Pepper* played on the hi-fi. Candles and incense burned nearby. Susan and I, now oldie-weds of a year, sat drinking wine and passing a hash pipe with our hippie pal, Mark Brandow. We lounged on cushions in Mark's crash pad located in the artists' quarter of Minneapolis overlooking the Mississippi River. Susie giggled, having a great time hearing Mark's and my stories and jokes.

Mark and I were reminiscing about our pranks and practical jokes as high-school buddies, especially when on ski trips. The bonding power of doing mood-altering chemicals functioned in full force, creating a warm feeling of belonging the more stoned we got. The combined power of the two drugs lowered our inhibitions and generated a serious case of the giggles. Nothing, absolutely nothing, felt addictive or destructive about this magical moment.

"Can you believe how brainwashed people are?" Mark asked, having just told us colorful details about his two years in Malaysia serving in the Peace Corps. "The only thing most people ever do is follow a stupid, predictable script. They go from high school to college to working at some job to getting married and having kids to paying for a home with a 30-year mortgage to sitting in a rocking chair at retirement. How boring!"

"Right on," I replied, taking the hash pipe passed to me and puffing on it. "They're like robots, blissfully unaware of more exciting choices."

"Like lemmings," Susan added, taking the pipe from me and puffing on it.

Mark quietly nodded his head. "Yep. They practically trip over one another running for the edge of the cliff, where they fall headlong into the sea and drown."

We talked in this vein until Mark got up to flip the record on the hi-fi.

"When I lived in Taiwan as a college exchange student," Susie added, puffing away, "the people did everything based on their ancestors, and their customs were so different. The Taiwanese managed to be happy with so few material comforts. Compared to Americans, they were poor. I'd do anything to travel there again. They seemed so much more contented than we are."

These idealistic ideas and glowing memories, combined with Mark's lively adventures, triggered my desire to travel. Except for our paying jobs and a rented home, Susan and I fit the hippie counterculture scene more than the Establishment's mold. "Wouldn't it be something if we could just pick up and travel like that?" I suggested. "Not when we're old or retired, but right now."

Mark nodded, took a long drag on the hash pipe, then handed me a baggie containing Mexican marijuana, so I could roll a joint. "What's to keep us from hitchhiking overseas together?" he asked. "I'm headed for Amsterdam and France in two months to see Peace Corps friends, then on to Africa. Like, what if we three met afterwards this summer in Morocco or Cairo?"

Susan and I glanced at each other, tantalized.

"Let's take him up on it," I said. Noticing Susan's face turn incredulous, I asked, "Well, why not? Before we settle down and have kids, how about it?"

Her eyes grew round, then she sat straight up. "Sure, why not!"

Our dream to go traveling together took form in the next few minutes. I wagered $25 with Mark that we'd meet him in Tangiers, Morocco, on the upcoming Fourth of July. He shook hands, assuring us that the then-current trend of "Europe on five dollars a day" was feasible, especially by backpacking—no respectable hippies dared travel otherwise.

"Love, peace, and flower power!" we all exclaimed.

Back home, Susan and I pinched ourselves to make sure we'd really made such outrageous plans. We vowed to continue building our careers and to save as much income as possible until our departure six months away. We kept it secret from both of our families for as long as we could, knowing we'd take considerable flak for exercising our freedom once they heard about it. They just weren't into wild, extravagant ideas.

At work my new boss seemed to appreciate my contributions as a film editor and encouraged me to collaborate closely with clients, although he kept nagging me to cut my long hair so as not to alienate the corporate types. I also undertook making other short films, among them *Hero*, about free-thinking hippies (played by Mark and his girlfriend) encountering stiff-necked Establishment-type strangers while strolling on a sunny day. It reflected the conflicting contradictions of the civil rights era, the war protest demonstrations and marches, and the general anarchy on college campuses that swept the nation in the early 1970s. Both *Hero* and *Hitchhiker* circulated among local film festivals and re-affirmed my calling to make movies.

To keep my performance level high at work, I made a rule for myself never to smoke grass during business hours or in and around the building—and I honored the rule without fail. The owner/boss of the company looked the other way whenever staff members went out for drinking lunches, about every two weeks. I gladly joined in and drank my share of beer and cocktails along with jovial colleagues.

In a sneaky sort of way, this ritual of drinking lunches embodied a kind of secret-keeping in that it was a group "wink-wink" experience, despite the boss's tacit knowledge. It felt much like when we high-school buddies sneaked in to watch X-rated movies at the Avalon and the spinster lady pretended to believe we were of age; or much like the secret "males only" society who get their kicks by ogling centerfolds. Once again, on both an individual and group basis, it demonstrated the secret-keeping principle that stealing hours is something one believes is required to feel good.

Susan's progress at the art museum advanced splendidly, and we attended wine-and-cheese openings as a fun part of her job. At home, however, after fifteen months of marriage, I'd come to the disappointing realization that Susan's and my love life was fizzling. Our original pace of making love once or twice a week had slowed to once or less a month. I'd grown tired of initiating sex and waited for her to, but it never quite happened, nor did it come up in conversation. What did the lack of interest mean? Was she rejecting me?

At a conscious level, I eventually made attempts to talk to her about it, but heard back little other than "Not right now" or "When I have more energy." At a subconscious level, I sensed that Susan felt afraid, almost paralyzed. She seemed only to be interested in what was conventional, and I wondered if she had just pretended to have the feelings of adventurous joy that were expected of a new bride. Maybe they'd never really been there at all.

The free and easy way we'd made love in Kansas City before the wedding confused the current situation and made it all the more ironic because we'd vowed to love and cherish ourselves as one body and soul at the altar. The rare times we did have sex, it felt awkward, forced, and mechanical. I'd anticipated our love life would get *better* after our vows. Now, facing the very opposite, some wisecracks from older married men echoed in my brain. They'd scoffed about "great sex during courtship, but once the knot is tied, you're done for . . . You're left high and dry 'cause wives don't have to put out."

In this moody frame of mind, I arrived at work one morning and there at the front desk sat a gorgeous young woman. Simone was a knockout in her early twenties, a temporary worker filling in for our vacationing receptionist—and, as time made clear, a huge flirt. She had a centerfold's body and generated the same sort of spell that Bonnie Witten and Cindy Foster had done when either of them wore a tight-fitting sweater. And she had incredible chocolate brown eyes that radiated mystery. Two-timing fantasies swirled in me. My hormones raged again, and I felt like a single guy stuck in marriage. Each time Simone slyly rolled her eyes or jiggled her hips, fantasies of making out with her bombarded my imagination. Other men in the office reacted the same way.

Does marriage really mean faithfulness and not free-wheeling sex between consenting adults? I asked myself. I'd made a promise of fidelity to Susan and meant to keep it, but could I? A replay of the old two-timing dating pattern resurfaced, this time bolder and stronger. The steamy, stormy urges within me now surged and swelled. The main question became whether I should act on them or not, which I carefully kept secret. I held back all week, then caved in on Friday and made my intentions known to Simone before she moved on to the next temp job.

"So . . . ?" I asked, having rehearsed the line and timed my approach to coincide when nobody was at her desk. "Are you interested in a little action this weekend?"

"What?!" she replied. "You're a married man, John!"

"Yes. Why does that make any difference?"

"Well, haven't you ever heard, 'Never get involved with a married man'?"

"Of course, who hasn't? So then, what have all your suggestive glances and jiggles been about? Were you just stringing me on?"

"I . . . I admit you're attractive, John, but I have no idea what you're talking about. If you think a little flirting means I'm available, you're greatly mistaken."

I glared at her. "*Really*, Simone. I can tell the difference between flirting and just being friendly. There's not a man here who doesn't think you're hot to trot."

She looked down slightly, finding this appealing but pretending not to, refusing eye contact.

I sniffed, turned on my heel, and marched away. "You sure had me fooled!"

The surprise of surprises came the following Monday when Simone returned to duty because the receptionist had extended her vacation. My hopes of action with Simone kept hounding me. The maddening part was that Simone still fanned the flames with more flirting, including playing up to other men in the office who obviously soaked up her attention. It wasn't long before our office manager, a lady my mother's age named Gladys, deciphered the dynamic displayed by me and the half dozen other men hovering in Simone's vicinity.

A snowmobile party hosted by the company's cameraman that weekend included Simone. And Gladys. Susan and other spouses had been invited as well, and my fading hopes of coupling with Simone stayed dormant. Susan and Gladys, already introduced and chatting like old friends, took notice of Simone who was basking in the attention of two other men, drinking and laughing lustily. Susan looked at me, as if to catch whether a sparkle in my eye glimmered for Simone as well. I didn't display any, but when Susan looked back at Gladys, they shared a female-to-female connection that condemned me.

On the way home in the car, Susan probed, "You're captivated by Simone, aren't you?"

I decided not to lie. "She's a turn-on, all right."

"And I suppose next you're going to tell me you want to go to bed with her?"

I paused. My imagined near-affair was turning into a real-life fiasco. "Nothing's happened except a little innocent flirting, that's all."

I had hoped my attempt at a half-truth would lead to a better understanding between us, but she acted threatened, and news of my flirting triggered a gigantic disappointment in her. I saw an opening to bring up how to improve our own inert love life, but no amount of explaining boosted her spirits or minimized the damage. Instead of a conversation about *us*, she reacted by closing down. The topic went underground, way down. Deep doubt plagued her in the days ahead and became a wedge in our marriage from then on.

So much for disclosing secrets and revealing real feelings!

In late April, now heading to Europe and Africa, Susan and I drove to New Jersey in the Chevy Nova, where we parked it for the upcoming months in Susan's parents' driveway. Her folks objected strenuously to our fancy-free itinerary, complaining it was entirely too open-ended for their conservative sensibilities, but we'd bought one-way tickets regardless and boarded the airplane at JFK for the international flight. At the Jetway, we tried again to level with them and convey our motives.

The bottom line was that we were skeptical about American values and were groping for an identity. Unsettled by the national tide of social and political upheaval, we wanted them to understand our need to air out our '60s-sogged brains. We hoped that the adventure, the experience of traveling in foreign lands, would replenish us. We wanted to find a new lifestyle. We were looking for a better way.

But the Troellers could not hear us. Sour-faced, her parents bitterly waved farewell.

Carrying backpacks of 35 and 50 pounds respectively, Susan and I tramped the quaint counties of Ireland, the shires of Britain, and the byways and villages of the continent, meeting extraordinary folks as we "auto-stopped" on our trek to meet Mark. Sure enough, on July 4th we rendezvoused with him on the ferry boat from Spain to Morocco and landed that afternoon in Tangiers. Being paid $25 never seemed so rewarding!

A sample list of the wonderful folks we met who influenced our values and outlook as world citizens included:

- *Aschille,* an architect from Switzerland who drove narrow mountain roads more than 1200 kilometers to deliver us on time to meet Mark;
- *Moulay,* a Muslim peasant in Morocco who saved our lives when drunken Arabs stranded us at night on the steep back roads of the Atlas Mountains;
- *Paula and Chico,* an engaged couple in Portugal who befriended us for four months while we dwelled in their seldom-visited land for $3 a day;
- *Monsieur Filattre,* a French driver who invited us into his family home for a week after finding our 35mm camera in the backseat of his car and who graciously showered us with provincial hospitality;
- *Vince,* a French-speaking German émigré to the British Isles who embraced the rhetoric of America's counterculture and opened our hearts to other free-spirited, youthful contemporaries in London.

Our plans to stay abroad shifted from 3 months to 12 months because of our enthusiasm for embracing foreign cultures everywhere we traveled. We wired home to our bank in Minnesota for $1,500 in savings that we had reserved for our return. "Let's go for broke!" we cried. It felt scary and freeing at the same time, but fully worth it. The friendly strangers we met proved easier to get to know and love than our friends and families in America, it seemed. We wanted our heyday to never end.

The extra months also afforded me the time to try my hand at writing a movie script, a dream that emerged from my growing sense of calling and my love of movie classics. Since high school I'd thrilled to stories such as *The Pawnbroker, Last Tango in Paris, Mutiny on the Bounty, I Am Curious-Yellow,* and *Cool Hand Luke.* More than anything else in the world, I wanted to originate movies like them, because they had moved my emotions so profoundly. That meant, I decided, creating the stories and writing the screenplays.

While in Morocco, Mark had given me a paperback novel by Herman Hesse about a precocious student in medieval times who finds and follows his calling as an artist. It moved me thoroughly, unlike any book I'd ever read. In a burst of passion, I started adapting it in Portugal, wearing out pencils and filling up legal pads, groping hour after hour to get the rhythm and feel of screen language. I titled it *The Scholar* and finished the script in England, where we landed three days before Christmas and rented a one-room flat in London. I fretted at times about securing the film rights, but reasoned that producers would—if they really wanted to film it—seek and pay for the rights themselves. Susan typed the screenplay until it reached 196 pages, amounting to a four-hour movie. I immediately began cutting it. Susan, bless her heart, retyped it from page one until we both believed *The Scholar* was the right length and ready for Hollywood.

The three main outcomes from our year of globe-trotting were: (1) we pledged to move to Hollywood upon our return to the United States; (2) we discovered that everyday people throughout the world have more similarities than they do differences—an old truism, certainly, but still true; and (3) Susan and I proved to be a fantastic team whose teamwork as travelers forged us into life mates committed to spending our lives together. The continual flow of adventures stretched us individually and bonded us as companions, allowing the sexual tensions between us to fade and my addictive double-life to dwindle to temporary nonexistence.

We returned to New Jersey and met with culture shock and hostile in-laws. Litter, gaudy billboards, and harrowing noise greeted us. Everything from cars to buildings were too big, too much, in our post-Kent-State-massacre homeland. Susie's parents objected furiously to our bellbottoms, hairstyles, lack of money, carefree attitudes, and Hollywood career plans. Her father, now a higher-level executive and still a heavy drinker after 50 years, got verbally abusive: "When the hell are you kids going to get serious? Quit ruining your lives! And you, mister, had better start treating my daughter in the manner to which she is accustomed!"

I quietly defended both our trip and my intentions to write screenplays and try filmmaking in LA. Susan's mother, the timid caretaker and peacemaker-at-all-costs, intervened on our behalf—"Bill, just give them a chance to get settled"—and received a tongue-lashing that shamed her into silence.

Susie reminded them, "You raised me to settle for nothing less than the best, and I'm firmly behind Johnny and his plans."

Bill slammed his fist on the table, rattling the dishes. "No!"

After dinner I insisted we pack up our Chevy Nova and leave immediately, and early the next morning we departed.

Our journey from New Jersey to California paused for a layover in Minneapolis, where we informed my family of our Hollywood plans. They were aghast, but less so than Susan's folks. Nobody wanted to hear about our overseas adventures. Mom urged us to stay in Minneapolis, Tommy called my moviemaking plans "bombastic," but David—dear David who knew me to the core—saw through to the "artistic me" and quietly gave his approval: "Johnny, just do it. You have the freedom, use it."

Susan and I rented a four-by-six-foot U-Haul and loaded our few stored belongings into it. Mom had the decency to invite us over to her house for breakfast on the day of our departure. That same morning, May 3, 1972, which would have been her and Dad's 37th anniversary, the phone rang and David announced the news of his daughter Katy's birth just moments before. After making a quick stop at the hospital, Susan and I headed west in our Chevy and hitched-up U-Haul, "California Dreamin'" playing on the radio.

Two months of getting settled in smoggy LA followed. An unknown without contacts, I peddled my script to agents, but nobody cared to even open it. One of thousands of aspiring hopefuls, I had no track record. Forced to regroup, I went seeking production work, finally landing a film crew job as a utility man, the gofer guy, running for anything and everything at everybody's beck and call.

My first assignment required waking up at 3:30 A.M. and driving 40 miles to Zuma Beach, where I labored from 5:00 A.M. on a TV commercial for camping equipment. From predawn to twilight, I unloaded heavy cables and lights from a huge truck, carried the equipment across acres of sand to the camera location overlooking the shoreline, ran to the catering wagon for the director's coffee and donuts, lifted and moved dolly track for the camera crew, helped the prop men prepare the client's tents/lanterns/coolers/stoves, and "wrapped" everything back to the huge truck at dark when the shooting ended. All this for $3.50 an hour and a 20-minute free lunch on the fly.

After nightfall the production manager, who had observed my gung ho efforts for sixteen hours, walked up and asked the magic question, "Are you available tomorrow, John?"

Exhausted, eyes sunken, I replied, "Yes."

"Good. See you tomorrow, bright and early." He gave me a map to the next day's location, a call time of 6:00 A.M., and patted me on the shoulder.

From that moment on, Tinseltown and I became officially linked. I'd passed some very important tests and learned some crucial lessons. By showing up on time, eager to work; laboring patiently and reliably without belly-aching or slacking off; and striving to act as professionally off-camera as many of the performers did on-camera, I was able to earn a spot as an actual crew member, leaving my gofer days behind. I also learned that being asked to work another day by someone in power engendered good will for me as a freelancer. This in turn led to more future gigs.

At a gut level I'd experienced three basic axioms:

→ Freelancers earn a reputation one gig at a time.
→ You're only as good as your last day's work.
→ Every opportunity to "perform" counts.

During the next months, I worked hard to establish myself and succeeded most often in the art department. I earned a promotion to prop assistant after a year, then to property master months later at $100 a day. My skills at making things and my inborn artistic talents proved useful in the studio, where setting up shots meant collaborating with the cameramen, looking through the camera viewfinder, and helping compose "the look" of each shot with grips and gaffers (construction and lighting technicians). My ability to make quick and confident decisions led to another promotion another year later—that of set decorator, earning $150-200 a day plus overtime.

Between gigs, as exciting as these on-the-set growth opportunities felt, the primary purpose of coming to Hollywood—marketing my screenplay and myself as a writer—gnawed at me. No matter how cleverly I tried to crack agents' or producers' indifference, they flatly, even rudely, rejected my writing. My feelings got trampled on often and my dream of screenwriting success dimmed as my hurts increased. I wrote two new scripts, but neither went anywhere.

Doubts mounted, as did my drinking and drugging, and my insecurities about becoming a storyteller only intensified. The nagging need for recognition, celebrity, and fame lurking in my psyche haunted me—the very same ambitions that had driven my vain attempts to star in hockey and school plays. Fearing a similar fate, my insecurities fed my addictions, and ongoing attempts to write failed to overcome these insecurities. Doubting what was inside, I strove for external achievement to validate me. I developed an ulcer, started brooding, spun in a downward spiral mentally, and lost my moral bearings.

And drank. And smoked. And searched for new ways to numb the pain.

Pushing limits showed up in Susan's and my lifestyle. Our first friends turned out to be gay, a group of slaphappy men that we met by chance one night when we ordered beers at a neighborhood bar called the Rusty Keg. We'd rented a one-bedroom apartment a mile from Paramount Studios, and the Rusty Keg was only five minutes away. We picked the bar at random because it looked harmless and cheery, like the one on *Cheers* itself. As we drank a pitcher that first night, we looked around and realized that every customer was male. Rather than freak out, we flowed with the situation as we'd done so often when traveling abroad.

Voila! We soon became fast friends with Ken, Larry, Cal, Snoopy, Jimbo, and Little Larry. Outings with these "fairies," as they liked to call themselves, meant lots of barhopping, parties, and fun. Susan felt respected and entirely safe, and so did I. Many times we drove home drunk to our one-bedroom apartment, but never got pulled over or arrested.

Pushing limits also prevailed whenever film friends like Jack Dunn and Benny Jacobs, coworkers of mine from the art department, invited us to parties where dope and flirting with their wives were common. None of this really led to secret-keeping because our parents or family members weren't around to notice or hold us accountable. Susan showed more reluctance to indulge in getting wasted or fooling around than I did, but she went ahead anyway.

The alcohol and drugs flowed. My dope smoking and drinking soon expanded to experimentation with cocaine. Anyone who worked on a film crew snorted a line now and then, encouraged by the pervasive unspoken creed among workers to be seen as cool, similar to "honesty among thieves."

Pushing limits also showed up in our marriage. Boredom in bed fostered a climate as arid as the dry desert surrounding Southern California. My solo, secret activities—that old double life—gained control again as the search for intimacy and fulfillment reasserted itself. I began amassing magazines, a harem of naked ladies on the pages of *Playboy, Penthouse,* and *Oui* that piled up in a closet over numerous months.

Naked female flesh became so pleasurable to look at that my moods improved about the same as when I'd get high on Jack Daniels or Acapulco Gold or Colombian Coke. But the highs lasted only for a moment, I discovered. Then the nasty cycle repeated itself. Cravings. Waiting for the next month's centerfold. Biding time until the next supply of grass hit the street. Having only enough money for drugs sporadically. Going without. At times I started to panic whenever my supply ran out or an opportunity to indulge got squelched.

Anticipating new female models to ogle, I felt numb to the fact that my search for fulfillment focused entirely on the external, instead of looking for fulfillment from the inside out. It was just like booze and grass—an external catalyst for mood-altering effects inside my brain. Basically, I mistook intensity for intimacy in both cases, drugs and sex. The pleasures I'd chosen had me trapped, and now masturbating while flipping full-color pages of seductive women joined the list. Again, I was stealing hours doing what I thought was required to feel better.

These masturbation episodes became sensual, solo sessions, carefully timed and orchestrated, much the same as my running naked in the woods had once been. When Susan left our apartment on errands or other business, I'd steal hours outside the bounds of our vows.

Occasionally I sneaked out and visited nude beaches and porn movies, where women exhibited themselves and flaunted their bodies—implying they had ravenous libidos. I told myself that men could not be the sole culprits at this game because women participated as complicit partners by showing off their nudity. At times I encouraged Susan to go along and be complicit too, but she resisted.

In addition to my "lust of the eye," I indulged in erotic literature—books that inflamed my fantasies. Debauched perversity through the written word entered my imagination and took hold. I stole more hours alone, in order to numb my nameless distress, while risking the shame of being found out by Susan. Yet the risks of being found out became part of the game and heightened the exhilaration. Once more I tasted:

➻ the *excitement* of breaking rules,

➻ the *pleasure* of admiring, or reading about, naked women,

➻ the *delight* of getting away with it.

On film sets and television locations, I continued working long, exhausting hours—often 5:00 or 6:00 in the morning to 9:00 or 10:00 at night—many days in a row. I performed at light speed, an ingrained work habit by now, and the challenges stretched me professionally and artistically, as well as paid buckets of overtime. My streak of steady employment served as a great outlet for my artistic talents and boosted my ego. But Susan felt uneasy about the intermittent spells of nonwork and lack of guaranteed financial earnings, unlike her highly paid father whose corporate career paid dependable wages and was still going strong after 40 years.

I remained secretly self-centered sexually, ignoring Susan's insecurities, which my two-timing dating history had once amplified, as had my bad-faith dalliance with Simone and lame promises never to do so again. Susan's insecurities manifested enough to shut her down, and my coming home often after 14- to 16-hour workdays didn't bode well for romance.

Demands at work reached new levels when I became an art director in charge of assistants and pricey budgets. Despite earning even more money and prestige, I still endured frustration. My screenplays had recently reached the offices of more favorably-minded agents and had generated more positive comments, yet still garnered only verbal interest and no paid offers. I decided to spend money and put forth the effort to attend seminars and screenwriting classes in order to improve my writing techniques and contacts. Then I planned to write yet another script. The addictive cycle of seeking fame and acclaim—this time via an Oscar, my avowed goal—loomed in my ego. Susan acted lukewarm at first about the classes and the prospect of another year spent writing a new story, but she slowly came around and supported the effort.

Then the day came when I met a stunning production assistant named Betsy. My womanizing with a real person rekindled in earnest—on the sly, of course. Betsy and I flirted while on the set of a B-movie western, and then one afternoon the director called "Wrap" early. Betsy and I arranged for a quickie, and later that afternoon, I knocked on her door with three full hours of free time before having to return home.

This was one secret I meant to keep forever.

**"Don't sit on your feelings.
Listen to them and be brave."**

Alice Walker

≈ Chapter Eight

The Marriage Circle

I stood outside Betsy's apartment door, shaking. My finger pushed her doorbell. Instantly my breathing rate doubled, sweat droplets formed in my palms, yet dryness like sun-scorched sand parched my throat.

The door opened. Betsy's face smiled. "Come in, John."

I stepped inside, almost trembling.

She was dressed in tight jeans, tall boots that came to her knees, and a green sleeveless pullover top. Her skin shimmered dark and smooth, her entire body sleek and well-proportioned. Her hair seemed curlier than I remembered and her face prettier. Her apartment, overlooking a hill streaked with orange sunlight, afforded the perfect setting for an intimate, uninterrupted sexual encounter.

"How good to see you," she said, squeezing my hands, unable to contain her excitement. "Some beer? No? How about some wine?"

"Anything you have will be fine."

She went to the refrigerator, took out some inexpensive rosé and poured two glasses. As I watched her, I knew I was taking the kind of risk that could get me into huge trouble, and I knew that if I did get into trouble, I would have to pay for it dearly—"heaven hath no fury like a woman (a wife!) scorned." But I also knew that what I was risking could lead to something bold and new, a different kind of experience unthinkable until now. Betsy was the first woman besides Susan since our wedding four years earlier who had consented to be my bed partner.

"You can see I'm a dyed-in-the-wool romantic, can't you?" she giggled, waving her hand around her hippy pad.

"You and me both."

"Come on, John, let's sit under the loft and talk a bit." She took my hand and led me to a perch under her sleeping loft where we started sipping away. The touch of her fingers on my palm thrilled me, the same kind of hot chill that had raced through my arteries when we'd met at the movie studio ranch in the hills west of LA.

"How would you define a romantic?" I asked.

"Well, I guess it's a person who works hard at making their dreams come true."

"I like that. I'm that kind of person."

"About five years ago, just after I turned twenty," she went on, "I spent a whole summer on the prairie in Montana. Just me, alone, in a farmhouse. It was wonderful. There was this horse named Prince. Prince and I went riding every day. I'd stop every once in a while to pick herbs or watch thunderclouds, and he would nudge me when he wanted to get going. At night I did a lot of reading. The whole experience really expanded my life, my dreams."

"Sounds like a romantic dream, all right. The reason I'm here in Hollywood is because I love movies. I practically grew up in theatres. Practically every time I've experienced something really deep in life, it seems there was a film that helped me deal with it. *Rebel Without a Cause, Cool Hand Luke, Mutiny on the Bounty, The Pawnbroker,* you name it. Watching them changed me and made me want to come here to make great movies like them."

"Where did you grow up, John?"

"Minnesota. 'Land of sky blue waters,' like the Hamms beer commercials say."

"It must be beautiful there."

"Oh, it is. But there's no film industry in Minneapolis like here in California. Hollywood is where I had to end up if I was to fulfill my calling." I paused to let this last remark sink in and made eye contact. I wanted her to understand that another of my dreams-to-come-true was the reason we were together right now.

She interpreted the glint in my eyes and smiled. As if to prolong the suspense, she clinked my glass and reached for several eight- to ten-inch tree twigs the diameter of a thick pencil and a small green book entitled *I Ching*.

"Do you know about yarrow sticks?" she asked, fondling the twigs.

"Not really."

"Have you ever read the *I Ching?*"

"Nope."

"They're connected, sort of like astrology and the future."

"Interesting. Very interesting."

She smiled, as if this remark made a significant difference. I was pleased because I thought it foreshadowed a knock-out time with her shortly. Gathering up the yarrow sticks, she chanted something in a whisper and "threw" them between us. They landed in a heap.

"Before I read these," she said, "tell me a little about your family. What are they like?"

"Uhh, shouldn't we move on to other things first?"

"We still have time. Go with me on this."

"Okay. My brothers and I grew up in suburbia, got along pretty well. Fairly good grades, some sports in high school. No sisters. My mom and dad loved us, although there were some pretty nasty times when bad things happened and we kids took it in the shorts as teenagers. My dad's dead now. My mom still lives in Minneapolis."

I stared into her eyes. I was curious about how we would get to bed.

"My own situation?" she responded, interpreting my gaze. "I really love my folks and they love me. I'm very lucky. We all love each other. Now then, these aren't just normal sticks . . ."

Behind her, tacked on the wall, were several pen-and-ink sketches. She reached up and removed some of the drawings, putting them on the Indian blanket spread beside us. I looked at each carefully: excellent technique; bold depictions of unicorns, satyrs, and Minotaurs. I liked them and muttered something about their quality.

"Thank you. They're mine."

But I was burning inside to get down to business. Time was ticking away. The inevitable moment was approaching. We exchanged soulful looks. She was apparently in no hurry, but I sighed, eager to initiate the ritual we'd both agreed to enact.

"Let's get onto other things," I ventured during the lull.

"You're married, aren't you?"

"Yes. But you knew that."

"Of course. What I don't know is anything about your wife. Are you separated?"

"No."

"Are you going through something negative right now?"

I laughed. I insisted that my mate of four years was a sweet, lovable soul. "She provides a warm home, delicious meals, challenging conversation, and is deeply committed to our marriage and cares about everyone."

"Are you as committed?"

"Yes, definitely."

"Then why are you interested in other women?"

I sat back. "I . . . I guess the idea of making love to only one woman my whole life seems so limiting. I'm not sure I'm a one-and-only kind of guy."

"You sure nothing's wrong? Why are you looking outside your marriage for fulfillment?"

Feeling provoked, I leaned forward. "You're single, Betsy. It all changes once the knot is tied. It's an old, old story."

"But I thought marriage partners were supposed to be faithful?"

"Look, I see a girl like you and get turned on. Does that make me a dirty old man?"

"But unless you're faithful, you won't have a good marriage."

"Oh? How come I can't be married *and* spend an hour or two with somebody as sexy as you? Where's the harm?"

We talked in this vein for several minutes. She became increasingly adamant about my fidelity, and I became increasingly defensive. She argued that a single girl getting involved with a "happily married" man was psychic suicide. I argued that two consenting adults—whether married, single, separated, divorced—had the freedom to choose any form of relationship they wished.

Stalemate. The tense moment of truth arrived. She acted distant; I felt betrayed. We searched each other's eyes. Only moments before, she had exuberantly invited me in. Now we faced each other like political candidates opposed in a debate. I leaned to kiss her. She backed away. I leaned closer. She allowed a peck on her turned-away cheek.

"Unless you talk to your wife and she tells me she fully approves, no dice. Sorry."

I pulled back, angered. "This is too weird." I swallowed. "Should I stop by again?"

"Not unless it's with the understanding that we're just friends."

Cheeks burning, indignation rising like hot vapor within me, I held back swearing profanities and stomped away without saying a civil goodbye. Storming to my car parked outside, I got in, slammed the door, and stewed. Thoughts of sexual fantasies coming true collapsed from the stinging pain of our actual interaction. Feelings of eager anticipation clashed with the blunt reality of rejection. I cursed myself for ever getting married, for ever being so stupid as to vow "till death do us part," for the hypocrisy of having to act faithful when inside I was burning with lust.

An all-too-familiar pattern repeated itself, with slight variations, during the next several months. Outwardly maintaining a happy marriage, inwardly I churned with profound desires to steal hours and sleep with every attractive girl who crossed my path. The familiar acting one way while feeling another hardened into putting on appearances while masking reality. The scenario always played out the same: I would get turned on, determine that the young lady was also turned on, make tasteful hints or suggestions, confirm her interest, ask her to have sex, then go to her house and interact as naturally as possible, seeking a happy coupling as consenting lovers.

Time after time I was disappointed, set up for the best and handed the worst. In all, I estimate that for the few tantalizing promises of sexual thrills, I incurred dozens of stolen hours of phoning and visiting, scores of times being told no, and interminable months of marital strife and hurt.

One day, exhausted, I sat and pondered, "Why am I consumed by lust?"

Not because I didn't love Susan. We were a team, a solid pair; we fit each other in so many ways. Nothing about our backgrounds, socially, economically, racially, was a mismatch. We were nice middle-class people, from mixed-up dysfunctional homes like so many of our generation. Susan was good-looking, trim, likeable, intelligent. According to her standards, I, too, was good-looking, fit, likeable, and intelligent. Nothing was basically amiss.

But something *was* wrong.

Marriage itself was the problem, I postulated. The rules were all messed up. How could any red-blooded person reasonably limit his or her sexual appetites and activities to one person? Complicating the problem was the phenomenon that many people were talking about, the much-debated free-love/consenting adult/communal living philosophies of the media-hyped '70s: *Playboy Philosophy, Open Marriage, Flexible Monogamy.* But talk was cheap, and in the end too few people acted upon their spoken convictions. Biologically, marriage seemed unnatural. Males of every species roamed from female to female, switching mates and oftentimes collecting several. Weren't we all animals at the core of our beings? Why deny the imperatives of our physical nature?

I wrote these thoughts in a kind of diary I kept called "Dailies," after the movie term for film that is processed in the lab overnight and made available for viewing the next day:

> Sometimes I get disgusted at the limits we place on ourselves. It isn't fair. The most difficult thing in the world is to touch another person's soul, because doing so means that someone has given their approval to enter private territory, sacred territory. With Susan that approval was granted

years ago, and sometimes it has led to love and companionship. But often it hasn't. If my wanderings outside the perimeter of our marriage ever become known to her, I hope she reads the next sentence and burns it into her heart forever: I did it because it was a need of mine, a compulsion that I couldn't find a way to stop or prevent.

I became increasingly aware of a concept I came to call "The Marriage Circle." It was the notion that marriage, like a circle, is self-contained. To step outside it is to endanger it. To stay within it is to expand it, strengthen it. Love is the line surrounding married couples. It protects, but is fragile; it is flexible, but oh-so delicate.

This same circle is a boundary, a constraining limitation. It limits movement, freedom. It denies one's built-in animal urges. It is a barrier over which many a war between spouses, and within spouses, is fought. Daily. Over the centuries. In me, for the present and beyond.

Once lust took hold in me, it wreaked havoc like an earthquake reduces a rushing freeway to massive rubble and deathly silence. It became a raging beast dead set on demanding its way, a prowling monster on the loose.

You could say that I let temptation dominate my decisions and actions, but that presumes a moral view that I didn't share at the time. A view that the drive for pleasure, which I believed was my right, needed controlling. In my search for answers, I'd concluded, (1) marriage itself was the problem, (2) my own inbred testosterone nature was a contributing factor, and, bottom line, (3) Susan and I were mismatched sexually through no fault of hers or mine.

This painful fact we both sensed deep down, but struggled talking about. We spent a lot of time individually burying it in silence. If asked, she would have said our poor performance in bed was because of her suspicions I was playing around; I would have said that my playing around was because of our poor performance in bed.

In truth, I tried to get us to openly communicate our feelings, our needs, and wishes. But her fear of my passionate overreactive tendencies (my basic intense nature and tendency for drama, exacerbated because of my frustrations), along with my anger at her for clamming up, led to an impasse. It's hard being romantic and afraid at the same time (Susan), just as it's hard being romantic and angry at the same time (me).

Had we managed to discuss it successfully, we possibly could've drawn closer together in our mutual disappointment over our lackluster love life. Instead, pessimism doomed improvement. Nothing I did to spur excitement in our love life worked. Our opposing inclinations translated into hostility, into resistance, although we denied it and covered up the ugly truth for the sake of keeping peace at home. Every so often I hinted about my vision for an adventurous marriage and tried to justify to Susan my desires, my rationale. She responded with blank looks and shrugs.

So I turned away and became tempted by other women. I felt reluctant to bend our vows, but went ahead anyway. I hated the deception involved in calling and hustling "prospects" whenever Susan wasn't home or when coworkers weren't within earshot. In desperation late one night with the lights out, I told Susan of my need to sleep with other women. As we were lying under the covers I whispered, "I feel it's only honest to tell you that there will probably be other women in my life I'll go to bed with."

"What!" Her hand grasped mine like a bear-trap snapping shut.

"I said, there will probably be—"

"I heard what you said! What do you mean?!"

I sighed. "Susan, we both have a pretty good idea of how we feel about this. I don't mean to hurt you, I really don't."

She sat bolt upright in the dark. "Hurt me? That's cute! What do you call what you said just now?"

"Please, just listen. I want us to stay married and be happy. But I can't see any other way out of it. I'm only talking about the occasional fling, nothing more."

"Happy? How can we ever be happy if you're out having sex with other women?"

"We can. I know we can."

"No way! Sharing you with other women is not my idea of happiness."

"And nursing grudges the way we have been is not mine."

Silence.

I added, "I think it would help for us to see a counselor."

"I'm not willing to put up with you hopping from bed to bed every time a sweet young thing gets you all hot and bothered!" She argued fiercely against the idea. My suggestion to get counseling went ignored. I also tried to get us to mutually admit how ice-cold our love life had become. No such luck. I'd touched off a firestorm. In attempting to communicate a sensitive issue, I'd stirred up her primal emotions. By 3:00 A.M., we were irrevocably apart.

Irreconcilable differences.

Over the next several weeks, an even deeper wedge lodged in our marriage, resulting in her short-term and long-term paralysis. My intake of alcohol and marijuana increased. As tensions mounted, Susan might ask me a simple question and I'd snap. When driving, if the traffic in front of me moved too slowly, I'd curse a purple streak. The fear of not selling a screenplay provoked me to chew my fingernails. In a rage, I once flung dishes on the kitchen floor and smashed my fists into the wall, frightening Susan. My search for answers, lately in books on Scientology, astrology, and numerology, uncovered nothing.

Another drink. Another joint. One more escape attempt. One more mood swing that ended the next morning when I woke up on the floor with a hangover from having passed out the night before.

Loneliness develops in marriage when either or both partners avoid telling the other about negative thoughts and feelings. After many attempts to communicate, after reaching no agreement on the issues of sexual freedom, the tendency to bury these conflicts became operative. Emotional walls and armor cut off meaningful communication. We'd convinced ourselves that things would get better if we just didn't talk about it.

Despite the undercurrents between us, we found occasions to pop open a bottle of wine, cook some steaks, crank up Steely Dan on the stereo, and enjoy ourselves. Then came the evening when Susan and I conceived our daughter—a joyful act of intimacy that spiced up our sex life and served to verify Susan's fertility and my virility. We took natural childbirth classes, spent enjoyable hours decorating a tiny room in our apartment for the new arrival, and celebrated the newcomer's entrance into our lives.

As the pregnancy of our first child became a focus in the weeks ahead, some of our homosexual friends dropped away, and I anxiously kept looking outside the Marriage Circle in hopes of grander gratification. I had no concept of sin to muddle my inclinations. There were no taboos, given my spiritual state. There was just a do-your-own-thing type of conviction and the dull, numbing decision to avoid the topic entirely.

Despite my vows to love, cherish, and honor Susan, I focused on my own needs rather than our mutual ones. Seeking oneness, I sought to combine my half of the whole with the half of another woman, especially a beautiful woman—to become "one flesh" with her. I sought cosmic bliss, timeless significance.

Could such an ideal be experienced this side of one's grave?

Thus, I romanced Jennifer, a makeup artist who turned me down after intense soul-searching and inner turmoil because she'd already divorced twice. And Leslie, a production manager who turned me down because she was seeing another man and lived too far away. And Denise, who kissed me at a party one weekend, in greeting only, but a spark flew between us.

Denise, the wife of my work acquaintance Benny Jacobs, lived three short miles from our apartment. Within twenty-four hours after the party, she and I frolicked in her bedroom, wearing not a stitch of clothes, like wild children free of parental restraints. Her husband was safely at work on a film crew, and Susan was safely at home nursing our newborn daughter, Emily.

I had crossed the line and ruptured the Marriage Circle.

MetaViews to Muse #4

To help you recognize and confront secret-keeping tendencies and habits, these reflections on what you've read in the past several pages are meant to encourage you to consider your own life's challenges and choices.

✳ A secret life boils down to seeking an external solution to an internal dilemma. It leads to the Lie of Addiction: "something outside me can fix what's wrong or missing inside me." In my case, the self-defeating behaviors I repeated to relieve emotional conflicts led, ironically, to the very consequences I was trying to avoid.

Are you caught in a similar trap? If so, please explain.

✳ Another mistake in thinking occurs when Secret Keepers confuse intensity for intimacy. They push the limits and live on the fringes in order to feel alive. They believe the risks and thrills will replace the missing contentment and fulfillment inside them—that is, if it's worth doing, it's worth doing to excess. Intimacy, on the other hand, results when an individual shares with another person what's worthwhile within him or her, bonding the two together.

What motivates you, intensity or intimacy? Are you pushing any limits? Does pushing those limits cause you to feel more alive?

✳ Leading a double life generates rituals that grip and overwhelm the Secret Keeper. Highly developed skills at hiding and covering up become habits as well as sources of pride and even add to the thrill-seeking fallacy. In my case, the risks of my secret life were part of the high.

Do you have rituals that grip or overwhelm you? If so, what are they?

* Secret lives can be an attempt to make ourselves whole, strong, and healthy. This belief can be part of the delusion, that one's ambition is mistaken for one's calling—as was the case for me by my trying to make movies in Hollywood at all costs. When we strive too hard at our ambitions, it may be that we're compensating for nagging doubts/pain/grief/self-loathing, rather than using our talents to fulfill our genuine purpose in life.

Are you driven by ambition? Trying to reach a goal regardless of the cost? Or are you motivated by the genuine purpose you believe you were created for?

* Hundreds of miles away from home (from accountability), the secrets I held came out in the open and lost their power as taboo. Once a behavior loses its power to generate guilt, the perpetrator is on the fast track to disaster. This, too, is part of the delusion. It is easy to be fooled into believing that as anonymous strangers, when nobody is looking, wrong behavior therefore doesn't matter. But it's really just another form of disconnection or isolation and can easily be misunderstood as permission or license to misbehave.

What role, if any, does anonymity play in your deeds? Do you feel guilty about things you do when nobody is looking?

* **The following are two of the eight splintered mindsets of a Secret Keeper:**
> + Living from the outside in.
> + Getting one's way, any way possible.

"A slave is one who waits for someone else to come and free him."

Ezra Pound

 Chapter Nine

Despair

The birth of Emily Louise Prin brought great joy. I witnessed her birth as Susan's breathing coach, taking part in the miracle and soaring four feet off the ground for days. Emily was soft, cuddly, cute. I'd never grown up with a girl in the house, and it pleased me that she was a girl and not a boy. Bathing Emily was fun. Diapering Emily was fun. Burping Emily was fun. Susan and I took care of her the first several days, both of us sensing deep down the presence of a Supreme Being, grateful that our daughter was healthy and whole. Secretly, I felt relieved that my manhood was not going to be an example for a son.

Both our families greeted Emily as their first grandchild, and Susan's mom came out to help us for a month. Martha offered much-needed help, and we all got to know one another better in the process. Away from Bill, Martha smiled more and spoke her mind less guardedly. In my family, Emily was the second girl after her cousin Katy, Dave's daughter. In both of our families, her arrival confirmed to skeptics that Susan and I were no longer wacky weirdoes living outside the so-called American dream.

As any parent knows, having kids makes you aware of the need to clean up your act. A two-pack-a-day Old Golds smoker, I coughed and wheezed and huffed and puffed too often. My gut warned me that the consequences of this addiction to tobacco were too high. For once I listened. As my 30th birthday approached, I battled this nasty habit. Of the many drawbacks, it felt like every cigarette fouled my breath, ruined my lungs, polluted the atmosphere, and caused throbbing pains under my left arm. I'd considered quitting this enslavement for two or three years and now resolved to stop once and for all. Mark Twain once said, "Quitting smoking is easy; I've done it hundreds of times."

My willpower, or as Susan said "won't power," was shaky. I thought back to my boyhood days when I became a slave to candy and stole coins from Mom's purse to maintain my "habit." I reminded myself that I'd lost sixty pounds of fat as a teenager and kept it off. I'd also learned recently that Tommy had kicked his two-pack-a-day Pall Mall habit, and his example inspired me. One more ugly thought motivated me: the air Emily breathed in our home was contaminating her little lungs!

With my birthday just five days away, with the insight that my 30s and beyond could be free of nicotine, I vowed not to smoke for 24 hours. It was nerve-racking but I managed not to give in. Then a week passed and I told myself, I've *stopped, not quit. Quitting* sounded insurmountable; *stopping* sounded more doable. Three more weeks came and went. I celebrated, wildly excited. Another month went by successfully, then the next month and the next.

I've never smoked since. Immediate benefits: clean air for Emily, higher self-esteem, a jolt of personal empowerment, and assurance I *could* do what's right *and* make it stick. Triumph came one day at a time, from slavery to victory!

In my quiet moments, I once again pondered Dave's uncanny ability to stay unhooked by addictions and never become enslaved to a secret life. Our differences in these areas amazed me. Always the first one to experiment with anything that might help me feel better, I questioned why he seemed to feel good enough already, to not have the emotional lows requiring his having to experiment in the first place. He was of one mind; I was of two.

When we talked on the phone or during holiday visits—he was now a traveling salesman for 3M company based in the Houston branch office—he said, "It's because of my parental pressures and responsibilities that I've disciplined myself away from excesses. Instead of the emotional rush from gambling," he claimed, "I've channeled my energies into work, Johnny. That's where I get satisfaction nowadays, from making bigger sales." He talked about the ways that achieving his high-level productivity goals served his family of four. "I've found my passion and don't need the artificial highs, don't need to push the limits."

I envied his being single-minded and happy about it, while I remained multi-minded and seldom satisfied. One mind at peace, the other mind in pieces. Whether it was "nature" or "nurture" or some other force, the plain fact was that we'd turned out the way we had despite being identical twins.

Turning 30 proved hard for me in other ways. I could hardly think of myself as young anymore. My career goals were not remotely close to being met. Whenever I took stock of my predicament, I came out the loser. Often I felt alone in the world, in my marriage, and in my own skin. My fling with Denise had lasted just two stolen afternoons, then fizzled. Heartache. Disappointment. My screenplays had bombed. My fifth script was underway, but I felt hounded by doubts and insecurities and foggy thinking from a pickled brain. Nail-biting anxiety. Satisfaction deferred.

Although a proud daddy, I was a sick husband. Although a thriving art director, I floundered as a screenwriter. Brooding became my life. Suicidal thoughts crept into my consciousness. My feeble concept of God meant I only had Fate to rant and rave at. I began to ask myself whether life was worth living. In tears, I admitted to myself that I felt desperate, defeated, dejected.

In a determined effort to further my writing career, I rented two spare rooms from an elderly neighbor lady where I set up my typewriter and files. She reminded me a great deal of Mrs. Russell in Kansas City. In addition to my fifteen-dollar-a-month rent, I went grocery shopping and ran errands for her. The rooms, which I dubbed the Little Place, reminded me of my bachelor days in the attic, those free and footloose days. Like my star rising at Gorden Film Labs, so now did my hopes that my star would rise in Tinseltown.

A would-be producer friend, Steve Navin, called one day and raved about my script *The Scholar*. "I've finally scraped together a few thousand dollars of seed money," he announced, and several meetings later, we'd hammered out an option deal: I was to rewrite the story as an American period drama set in the 19th century, and he agreed to pay me $2,500 for the right to produce it for one year after its completion. We signed the contract and he paid the first $1,000. My dream of being a paid writer had finally come true. I eagerly plunged ahead on the script for the next few months. I'd never been so excited in all my life. Susan and I celebrated at Musso & Frank's on Hollywood Boulevard, a classic eatery frequented by movie stars, and jabbered until closing time about the vistas that had opened up.

"Our gamble of coming to Hollywood has paid off!" I exclaimed.

We clinked glasses in a toast and Susan roared, "We're on our way!"

Steve paid me the final payment the day I delivered the revised *Scholar* script and immediately shopped it to legendary producer Dino de Laurentis. After waiting weeks to hear back, we were told "it's not commercial." To my knowledge Steve never tried anywhere else. Once more I felt a slave to feelings of failure.

Sour, depressed, determined to have what I wanted when I wanted it, I became disoriented. One day I got arrested for shoplifting. I'd been prop-shopping in a Sears store on Santa Monica Boulevard and walked out with a $2.98 tape measure, unpaid for, which I told myself I needed for my tool box. Yes, I knew I was stealing it. My moral standards had sunken that low. Two security officers nabbed me outside the entrance, escorted me back inside, and grilled me. The older one handcuffed me to a bench in a cramped office while the younger one took my picture with a Polaroid camera, then showed me countless snapshots like mine in three-ring binders. They rattled off statistics, fines, court dates, and all the messy procedures that would follow. No longer protesting my innocence, I signed a short legal document admitting my guilt.

"You don't realize how close you came to being booked just now," said the older officer. "If I'd have finished writing out this report and called the police . . ."

The younger officer added, "You should have been here a half hour ago. A widow lady, $.89."

They informed me that I was free to go, that they wanted me to come back and shop, and that news of what happened would be limited to the three of us. A wave of relief, of forgiveness and gratitude, surged through me. I was guilty, but not condemned. I breathed a huge sigh, shook hands, and left.

Though a free man, I was a very troubled soul. By the grace of God I'd gone unscathed, but I knew deep down that this brush with crime was symptomatic of my overall disorientation. My mind wobbled and teetered. Losing my grip on my sanity, I felt helpless to do anything about it. For days afterward, I questioned my insane misdeed and choked with self-loathing.

As with all my secrets, I kept it carefully hidden from anybody's knowledge.

One more sad attempt at another stolen-hours affair followed, this time with Janet, a blond production assistant working on a commercial for a toilet bowl cleaner. Arrangements with Janet led to plans for a Saturday-morning rendezvous. In my undiscerning, drug-induced, disoriented state, I brought little one-year-old Emily along. Janet saw me coming through her window and, for good reason, didn't answer my repeated knocks on her door. Another fizzle. More dejection.

What is wrong with me? I kept hounding myself.

My suicidal thoughts turned to plans. I envisioned driving the Dodge van I used for work—purchased with funds generously gifted by Susan's folks—at 90 miles per hour off the edge of Pacific Palisades, plunging into the ocean below and crashing to smithereens on the jagged rocks. Similar scenarios, equally dramatic but never involving Susan or a loved one who would find me bloody or stone cold, crowded my thoughts. Recognizing drugs as my adversary was impossible.

Plainly, life was not worth living. I remained stuck in the victim's mantra: "Life sucks, then you die." The books I read at the time often depressed me too, like *Animal Farm, 1984, Catcher in the Rye,* and *The Bell Jar.* I identified strongly with poet Sylvia Plath's suicide in *The Bell Jar* and began viewing suicide as a possible solution to my misery. Maximizing pleasure and minimizing pain became my one remaining strategy.

Spurred on by my momentary—and monetary—success with *The Scholar,* I contacted Steve Navin and proposed a more commercial script entitled *Queens Wild.* A rip-roaring Western tale about sexy women heroes, the story told how they faced down villains in gunfights and enjoyed scintillating sex. We agreed on another $2,500 deal. To research it, I decided a trip to Texas was in order. Promptly I made plans to drive east in our Dodge van, solo, leaving Susan for two weeks to care for Emily. When she voiced skepticism, I added that I needed space to find myself. Having observed my dark moods, she shrugged and grunted, "If you insist."

In Austin, I visited Melanie on the sly, still another production assistant I had flirted with months before who'd tired of Tinseltown and had moved back to her hometown. We had a dissatisfying one-night stand. Again, I was left alone with more depressed thoughts.

Bereft, I drove up to Colorado and visited Karen Iverson, my former fiancée who was now married and lived near Boulder. We spent hours reminiscing about the good times, but our visit turned bittersweet. She admitted to marrying on the rebound, and while regretful about us, professed loyalty to her husband. I ached to wrap my arms around her and reignite the fire that had once burned between us, yet I kept my distance. Instead I drove away frustrated and defeated at the deepest levels, raging at my bewildering destiny and combating intense cravings to experience the love connection I so longed for. Returning to LA seemed hopeless—scriptwriting was going nowhere, making love with Susan was pretty much nonexistent, I could hardly control my own compulsions, and the jagged rocks below Pacific Palisades loomed ever nearer.

My two stolen weeks had netted nothing.

Arriving back home, I maintained a stern distance from Susan, partly for her own protection because I was ready to blow up violently like a geyser and partly so I could indulge in a drug-laden bender. As I downed vodka and inhaled weed at record amounts, the internal pain became greater and greater. The addictive promise of relief was no longer working. I smoked eleven joints in one day and felt nothing. My true Self hated the Addict inside who was making me suffer.

Once addictive thinking takes over a person's behavior, I was to learn, the Self (genuine, emerges from birth) and the Addict (an imposter, emerges from the onset of substance abuse) wage a constant battle for supremacy. Mentally I listed reasons for committing suicide: Profound sense of failure. Violation of my own values. Living according to society's stupid standards. Erosion of my personal power. Inability to find happiness. My distant, absent father. My slave-driving, narcissistic mother. My wounded, fragile wife . . .

Everything was to blame but my secret double life of addictions.

The only bright spot in this ever-darkening picture was Emily, the light of my life. Now two years old, she and I reveled in all sorts of daddy/kid-things together, like my lifting her high in the air, carrying her on my shoulders, twirling her while holding her ankles, tickling her bare feet, and chasing her through the house yelling, "I'm gonna catch you!" She'd giggle with glee and pretend to hide, so I'd play along pretending I couldn't find her until she'd holler, "Boo!" From this little game, all sorts of silly nonsense names arose for her like *E-boo*, *E-bunna*, and just plain *Em*. One day after I rattled off a dozen or more nonsense names, I asked her, "What do all these names for you mean, Em?"

Instead of a silly nonsense answer, she replied in a heartbeat, "They mean you love me, Daddy." My heartbeat soared hearing that! We also played word games, and one day she learned the word *sock*, which she pronounced "gock," and also the word *truck*, which she pronounced "guck." About a week later, we were driving down the Hollywood Freeway and a huge truck passed us. She pointed out the window and announced, "Gock!" I gently reminded her, "No, Em, 'guck.'"

In terms of my relentless downward spiral, it's clear that she helped me stay sane and kept a glimmer of hope alive in me.

⚬⚬⚬

In Alfred Hitchcock's movie *The Birds*, the opening scene shows the main character walking along a peaceful street in sunny daylight. Out of nowhere, evil appears in the form of thousands of ruthless gulls that attack her with deadly force.

In a similar way, one balmy Sunday afternoon a year later in 1977, Susan and I were walking along the sandy shore in Newport Beach, California, feeling the hot sun on our bodies and cool wet sand on our bare feet. As we licked peppermint ice cream cones, I spoke of the darkness I felt inside—no longer a secret I deemed necessary to cover up.

"More and more nowadays I'm thinking of ending my life," I told her almost casually.

She looked at me as if I'd splashed ice-water on her. Our bare toes squished the wet sand from the lapping waves. Reacting to my out-of-nowhere statement, which came out of nowhere like the gulls in Hitchcock's film, she turned and stared. "You're actually thinking of doing it?"

I nodded.

"Why?"

"Life really sucks. Simple."

"Come on, John. Don't be so dramatic. It can't be as bad as that."

"Afraid so. I'm no longer sure it's worth it."

"Worth what?"

"Worth living."

Susan looked at me oddly, as if I might be joking, then frowned. "You're serious!"

"Yes, dead serious."

Neither of us laughed at the accidental pun. I doubted if she or anybody could convince me of a sane reason for believing otherwise. It was time, I thought, for her to start adjusting to the idea. After a long silence, she said, "We're so opposite, you and I. What could possibly make you think that?"

I rattled off my list of reasons and added, "We mortals are condemned from birth to never know satisfaction or fulfillment. The odds are stacked against us and always have been. Generation after generation, people are born to suffer, sometimes horribly. Justice? There is none."

"Such negativity, John! I'm sick of it! Is this happening because you're unhappy about your screenwriting?"

"Not entirely."

"What then?"

"Oh, a million things. Civil rights atrocities. Sky-high gas prices. Kent State. Redneck nigger-haters. My high-school hockey coach. Mom. The Kennedy assassinations. Dad's dying. Concentration camps. Our sex life. A god who sees misery but does nothing. Stuff like that."

A very long silence followed.

She pulled me by the hand toward the water where we put our feet into the squishy wet sand. "How can you be so depressed?" she asked. "Look all around you. Look at this huge, wonderful ocean, right here for us to experience. We're part of it all and get to marvel at it. Doesn't this make you excited?"

"I guess I'm a big party pooper."

"No lie! Feel how good the water feels." She waded in a little farther, reached down, and splashed her arms with seawater, then splashed me. "Try looking on the bright side of things and just appreciate what *is*."

I tried to think of a clever answer but none came. "It stinks," I replied. "It all just stinks."

"Always wanting, wanting, wanting. John Prin, the wanter. Your endless wanting makes you miserable, Johnny."

From that moment on, my will to talk faded like the last toke on an empty bong. I blanked out. "Maybe so," I mumbled.

She looked at me with the sorriest expression I've ever seen, then turned and peered at the placid Pacific. I knew I'd hurt her, again, and was tired of making her suffer. One more reason to add to my list of reasons to hate myself.

We walked on a ways, several feet apart, glum and wordless, then reached the spot where we'd left our beach bag and headed for the car.

"Nothing like a ruined Sunday stroll on the beach," she said. We drove home to our apartment in sullen silence.

I worked the next day at my improvised office, the Little Place, writing *Fortuna*, my latest stab at a spec movie script. By now *Queens Wild* had gone unnoticed. *Fortuna* was another attempt at success, this time a collaboration with a screenwriter friend, a futuristic drama about the inventor of a pharmaceutical pill that increases humanity's intelligence to the 500 IQ range, but inadvertently causes the world to divide according to those lucky enough to get the pill and those who don't.

I put thoughts of suicide out of my mind and devoted my efforts to the screenplay, exerting all my powers to make it a masterpiece. I told myself, "The harder you slave at it, John, the more it will be a script worth the world's attention, maybe even an Oscar-winner." I wanted to believe this so much that I repeated it silently like a mantra and committed to its excellence as I had once done as a boy making Indian artifacts, the canvas canoe, and my hockey goalie pads. I wanted it to be something my former English teacher Mr. Anderson would be proud to read.

In the most secret part of my soul, I forged a Faustian pact with Fate: If *Fortuna*'s success launched my dream, it would be a sign that the "gods" approved of my calling to be a filmmaker. If it failed, it would be a sign that my dream was doomed and my life should end. On this outcome hung life and death, as absurd and outlandish—as bombastic—as it sounds. The result would determine whether I was blessed or cursed, whether I was slave or master, whether my life deserved to be lived or not.

One afternoon, after ten straight hours of drafting *Fortuna*, I stopped typing at 6:00 P.M. in order to get home on time for cocktails and supper. I wanted Susan to feel appreciated and knew that arriving on time would send this message. But because I had another camera shoot the next morning to film a commercial, I headed home chafing with resentment for having to postpone more of *Fortuna*'s progress. Once again I was caught in a bind—another double identity. By day I was the hard-at-it set decorator, caring deeply about my film work; by night I was the hard-at-it screenwriter caring deeply about my script career. Though I had climbed the ladder of success working on camera crews, learning in the world's premier entertainment center and gaining invaluable expertise, inside I was fuming. There was never enough time to write.

Make time. Take time. Do it, John, do it.

As I walked home, frustrated and feeling powerless, I noticed a neighbor man just a stone's throw from the narrow pathway between the Little Place and a flowering poinsettia tree. He was hammering loose boards on his porch. A husky fellow with a barrel chest, he wore a cowboy shirt and sported a bushy red beard. I'd seen him often, an outgoing guy my age who lived half a block down the street from our four-plex apartment building in a tiny bungalow shaded by a towering avocado tree.

"Hi, Joe!" I called out. "Any good auditions lately?"

Joe looked up. "Nothing but a two-bit drunken friar role. Had to tell my agent I wouldn't even try out for it, John."

Joe Conner was what they call in Hollywood a character actor, a non-leading man who played stereotyped supporting roles such as hit men in gangster movies or cowboy sidekicks in Westerns. We'd met two years before and had traded hard-luck stories, his about going nowhere in his acting career and mine about a dead-in-the-water screenwriting career. Being husbands, we'd talked about our marriages. Being Midwesterners, we'd talked about our former lives in the smog-free heartland. Being transplanted Southern Californians, we agreed that Hollywood was a polluted paradise.

"An actor refusing an audition?" I replied.

Wiping the sweat from his forehead, Joe stopped hammering. "Had to. It ain't right portraying a man of faith as a drunk."

"Run that by me again, Joe."

"You know, the Robin Hood/Friar Tuck kind of character?"

"Yeah. So?"

"So, he represents God. No matter what folklore says about such a man, I don't think it's right to perpetuate the stereotype."

I'd heard Joe come up with some interesting twists before, and this time was no exception. "But, Joe, some other actor is going to get hired. And *he'll* get paid, but you won't. There goes your career."

"That's show business. My job is to be true to what I believe."

I paused. Here came the twist. I asked, "And what do you believe?"

He walked over and looked me in the eye. "It's not right to portray a man of faith as a buffoon. Religion is lampooned too often in the media, you know, and I don't want any part of it. It'd be hypocritical."

During the past two years, I'd listened to Joe's conservative ideas about the Old West and the Civil War, favorite topics, and his belief that Watergate should never have toppled Nixon. I took it all with a grain. "But are you saying people in religious orders never drink?" I probed.

"Irrelevant! I'm not going to perpetuate the media's disdain for God's servants no matter how much it pays or what it means to my career."

"Well, you definitely have high standards." And for that I respected him. We talked in this manner awhile longer, then I hinted that I needed to get home for supper and, for a change, be on time. He asked in a polite way about my work, in particular what I was writing.

"Another screenplay. It's called *Fortuna*."

"For—what?"

I explained the title, which meant "fortune," and that I'd teamed up with a collaborator. "We concocted the story together and he agreed that I should write it." In our two minds it was the perfect high-concept commercial screenplay, I went on. *High-concept* meant a must-see, one-line description of a movie that would motivate audiences to flock to see the film, a term I'd learned in costly writing seminars. What I didn't disclose to Joe was the bargain I'd made with Fate, the win-live/lose-die pact. Instead, I said, "Gotta go, Joe," then asked him. "Would you read *Fortuna* when it's done? And give me your feedback?"

"Sure. Be glad to." He then promised to pray for me.

"Pray for me?"

"Yes, I can see you're rattled by this project for some reason."

That seemed both strange and insightful, but I let it pass. As we parted company, he gave me a handful of avocados from his towering tree to take home, so I could impress Susan, a guacamole lover.

The next morning I dragged myself out of bed at 5:00, having indulged in too much booze and wine the night before. My enjoyment of Susan's authentic Taiwanese stir-fry dinner had been dampened by my overdrinking, which in turn had dampened her feelings of being appreciated. Not much new there, despite my honest intentions and the delicious guacamole made from Joe's avocados.

When I arrived on the film set that morning, however, something *was* different. It was August 19, 1977, my 33rd birthday. Not only that, but I was working again for the boss I loved to hate, director Sergio Borloff, the same guy I'd goferred for my first day as a utility man at Zuma Beach on the camping equipment commercial, five years earlier. Also, the advertising agency came from my very own Minneapolis/St. Paul, not New York or Chicago as usual. This agency represented one of Minnesota's national name-brand manufacturers of breakfast cereals, and I was the highly paid art director in charge of making the product—in a new-and-improved package—look sensational on camera.

My spirits should have soared to Nirvana levels, but as usual I was vaguely hungover, so I put on an upbeat mask to fool everybody. Secretly, I felt bored from the sheer redundancy of yet another copycat commercial for the American viewing public who could care less about watching it. My spirits also felt low because my dream—what I believed was my future and best hope for happiness—sat idle at the typewriter in the Little Place waiting for me to write the next memorable scene about millions of supersmart world citizens acting out of sync with their primitive emotions because they'd swallowed *Fortuna* pills.

As always, I was walking a tightrope between two opposing worlds and acting one way while feeling another.

"John, are you and your good little elves going to make everybody happy today?"

Hearing Sergio's voice, I turned as he strolled up to my prop table with a cup of coffee and eyeballed two of my assistants who stood handpicking the largest cornflakes for the close-up shots later in the day.

"Anything for you, Sergio!" I replied. "We exist to make you and your high-paying guests ecstatically happy." My sarcasm was part of our banter. As with all film production companies, Sergio's firm courted favor with the most prestigious and high-paying agencies, and part of my role was to deliver on the exalted promises he'd made—or risk loss of the agency's future business.

He rolled his eyes playfully, but there was a stab of seriousness in his glance, perhaps his way of reminding me to gear up for the critical product shots to come. So began the organized chaos of that day's 15-hour shoot involving 53 superbly trained professionals whose coordinated efforts combined to put 30 seconds of advertising on a 21-inch screen, so viewers could get up from their sofas and turn their backs while going to the bathroom or refrigerator before the next segment of their interrupted sitcom or talk show resumed.

Film shoots are a study in opposites. On the one hand, the skilled workers cooperatively create an elegant symphony of efficiency: muscle-bound men called "grips" pull wheeled dollies that carry camera operators who focus lenses on actors who in this case play an All-American family, mouthing their lines as sound techs record their dialogue and gaffers aim lights on their faces in stage sets designed by art directors like me, while production assistants bring coffee to the agency "creatives" who observe every nuance of these screen performances on video monitors positioned for their critical viewing.

On the other hand, the numerous cables on the floor make it easy to trip or stumble while the noise of airplanes overhead spoil sound takes or idle crew members carousing at the fully stocked snack table get in the way, or fuse boxes explode from high amp lights that spook the actors who blow their lines and make the on-camera family dog pee on expensive kitchen furniture—all of which were my responsibility to have purchased, transported, set in place, and now clean up and reset for a new take.

Amid this mayhem, hour after hour, I thought of having reached yet another birthday without career, sexual, or emotional satisfaction. I allowed my miserable thoughts to hatch miserable feelings that magnified my suffering—my own secret hell amid preparations for another splendid off-camera performance for the sake of American television commerce.

In the end, I managed to visit for a few minutes with one of the agency producers about his interest in reading my hot new screenplay *Fortuna,* and, joy of joys, he handed me his business card, so I could send the script to him. As Sergio called "Wrap!" for the day, I packed up equipment with my assistants for an hour, drank three beers, and smoked a joint along with my crew buddies. Just after 9:00 P.M., I left the studio and arrived home a half hour later.

Susan and three-year-old Emily were waiting up for me with a cake and 33 burning candles. They sang "Happy Birthday," gave me huge hugs and kisses, presented me with a card and a gift, and we all went to bed. As grateful as I was to Susan, I fumed within, angry at life because I felt one year older and could not reverse the feelings of failure. In my mind, I'd spent this special day toiling on trivia, a slave to breakfast cereal rather than forging ahead on my dream. My paying work, including double overtime, meant nil. My dream meant all, despite its never having benefited my family with even poverty wages.

As Susan turned out the lamp beside the bed, I grumbled, "Next year by this time, I hope these stupid commercials are ancient history and cameras are rolling on *Fortuna*."

Susan sighed. "Right, John."

"What's that supposed to mean?"

"Never mind. Oh, okay. It means you're wanting, wanting, wanting again. Do you have any idea how awful it is to wish you happy birthday and minutes later hear you moan and groan?"

I felt boxed in, trapped. Again, I was hurting her. As if my aspiring for lofty goals inflicted anguish on her. *If only lofty RESULTS matched lofty goals! I'm only trying to live out what I'm called to do!*

I tossed and turned until midnight drew near. My ulcer flared, aching and burning. It felt as if a rodent kept gnawing away inside my gut. I debated whether to get up at 2:00 A.M. and pour a stiff one—"poor me, poor me, pour me a drink"—but decided sleep had to come naturally this time. An hour later sleep finally descended upon me, but no peace came with it.

⌒∞⌒

My efforts to write a blockbuster screenplay resulted weeks later in a honed, refined, winner of a script—so my partner and I told ourselves. *Fortuna*'s launch day arrived. My partner, Dale Thompson, and I personally delivered script copies to a dozen hand-picked agents and producers on a Monday. With tempered optimism, we rolled joints and waited. The suspense mounted hour by hour. Of course we knew it would take days or weeks to hear anything, but in our excitement we kidded about miracles happening and puffed billows of hazy smoke in hopes of hearing sooner.

Held at bay during this period were the stresses and strains from the tensions in my relationship with Susan. She had spoken the D-word, "divorce," recently. According to her, my attitudes and activities around drinking, pot-smoking, womanizing, and screenwriting were addictive, out of control. "Where am *I* in your life, John? I feel edged out. I don't know how much longer I can take it."

I realized something major was at stake, so I backpedaled, suggesting that we take a long vacation after hearing about *Fortuna*, so we could sort things out and hopefully find ways to come back together. After some sharp retorts, she agreed. We both enjoyed traveling, so plans emerged to take a month off once *Fortuna* was officially launched. We prepared to drive cross-country in our Dodge van with Emily, mainly to sight-see and visit our families. From these times of talking with her, I realized that I loved Susan and wanted to fight for our marriage rather than call it quits.

At the end of the same week while Susan, Emily, and I were eating supper, the phone rang in our apartment. It was Russ Oberon, one of the hand-picked producers, calling to tell me he had stayed late in his office to read *Fortuna*. "I've just finished the last page and couldn't put it down, John. I'm late for supper and my wife is going to kill me, but I had to call you. Your story is so moving!"

My soul leapt somersaults. I envisioned *real* results at last, results matching my Oscar-sized dream. Then came his magic words: "I want to read everything you've ever written, John, and everything you ever write. You are a masterful writer."

My pact with Fate had turned me into a winner!

"Great, Russ! Thanks for calling. Keep talking."

I listened, awestruck. Everything he said mirrored what I'd hoped for: "great plot . . . fascinating characters . . . worthy theme . . . high concept."

"So what about a deal?" I ventured. "When can we get together and discuss a contract?"

In an abrupt turnaround, I heard Russ stammer, "I . . . I love your story, John. But don't get me wrong, it's good, it's just not right for us. It's a little rough in spots. Sorry, but we have no interest in partnering."

I panicked. "No interest? How can you rave about my work, but not want to move ahead?"

"Don't shoot off at me," he protested. "It's purely subjective, okay?"

"I'm just asking! What you said doesn't make sense!"

"Stop attacking me! What I'm trying to say is you're really talented and are going to make a fine screenwriter. Not that we have a deal."

My blood pressure doubled. "Russ! Don't come off like you love my work and then cut me down. It took you two hours to read it. I took me two years to write it. I just don't understand why you won't discuss making it."

"Hey, mister, you're losing me!"

We got into a shouting match. My rage kicked in. His snooty attitude seemed just like Mom's. Somehow I knew this kind of response would be the same we'd get from the remaining professionals. I sensed he was setting me up like Mom used to when she'd compliment me before assigning another of her major fix-up projects. Had he and I been face-to-face, I might have attacked him with the same homicidal rage I'd harbored toward Mom. Instead, I called him horrible names and slammed the phone in his ear.

My pact with Fate had betrayed me.

The end of my life flashed before me like surreal fireworks against a black sky. I knew I'd lost him as a future resource, but it didn't matter. I wouldn't live long enough to worry about it. Enslaved to my passions, gripped by the morbid impulse to end it all, I bellowed in pain.

Startled, Susan shouted, "Are you all right?" Then she saw me reach for my keys and asked, "Where are you going?"

"Out!" I growled.

In a flash I stormed outside to our Dodge van to enact my suicide plan. Heart pounding, I put the key in the driver's door to unlock it but something made me stop. By some strange force, I turned away from the parked van and headed down the street . . . toward Joe Conner's house.

> "There is a proper time and procedure for every matter,
> though a man's misery weighs heavily upon him."
>
> *Ecclesiastes 8:6*[1]

∽ *Chapter Ten*

A Wheat Field in Nebraska

I found Joe standing in his front yard, watering his lawn. He looked up, surprised to see me coming. As I got closer, Joe lowered the hose in his hand. Earlier I had arranged for him to take our house key the next morning when we left for our trip. Instead here I was handing it to him now. His brow wrinkled in a scowl. Noticing my foul mood, he uttered, "Something's wrong, John. You're beside yourself. What is it?"

I pointed to the white H-O-L-L-Y-W-O-O-D sign on the hillside three miles away, visible through the palm trees lining the street, then burst into a tirade about "the vipers in Hollywood who kill aspiring careers." I felt livid with the same kind of rage I'd suffered from growing up as the butt of Mom's tricks and schemes. I repeated details about Russ's phone call to him, how it started off so well and then turned wicked.

"Do you know God loves you, John?"

Joe's question stopped me cold. "God? What's He got to do with it?"

"Do you know He has a plan for your life?"

"I'm . . . I'm not sure. A plan?"

Joe remained silent. I had no way of answering his questions. I stared at him. "What does any of that have to do with what's going on?" I asked.

"If you knew God personally, John, you wouldn't be going through all this turmoil right now."

"Get serious, Joe. What d'you mean *personally?* You're not any happier than I am. You've been jerked around by the system the same way I have."

"True. But I have the Lord."

I looked straight into his eyes trying to fathom his drift. I drew a blank.

"You're angry right now," he said, "'cause things aren't going your way. That's pride."

"Pride? I'm the least proud person in the world! I've got nothing to be proud of!"

"Pride is when our little plans don't go the way we want and we get all bent out of shape about it."

Bull's-eye. The impact of his words hit me hard and registered sharply.

Joe continued. "What He wants is for us to tell Him our problems."

"Problems? Yes! When are things ever going to break for me? The jerks who run Hollywood don't know quality when it hits them in the face. Five years of hard, uphill work with nothing to show for it. That's a long time."

"God is waiting for you to turn to Him."

I struggled to grasp his spiritual take on my dilemma. How could Joe, a country boy from rural Illinois with a barrel chest and an untamed beard, understand *me*? "Who . . . who says there's proof God exists?"

"People of faith all through the ages, that's who. I can tell you He exists. For me it's as plain as the nose on your face."

I balked, nearly gagged. "Sounds like drivel, Joe. What's your evidence? I see no reason for believing myths like that with so many unfair and evil things happening every day. I suppose you believe in Santa Claus and the Easter Bunny too."

Unfazed, he looked at me kindly and said, "Jesus is the sure way for anyone to have intimacy with God. God has provided a way for you to know Him through His Son."

Again I balked. I simply could not absorb what he was saying. Sarcastically, I pressed my point. "What about Santa Claus and the Easter Bunny?"

"Look," he added, "you have a choice, John. The reason you're frustrated is because you're not following God's plan for your life. It's that simple."

Deep down at some nonverbal level, I connected with his words and felt stirred by his confident attitude. The authority behind them hit another bull's-eye and registered sharply.

"For one thing," I countered, "Christ died 2000 years ago."

"Absolutely right, John."

"So how can you know Him *today*? You talk as though He's alive."

"He is."

"Please, spare me."

"He died two 2000 years ago, true, but He was raised from the dead three days later."

"What! You don't really believe that, do you?"

He took this last jab with a shrug. Joe's face remained calm. He, too, knew the same frustration I did professionally, but he was peaceful about it. It jarred me.

"Well, I'm glad you've got your little crutch," I went on. "Meanwhile I've got to finish packing for our trip. See ya." I started walking away—still fuming inside, but puzzled—still resolved that my life must end. My statement about finishing packing was a ruse.

A few feet later, halfway across the street, I stopped. "Pride? What makes you call it pride?"

"Have you ever read the book of John?"

I shrugged.

"When our little plans don't go the way we want them to, odds are they're not fitting into God's plan. Thinking that our way is the only way is pride."

That zapped me. I'd tried everything to find answers and meaning: hard work, alcohol, sex, drugs, the American dream, philosophy, Scientology, astrology, numerology, but nothing had worked. The riddle remained unsolved.

"If it's like you say," I continued, "what should I do about it?"

"Read the Gospel of John."

Something penetrated my mental armor. John, my own name. It stuck. It intrigued me. I was a writer. Writers write books and there was a book out there with my name on it. I asked Joe, "Why?"

"The Gospel of John talks about why Christ came to save us from our pride. If you want to go one better, read Romans."

"Why Romans?"

"John tells us why Christ came to us. Romans tells us why we need to come to Christ."

I stood there in the street, wordless. I knew somehow he might have a point. Joe kept watering his lawn, hose in hand, allowing me my space. I walked away, mulling over everything he had said, realizing vaguely that it was one angle I'd never investigated. Competing for my mind's attention was how and when to do myself in, but this new information interfered like crazy. As long as there remained one stone unturned, it seemed feasible to postpone my suicide plan. That evening, and all through the wee hours that night until dawn, I battled insomnia and ached, really ached, to end my misery and finish my time on earth. A very dark, dark night of the soul.

The next morning Susan, Emily, and I departed on our cross-country trip. Superficially everything seemed the same—another of my Academy Award performances of acting one way while feeling the opposite. We drove from state to state, the kind of mile-after-mile monotony that soothes one's nerves and makes you think. Three thousand miles later, we arrived in New Jersey on a crisp October day. Our visit with Susan's folks turned out to be the first affable time we'd spent with them since our wedding eight years earlier, largely due to Emily whose playfulness as a toddler consumed their attention and aroused their affection.

During the usual adult get-togethers over cocktails and dinners with Susan's parents and relatives, it dawned on me that something was amiss between her and her dad. Even more than his being a chronic alcoholic and rage-aholic, Bill Troeller was acting morbid one minute and joking the next. Volatile, then saccharin. Like Archie Bunker, he cursed "niggers" and Catholics in one breath, then the next breath cried tearfully about "my little princess who moved away and never came back home." Something was awry. Having always put Susan on a pedestal, having called her "my little princess" from childhood, he made a play for her sympathies by asking her to stay a few days longer. But she deftly avoided answering him and kept him at arm's length.

"I get the creeps every minute we're here," she confided to me privately later in her girlhood bedroom. She insisted that we limit our visit. As I listened, I noted her favorite wallpaper of cute dog figures, now faded and peeling. "We can't agree to his asking us to stay a few more days, John."

"Why not? Sounds okay to me."

"I just can't explain it. I get the creeps every minute he's nearby. There's no way I can get close to him; in fact I have to get away."

I probed, trying not to pry. "The creeps? How come?"

"I'm not exactly sure. All I know is I don't want to stay here a minute longer than we have to, and I think it's as much for Emily's benefit as mine."

Not willing to argue, I agreed and we left on the scheduled day.

In Minneapolis, we spent the usual get-togethers with my family—drinks, dinners, touch football, gin rummy, and chess games. When nobody was looking, I stole minutes sneaking extra drinks and smoking joints on the sly. With Mom, I was civil, but nothing more. We talked superficially, limiting ourselves to safe topics such as her adjustment to widowhood, her occasional dating of eligible widowers, and her retirement from full-time interior decorating. She had also learned how to drive a car. No mention of the Chippewa Hills years or Dad's death. Mainly, I felt a low-grade sorrow because these painful experiences went unaddressed, and I lamented the absence of healing that could have resulted.

One noon I visited Dad's gravesite to pay my respects. The sunlight shining through the trees intensified their leaves' brilliant reds, browns, yellows, and oranges. It was exactly the same kind of sunny day when we boys had toiled moving those god-awful birch trees. The beautiful grassy setting was situated alongside a duck pond with overhanging birch and pine trees. I knelt by Dad's granite marker, brushed the dirt off his carved name, and stood awkwardly silent.

Twelve years had passed since his death and my witnessing the miracle of his eyes shining with a supernatural radiance as he gave himself up to a divine, welcoming presence. I held back tears. I leaned closer, muttering, "Dad . . . Dad . . . Dad . . ." I began heaving with huge sobs and wet, flowing tears. He and I had seldom connected, or bonded, or had time to talk. I'd never heard him say, "I love you, Johnny." I'd never listened to him give me advice—how often I'd needed it! Something more important than his boys had consumed Toby Prin, had diverted his priorities and kept us apart. My sobs grew louder and the tears flowed stronger. My mind protested:

Nowadays is no better than then!
What model of manhood do I have to go by?
Who will help me make the decisions a man needs to make?
Why didn't we ever talk?

I sobbed, realizing that the precious bond between a father and a son, the assurance and belonging every healthy child needs, was never, was not now, and never would be.

In a surprise move on her part, Mom invited us to attend church with her that weekend, a whopping big change because she'd never behaved religiously a day in her life. I chalked it up to her being a widow and the new friends she'd met and possibly her loneliness, so we all tagged along to a Lutheran church of her choice on Sunday morning.

Listening to the preacher's sermon, I experienced the unexplainable again. Like Joe Conner's words, the preacher's stirred me exactly as Joe's had. The same authority and power rang behind them. The minister stood dwarfed in the pulpit, a little pip-squeak of a guy, but his message boomed with God's holiness. His theme: "God's loving eye is on the sparrow; how much more is His loving eye on you?" He spoke of God's caring for the humblest of creatures and that humans surely were more special than humble birds. His assurances of God's love and tender care pierced my mental armor and applied directly to me—an utter surprise, but one that felt very soothing and a whole lot like Joe's message to me days earlier. The same supernatural stirring now moved my spirit as I listened to the preacher.

When we left the church, Mom walked to the car as if nothing had fazed her, only to ponder, "Where should we go for lunch?" Susan whispered that she thought the sermon had been "a boring waste of time." I kept silent, wondering how I could have been so touched, but I held close to the wonderfully soothing feeling I still felt. Nothing could make me let "the stirring" go; shivers literally shot through my whole being.

Two days later, the morning after Halloween in 1977, Susan, Emily, and I departed for California. The soothing feeling had stayed with me. However, while driving through mile after mile of flat prairie on the South Dakota plains heading to "Lost" Angeles, the layers of oppression and confusion common to a suicidal, double-minded, alcoholic/addicted Secret Keeper like myself began to bombard me again. The prospect of returning to LA and facing all the garbage waiting there weighed me down. While I gazed out the window at the tall sand-colored grasses whizzing by, with miles of time to dwell on my thoughts, my mind and emotions warned me that I was in mortal danger.

Physically, my ulcer was worse, my sleep often fitful, and my fingernails regularly chewed raw.

Emotionally, I seethed with resentments, wallowed in self-pity, smoldered with blame, and lashed out too often in flashes of hot temper.

Mentally, I thought Fate had shafted me and made me a victim, doomed never to change. My grief over Dad and sorrow over Mom loomed freshly reopened.

Behaviorally, I suffered fretful bouts of ruminating for days on end, sometimes shattering dishes or smashing my fists into walls.

Sexually, my supercharged hormones spurred my attempts to become satisfied and liberated, but, in truth, they were hardly more than lustful promiscuity and another avenue of failure.

Professionally, my writing had netted only two options totaling $5,000, and I sensed that I was reaching burnout from years of grueling hours on film crews.

Spiritually, I felt like an unworthy dirtbag, shameful and unredeemable. My pathological obsession with self seemed irreversible and immutable.

In a farming region of vast wheat fields, we crossed into Nebraska on a narrow two-lane state highway. Susan mentioned Emily's need to eat, so we stopped at a roadside picnic area for lunch. Susan took out soup and sandwiches and positioned Emily on the bench to feed her. Disgruntled,

I barked, "I'm not hungry," then went walking up a gravel road, rudely leaving Susan on her own.

The curved road led me to an immense field of brown wheat stalks taller than my head, rippling in the wind like ocean waves. In front of me was no civilization, just brown wheat, blue sky, white clouds, and black birds. A cool breeze blew in my face. I gazed at the splendor of nature, but felt a bitter, wrenching, alienated feeling.

Why can't I enjoy this beauty instead of feeling totally out of place?

I stepped into the field, as if beckoned. My feet took me about a hundred yards toward the center where I stopped, looked up, then felt woozy and collapsed onto a mattress of dead stalks and rich, black soil beneath them. *Get up!* I told myself, but couldn't. My nose smelled the pungent earth, and my eyes peered at clods of dirt the size of golf balls just inches from my face. *This is ridiculous!* I scolded myself, aware that the farmer who owned the land could shoot me for trespassing.

Gazing skyward, I felt an ache worse than the ache to do myself in: the ache to live. Tears came to my eyes. My throat became parched. I wanted to scream out against the injustice of my life, against everything wrong and unfair and hurtful. Then I started sobbing and pounding my fists against the ground violently, the same as I'd smashed them against hard walls.

I wanted to change the direction of my life, but felt powerless and hopeless.

In a searing flash, I heard Joe's words again. If Jesus was alive like Joe had said, then He should have no trouble hearing me. "ARE YOU THERE?!" I hollered aloud, voice cracking, shaking my fists at the sky.

Silence.

"CAN YOU HEAR ME?!" I implored, sobbing louder.

More silence.

"DO YOU CARE?!" I waited for a reply, some kind of response. Then I cried out, "Jesus, if You *are* alive . . . if You *can* hear me . . . if You *will* help me . . . then please, please, *please* come into my life! Do whatever You have to do to make me okay. I need You. I'm going to end it otherwise. Please! Heal me! Fix what's wrong and make it right! You're my only hope!"

Still sobbing, I saw my life pass before me in flashes. From extreme exertion, I passed out. I lay crumpled on the ground. Several minutes later, I came to and realized nothing was different. No parting of the clouds. No angels with halos. No ladders from heaven. I felt like a surgery patient reviving after anesthesia, slow to reassemble reality. Flat on my back, I looked straight up, questioning whether I should even get up at all.

Thoughts of Susan with Emily at the picnic table jarred me. She had no idea where I was and might be panicky. I stood up. I looked back the way I had come and noticed a graveyard off to the side. Something about it drew me toward it, and I could tell by its geographical positioning that heading that way would allow for a quicker, shorter return to the picnic area where Susan and Emily waited. Vaguely disappointed that no miracle had occurred and still feeling anesthetized, I trudged toward the graveyard, noticing the gravestones on the periphery. One stone was so large that it dominated the others by several square feet. As I approached its rough-hewn surface of red granite that faced the field, I straddled a low fence and passed by it, observing the polished surface on the opposite side.

Immediately I stopped, astounded.

There in front of me stood Jesus Christ, a towering figure chiseled in relief, eight feet tall, hands extended toward me, eyes peering straight into mine. Beside him were chiseled the words: "The Lord is my shepherd, I shall not want . . ."

My mind whirled. In the next instant my soul exclaimed, "I just talked to You! I . . . I just made You my 'shepherd.'" The remainder of the 23rd Psalm was chiseled there, but my eyes glazed over. Feeling a warm shiver, my joy erupted within me, too enthusiastic to contain. My eyes went back to Him. Seeing the Savior gaze so gently, my spirit awakened and I threw doubt and hesitation to the wind. With everything in me, I let go of my lifetime of pain and joyously accepted the hope of a new life.

I BELIEVED!

I wholly embraced Jesus—and let Him wholly embrace me. Peace entered my weary soul and calmed the violent storm there.

For once I'd done something in secret that I wasn't ashamed of.

MetaViews to Muse #5

To help you recognize and confront secret-keeping tendencies and habits, these reflections on what you've read in the past couple of chapters are meant to encourage you to consider your own life's challenges and choices.

✳ Consciously curbing your secret life once or twice doesn't mean it's fully tamed. That's because within the Secret Keeper, the Self and the Addict wage a constant battle for supremacy. The Self is your genuine healthy identity from birth, and the Addict is that voice in you that develops later and whispers mean-spirited messages based on faulty conclusions you've made about life's experiences.

Can you identify with this struggle? If so, what messages does the Addict in you whisper? Do you heed or ignore these messages?

✳ Secret lives lead to delusional thinking, leading Secret Keepers to try to serve "two masters," but eventually they devote themselves to one and despise the other. This is because, as we face each new moment in life, we may fall back on a flawed strategy that worked to resolve emotional tension at a difficult time in our past, but now defeats the very satisfaction we seek—smoking cigarettes once calmed my nerves, but eventually made me much jumpier.

Are you trying to serve two masters? What are they?

✳ The person trapped in a secret life suffers layers of decay and dysfunction, contaminating the whole being inside and out. Secret Keepers eventually feel cheated and harbor a deep sense of injustice about their lives. They often seek to numb or escape this injustice by medicating frayed emotions through abuse of alcohol/drugs, compulsive gambling, indulgence in sexual addictions, or eating too little or too much. When core issues go unresolved, others in their lives take a backseat while self-absorption, victimhood, and self-pity become the norm.

Do you feel cheated in life? Have injustices been done to you? To what, or to whom, do you turn to numb your pain?

✳ Hurt and emotional pain make Secret Keepers attempt increasingly desperate solutions. The Self comes to hate the Addict because it wins again and again. Despair and suicide can seem to be the only alternatives. Once the individual exclaims, "I don't care! I give up!" his or her bankruptcy of resources prevents constructive change, and maximizing pleasure/minimizing pain becomes the main strategy worth repeating.

Does any of this sound familiar? Can you identify what percentage of the time the Self wins out? The Addict? Have you reached the end of your rope? If so, now what?

✳ Solutions for Secret Keepers work best when they incorporate the spiritual into their lives. Spirituality helps struggling individuals by providing wisdom, guidance, and a supernatural Presence to bolster the person's limited options. Spirituality offers reliable rituals and reconnection to fellow humans who follow a creed.

Do you believe there is a Higher Power? What role does spirituality play in your life? If not, do you view spirituality as a crutch or an irrelevant fairy tale? Are you trying to go it alone?

✳ **The following are two of the eight splintered mindsets of a Secret Keeper:**
  ✦ Maximizing pleasure and minimizing pain
  ✦ Treating others last and oneself first.

Part 3

> **"You aren't responsible for getting into the addiction, but you are responsible for getting out of it."**
>
> *Jack Hungelmann*
> *Author's friend*

∞ Chapter Eleven

Holy in Hollywood

Back in the van driving after lunch, Susan and I sat staring out the windshield. She drove and held the wheel rigidly, upset about my noontime absence. She had every right to be, although she said nothing directly about it. It was just another slight in a long list of offenses. "So, John," she said, breaking the silence, "what do you think about us finding a church when we get back home?"

My agnosticism was well known to her, so my reply—"Fine by me"—was shocking.

She jerked her eyes off the highway and exclaimed, "Did I hear you right?"

"Yes," I replied. Any mention of the topic of church until then had occurred solely in the context of Emily's future "religious training," and my answers never sounded positive. I weighed telling Susan about my wheat-field/graveyard experience right then, but it was too new and I wasn't sure what it meant yet, so I omitted saying anything.

"You mean 'yes, let's go looking'?"

"Yes, I mean yes."

"Well then!" she trumpeted. "Maybe this trip did some good after all!"

At bedtime that night when I settled into the double sleeping bag on the floor of the van next to Susan, I closed my eyes, expecting another bout of insomnia. For months my sleep had been erratic, too many hours spent trying to fall asleep, too many nights stewing and fretting. Now I felt frazzled at a cellular level, my weary soul exhausted, but the warm stirring felt even stronger. That night something very different happened. I felt profound peace and drifted off to sleep like a newborn baby.

At a cosmic level I *was* newborn.

Back home in Los Angeles, we opened a stack of mail and came upon a letter confirming our reservation to a seminar for married couples sponsored by the Catholic church. We'd forgotten about the Marriage Encounter retreat we had applied for months earlier and, because of our fatigue from traveling, we decided to call to postpone attending the three-day session.

The person on the other end of the line gently encouraged me to re-consider: "It's for couples with good marriages who want to make them stronger . . . child care is provided . . . you've already paid for it" Neither of us had any prior connection with Catholicism and we'd agreed reluctantly to attend in the first place at the suggestion of acquaintances, but I sensed this was somehow associated with my wheat-field experience. So I advocated our going. Susan, amazed at my willingness, agreed.

That weekend we sat among several couples, listening to priests and lay people talking about God's perspectives on the sanctity of marriage. Again, something stirred within me like the soothing feeling from Joe's words and the "sparrow" sermon. When Susan and I returned to our private room during one of the planned "couple's dialogue" breaks, I frowned as I heard her disclose this shocker:

"John, our marriage is crumbling. I think what this weekend is showing me is that it's time to throw in the towel. I regret what I'm going to say next, but I think it's time for a divorce."

My breathing stopped. I swallowed hard. "Slow down. Take a deep breath. Run that by me again."

She confided, tearfully, that she felt driven to get divorced as the only solution to the direction things were going. "I hate to, but I'm ready to call a lawyer. It's come to that." She listed my drinking, dope-smoking, fitful sleep, flashes of anger, brooding, and womanizing—but mostly the womanizing—as reasons.

Alarmed, I took both of her hands and stared into her eyes. "Remember when we stopped in Nebraska for lunch? Remember when I walked off and left you and Emily at the picnic table?" She nodded. I told her every detail about my wheat-field prayer and experience with Christ in the graveyard.

Surprised, she replied, "If what you say really happened, then your behavior will change." More cynically, she added, "Still, I don't think I can wait."

I stammered, "Ah . . . could you put off calling the lawyer for . . . ah . . . say two weeks?"

"Two weeks!" she cried. "I can't wait that long."

I pleaded, "If you're not convinced of my genuine change of behavior in that amount of time, then you have every right to go ahead . . . Please. Something really *did* change in Nebraska. Something real. But proving it is going to take time."

Reluctantly, very reluctantly, she mumbled her agreement. We stared at one another and wiped our tears with Kleenex, then returned to the large group and finished out the weekend.

During the next two weeks, I had no idea how to convince her, but I sensed a new Power at work within me. I went off to work cheerfully, without grumbling, and even whistled peppy tunes while doing chores at home and caring for Emily. My drinking and drugging continued, but with less of the usual urgency. I took the lead the next weekend and made good on our pledge to find a church. We piled in the van one Sunday morning, rather than sleeping late and reading the newspaper, and I drove us around to half a dozen local churches listed in the Yellow Pages. We watched the people coming and going at each church, trying to discern from their faces and body language any hint of "God."

At a church on Hollywood Boulevard around the bend from Universal Studios, we lucked out. A whole range of diverse humanity—couples, families, old folks, kids, blacks, Hispanics—milled about, talking and laughing and praying in the open. Right there in the van, we committed to attending that church the following weekend.

During the week leading up to the two-week deadline, I went to a Christian bookstore to buy a Bible. Before entering, I wondered if somebody might be lurking to ambush me with a tract or collar me with a fire-and-brimstone sermon. Walking inside, nobody seemed ready to pounce, so I ambled to the Bible section and browsed through the various translations, having only the vaguest idea of what to look for. I'd tried reading the Bible at times in my prior search for answers, and it had seemed as dry as reading the phone directory. I glanced sideways and caught the eye of a clerk behind the counter who warmly offered, "Can I help you, sir?"

The words *no thanks* formed on my lips, but instead I heard myself say to him, "Yes, actually. Can you recommend a version for a new believer? Someone who hasn't a clue about Scripture?"

He smiled and stepped over, then kindly gave me a Cliff Notes speed course describing the King James, Revised Standard, and Living Bible translations. I decided to buy the latter because of its everyday English and its soft cover and smaller size that felt comfortable in my hand. It was also the least expensive and had no gold edging or pretentious frills. I thanked the clerk and walked out thinking, *Now I can make good on Joe's idea about reading the Gospel of John.*

My reading of John occurred in one sitting. When I arrived home from the store, I flopped on the couch and finished it three hours later. It read like an exciting short story. I gained a firm understanding of who Jesus was and why He came to earth. My eyes opened to why his murderers hated him and how God turned evil into good on the cross, saving all of humanity from eternal death through Christ's resurrection. I actually liked the guy, this Jesus, and could imagine him as a friend. About all I questioned was his divinity, but my understanding about that would come in time and nothing else seemed improbable or hard to believe.

"Well?" Susan asked when I got up off the couch.

"It's a whole lot better than reading the phone book," I replied.

She appreciated my sense of humor, something rather new, then listened to my impressions spoken in an affirmative rather than antagonistic tone of voice.

"Let's have a drink before dinner and you can tell me all about it," she suggested.

Over cocktails, I informed her about my improved sleep, my healing ulcer, and my fading suicidal thoughts. I gratefully reported how my mind raced less when my head hit the pillow, how the gnawing pain in my gut raged less frequently, and how the black turbulence in my emotions was lifting. "I feel more rested, healthier, and more alive," I told her.

"I'll toast to that!" she proclaimed, raising her glass. It was clear that she took in all this information at face value—joyfully, but also with a dash of skepticism. Might I be "selling" her a bit in the face of the approaching divorce deadline?

Whatever hesitation she may have harbored melted during the first worship service at the church we'd picked out. We arrived for the late morning service the day before the deadline and slid into a pew as inconspicuously as possible—the first service I'd ever voluntarily attended. Before we settled in, an elderly woman noticed Emily, tapped Susan's shoulder, and offered, "We have a special class for toddlers. Let me show you where to go." Susan politely declined, but the lady's eyes sparkled and something moved Susan to accept the offer. The lady then graciously led Susan and Emily away. I stayed seated and held our places.

Glancing around the large, traditional worship area, I saw it filling up fast. Amid the sunlit stained-glass windows, worshippers mingled everywhere and exhibited the same kind of easygoing chatting and socializing we'd observed the weekend before. The impression on me was the very opposite of the kind of church members I remembered seeing at the Lutheran church back in Minnesota during my confirmation days. Here were lively folks, grateful to be spending their time in church, not tight-lipped Scandinavian or German descendents ceremoniously biding their time until the service ended.

Susan returned and assured me that Emily was in good hands. Just then the organ music announced the first hymn. We stood whenever those around us stood and sat whenever they sat, basically following along. Susan knew most of the words to the hymns from her childhood, but I needed the hymnal for every word.

The rest of the service became somewhat of a blur. I basked, more or less, in a state of amazement and awe—how could I have missed all *this* kind of worship for thirty-three years? Was this a church where religion did not block the spiritual, but opened the way to it? Nobody I'd grown up with had ever, *ever* enthusiastically gone to church. Nobody I'd known as an adult had ever, *ever* spoken of Jesus (without taking His name in vain), except Joe Conner. Yet here was a horde of happy worshippers, all raising the rafters in joyous song or sitting in hushed reverence listening to the sermon. The preacher spoke eloquently of God's loving and forgiving nature. When he reached the end of his message, something caught my ear as he declared, "If anyone here today wishes to know our Lord Jesus in a new, intimate, personal way, *today is the day!* With your heart, ask Him *in!* With your feet, stand *up!* Stand up, stand up for Jesus!"

A mighty force within me was so powerful that it lifted me off my seat. I shot straight up from the pew. A ton of bricks on my shoulders could not have held me down. Susan looked up at me, shocked at seeing me upright. Her face beamed wonder. She reached for my hand and held it until the last amen, at which time people around us congratulated me and patted my back or shook my hand.

"You've done a marvelous thing," they all said in one way or another.

Based on changes like these that Susan observed in me, she whispered as we walked to get Emily, "Well, John, the jury is still out." Then she quipped, "But don't stop now! Keep going! I won't be calling the lawyer tomorrow."

Relieved, I squeezed her hand and quipped back, "Let's hope that means never." She smiled and nodded. I smiled and added, "And to think none of these nice people asked us to donate money or to become members. Is something strange going on or what?"

"I'd say so. But I'm sure not unhappy about it. Not a bit."

When I reunited with Joe Conner later that week, he celebrated these developments. "John, that's good news. Welcome to God's family!"

Two months later, I had the privilege of telling Joe about Susan's conversion. He listened intently as I related how she'd opened her heart to Christ in her own quiet way while writing a letter to God during a new believers' class sponsored by the new church. Hers was a serene decision, the opposite of my desperate conversion drama.

"Just as valid," he replied. "Now both of you are in God's family!"

"Joe, how can I ever thank you enough?" I hugged him. "Without you saying what you did that day you were watering your lawn, I shudder to think of what would've happened to me. You're an angel."

"All in God's time," he said, chuckling and scratching his bushy beard. "All to God's credit."

We talked more, mainly about my euphoria as a new Christian and my sense of peace from the gloomy feelings that were fading away. "I'm no longer in charge of my life, but Someone wiser is, and the answers I'm getting are mysterious, but they work out better." Joe and I even discussed whether church membership was necessary and why belonging to a group of believers meant spiritual support more than obligation.

"God doesn't need your money or attendance in church," Joe explained. "God only wants *you*. And belonging to a worshipping group of believers helps that happen in so many ways."

In my quiet hours, I found new discoveries in each book of the Bible that I explored. The pages seemed to open themselves to whatever helpful information I needed at the moment. Reading what once was incomprehensible became enlightening, not a chore. I chanced upon Psalm 34 and read: "The Lord is near to the brokenhearted, and saves the crushed in spirit." [1]

That sure is me!

I flipped a few pages ahead and read in Psalm 40: "He lifted me out of the pit of despair, out from the bog and the mire, and set my feet on a hard, firm path. . . . He has given me a new song to sing, of praises to our God." [2]

That's me again!

I skipped ahead to Ecclesiastes and my heart resonated to Chapter 2: "So I hated life, because what is done under the sun was grievous to me; for all is vanity and a chasing after wind. For all their days are full of pain, and their work is a vexation; even at night their minds do not rest." [3]

My life in a nutshell!

Verse after verse, chapter after chapter, the statements and stories reflected my life. My personal journey on earth. The old misery and betrayals. The new salvation and hope. It felt like I'd stumbled onto treasure, like a prospector searching for gold who unearths a mother lode—wisdom written for *me!* Beyond knowing more *about* God, the hours I indulged in Holy Scriptures provided the bonus of *knowing* God directly, personally, in the present. To know *about* the president of the United States is one thing; it's quite another to *know* him personally and have him part of your everyday life.

These verses and passages gave me something to share with Susan that enlightened and modified the kind of hurtful conversations we'd had on Newport Beach or in bed with the lights out after my near-affair with Betsy. "See?" I exclaimed. "So much of what I was saying is right here in Scripture."

"Yes, I do see, John." She agreed verbally and meant it. But I thought I detected in her weary eyes reminders of those awkward times that were still too fresh to be regarded in hindsight. I puzzled over whether we would ever get past the past. I felt newness in each step, she—despite her own recent transformation to new life in Christ—seemed more hesitant. I closed my eyes in prayer, took her hands, and said softly: "Lord, heal us. Heal everything between us. And bring us to a new place. A place that we may only dream of right now, but will know as real one day. Amen."

To her credit, she worked up a smile, squeezed my hand, and kissed me. "Amen," she said. Then we hugged and she uttered, "Thank you, Lord, for my new husband!"

∞

On film locations and soundstage sets, my baby Christianity survived about as long as a newborn's dirty diaper—minutes, then straight into the toilet. I still swore and cursed, still laughed at off-color jokes. Little by little coworkers learned of my new relationship with an invisible supernatural Partner, discernable over time in my fewer outbursts of profanity or polite "no thank you's" to more than a beer at wrap time. One longtime colleague, a hardworking key grip, asked with lighthearted curiosity, "What's up with the faith thing, John?"

I replied lightheartedly that "a new person has joined me on my life's journey."

He gagged. "Oh? A wealthy producer? A lover? Who . . . ?"

"Think bigger than that, more cosmic."

He stammered and frowned when I finally said Jesus.

"John! *Really!*"

"Oh, it's real all right. Very real."

Whenever I would get into conversations like this, one of two things would usually happen. The person would either look at me in alarm and flee in haste, or make a joke such as humming the melody to *The Twilight Zone* and drift away. In this case the colleague pretended to page me over the intercom like a Star-Trek character, saying, "Earth to John, come in. Earth to John, we're losing you." Word spread quickly after others like him experienced similar conversations.

At parties, a more serious level of questioning occurred, especially once folks were buzzed on booze or dope. Jack Dunn, the gifted set decorator whose poetic sensitivity showed in his stylized designs, made an attempt at one of his parties to get beyond the biased "John got religion" mentality. Eager to bridge our minds, I welcomed a genuine exchange with Jack. As the stereo blared Jackson Browne and billows of marijuana smoke clouded the air, I said, "Ask anything, Jack. Anything at all."

Jack swigged some wine and launched in. "There might be something like a God force out there, but do you have to be so narrow as to name it, John? I mean, by doing that you're eliminating Buddhists and Hindus and Jews and Moslems and condemning them all to hell."

"Whoa! Not so fast! *I'm* not condemning anybody. What happened to me, Jack, is something I can hardly believe myself, even now. And the way it happened was totally unexpected. But it did happen, and at exactly the moment I needed it to. Of all the people surprised by it, I'm the most surprised. Like you, I never believed either."

"Really? Like the clouds parted and—bam!—there was the Big Guy?"

"Not quite. But one minute, nothing. The next, everything. And—bam!—I was alive and free."

"Free?"

I nodded. "I haven't figured out any other way to describe it. But, yes, free."

"Free of what?"

"Oh . . . free of insomnia, free of an ulcer, free of suicidal thoughts . . ."

"*You,* John? Suicidal? Come on."

"Yes, certainly I was headed that way." I continued listing, "Free of so much anger, free of being afraid of death, free of a divorce . . ."

"Hold it. Divorce? You and Susan are on the rocks?"

"We *were.* I suppose nowadays we're a few yards farther from crashing ashore, but the rocks are still there."

"You know," he paused, puffing a joint, "me and Lizzy aren't doing so hot. She brings it up now and then. Just what do women want, man? I don't get it. I work every gig I can, my kids love me, what? What?"

"I wish I could say. I think it has something to do with how differently men and women see things, like marriage or sex. Right now Susan and I feel less apart, and it's only been since Jesus came into our lives."

Jack covered his ears. "Jesus! That name, agh! Can we change the topic now? Here, have a hit." He offered me the half-smoked joint. "Guatemalan. Best weed I've scored in years."

I took the joint from him out of respect and, because I still loved getting high, puffed away. We talked more about his qualms, and I took no offense at his knee-jerk slur against Jesus' name, no more than Joe had when I'd done the very same thing. Without a hint of defensiveness, I realized that Jack just didn't know.

My inner-growth life loomed in my mind as Jack talked. I looked around his living room and picked out individuals whose careers had surpassed mine and felt contempt for them. They were getting ahead at the same things I'd spent six years aspiring to. Envy, although I didn't recognize it, was corroding my feelings of well-being and peace. *I* deserved success as much as they did, but comparing myself to them, I came up short, a failure.

Jack turned to me and asked something more about divorce. I "returned" to the conversation and picked up the thread of our discussion. Just then a young woman walked up and asked Jack for a cigarette. As he fished for one, she made eye contact with me and smiled—exactly the way Simone had at the film company in Minneapolis. Exactly the way Bonnie Witten had in biology class. Her huge green eyes glowed seductively and she carried herself with grace and ease, plainly delighted with her body and appearance. We'd caught one another's eye at other parties, but hadn't yet spoken to each other. I admired her exquisite figure, straight out of *Playboy,* which she concealed as little of as possible. Her entire midriff from below her braless breasts to her navel was bare, and only a blind man couldn't have noticed. When *I* took notice, her eyes lit up.

"Thanks, Jack," she cooed. "Who's your buddy?"

He lit a Winston for her. "Oh, hey, Rita. Meet John, the art director/screen-writer. John, meet Rita, the wardrobe mistress par excellence."

"Very pleased, I assure you," came her reply.

"Very pleased indeed," I said.

"I'm trying to quit these stupid things," she growled, inhaling in a manner that made her bust expand. "But every time I come to a party, I give in." She exhaled in an exaggerated way, then looked directly at me and added, "I guess there are just some things I can't say no to."

Both Jack and I caught her innuendo. "Hey, now!" said Jack, rolling his eyes.

"If you need lessons, Rita, let me know," I said about the smoking, the double meaning clear.

Rita frowned slightly, waited, then looked at Jack.

Jack nodded, then winked. "This dude said no to cancer sticks three years ago. He's got a big head about it."

"Oh, really?" She stepped closer, almost pinning me against the wall. "Is that so, Johnny-o? Any pointers?"

"Yes, that's so," I replied, delighted. "I'm available anytime." I wasn't the least put off by her little game and neither was Jack. We both knew the divorce conversation was over, though.

"Bye-sies, you two," Jack said, ducking away. "I'm gonna track down Lizzy."

For the next few minutes, Rita and I played word games dripping with innuendo. Rarely had a woman come on as strong and flirted so blatantly, but I loved it. I knew Susan was off on her own talking and smoking—she had continued to smoke cigarettes and puff pot at parties. After an entertaining volley of double entendres with Rita, I skipped ahead to the end game, looked her straight in the eyes, and asked, "Are you interested in going to bed together?"

"Oh, my, absolutely."

"Really?"

"Sex? Together? Absolutely. You're adorable. Especially if it means more 'pointers.'"

"When? Where?"

"What about your place?"

"I'm married."

"Okay. My place."

"Great. Where d'you live, Rita?"

We compared addresses and schedules. No easy matches. She handed me her wardrobe card. "Here's my phone number," she said. "Call anytime, midafternoon on. I'm usually home unless there's a late shoot."

"You got it. I can't wait." I looked deep into her eyes. "Sex together, right?"

"Oh, yes, I can't wait either!" She leaned forward, kissed me, and moved on. I stood in a daze, visions of pleasurable stolen hours with her exquisite body dancing in my head. I went looking for Susan and we tagged up, and the remainder of the evening I played along like nothing was going on—my upcoming fantasy rendezvous stayed a firmly held secret.

Making long-term change when it came to skirt-chasing behavior was far beyond me. I had no idea how to stop philandering. My struggle to gain victory over womanizing kicked into high gear. Although Susan had granted a divorce reprieve, it felt like a mere Band-Aid whenever I reflected on our love life and how far short of truly satisfying it remained. Although bitterness of heart about it no longer flooded my inner being, I still felt blasts of blame at times. Over time "a root of bitterness"[4] entrenched itself in me.

Recent Bible readings and sermons had made it clear that believers praise God in *all* circumstances, no matter how harsh or unfair, because they realize that "all things work together for good for those who love God, who are called according to his purpose."[5] In addition to my frustration over not finding sexual fulfillment and my envy of others' film success, there were my doubts about my calling to make movies. Had the Lord truly called me, or was the voice I'd heard my egotistical desire for prominence? Enough evidence pointed to the latter possibility.

As for Rita, whenever I called to set up a rendezvous, her phone rang and rang. Answering machines were just hitting the market then and she didn't have one, so I made lots of calls. Meanwhile, I worked on location or film sets all day, dashing away to make random calls during breaks. Or, I'd be driving and spy a public phone booth, jump out, and dial her number—until I knew it by heart. Once, she answered and we talked like we had at the party. But regardless of how we tried to schedule a two- or three-hour block of stolen time, it just never worked out. I began thinking that she was stringing me on, but her *words* . . . she'd played up to me and kept the fire alive, reaffirming our pact!

I became tormented by voluptuous images of us making love. These increased my feelings of being trapped in marriage—walking the tightrope again—acting one way while thinking another. My new faith gently warned me that I'd go crazy if I didn't stop. Yet I was doing something I'd never done before; I was praying about it. And prayer was helping. The more I sought answers in prayer, the clearer it became to me that I would have to stop chasing.

"But how? HOW?" I pleaded.

Depend on Me, came the answer.

"Okay, my life is now in Your hands, but the lust . . . it burns and burns."

Depend on Me, came the answer.

"Free me of lust," I implored. In Psalm 37, I read passages that boosted my hopes: "Delight yourself in the Lord and he will give you the desires of your heart."[6] "Commit your way to the Lord trust in him, and he will act. . . .[7] Refrain from anger, and forsake wrath. Do not fret—it leads only to evil."[8]

Two more weeks of phone calls, even a Valentine card to Rita, brought no rendezvous. I became desperate. I felt like the coyote in those *Road-runner* cartoons, chasing the elusive "beep-beep" roadrunner, getting banged up every single time. I reached the breaking point. The depth of my spiritual maturity as a newborn Christian was shallow, so shallow that I prayed, "If it's Your will, Lord, a rendezvous will happen." Then, at a deeper level, "If not, then something in me will have to change—please make Your promises come true."

The next day I did something unheard of. I brought my dilemma to a pastor at the Presbyterian church on Hollywood Boulevard where we were now attending, a down-home-guy in his fifties named Rev. Ralph Osborne. "Please just call me Ralph," he said, welcoming me with a firm handshake into his office. I made my case to Ralph about the eighth Commandment as we drank coffee, asking, "'Do not commit adultery' is terribly old-fashioned, isn't it? I mean, haven't things changed since thousands of years ago?"

Ralph belly-laughed, then *agreed* with me. I couldn't cover my astonishment.

"As a natural man," he replied, "of course I agree whole-heartedly. But once we are in Christ, we become spiritual men. As natural men, we can ignore the commandment. But as spiritual men, the commandment remains in force."

I couldn't hide my disappointment. "Aw, crud. Then I'm afraid I don't know what to do."

"Your hormones are telling you one thing, John," he added, "and the Holy Spirit is telling you quite another. You'll need to decide which to obey."

I held to my position and we debated the differing rationales. "It's just too high of a standard, that's all. To love only one woman in a lifetime . . . come on, Ralph."

He opened his well-thumbed Bible and showed me Scripture passages supporting his view, but continued chuckling.

"What's so funny?" I asked.

"John," he sighed, shaking his head, "you've just joined the age-old struggle—flesh versus spirit. Classic! And do you know how refreshing it is for me to help tackle your dilemma instead of ninety-five percent of what people come to me for, like complaining about the wrong color of candles on the altar?"

I left his office more informed spiritually and less secure selfishly.

The showdown came one afternoon when rain pelted Los Angeles. Though rare, when rain comes to Southern California, the sky rains pitchforks. Our shooting schedule that day ended by early afternoon due to the weather, and I saw an opportunity to steal hours from Susan after a rare half-day of work. I stopped at a public phone booth about 3:00 P.M. and sat in my van with the wiper blades swooshing, getting up the courage to run and call Rita once more, preparing to brave the downpour. I took a deep breath and, though misguided by the thought that it might be God's will, I prayed:

"Okay Lord, bring Rita and me together. I pray You will, because if she answers, I'm going over there no matter what. But if she doesn't answer, then You're going to have to deliver me of this crazy lust thing because I can't take it anymore. Please do something, either way, once and for all. You choose. I'll obey. In Jesus' name, amen."

I ran to the booth, jammed in my dime, and dialed. My heart pounded as I heard the first ring. Raindrops pelted me through the leaky door. Rivulets of water on the pavement soaked my feet. The second ring. *She's gonna answer any second!* The third ring, then the fourth and fifth. There was no Caller I.D. in those days, so I kept hoping. *Damn, where is she!* I kept letting it ring, determined not to hang up.

Miraculously, like the paralysis in Rosie Kowalsek's living room a decade earlier, I experienced an out-of-body miracle, a vision: From a distance I saw a strange man in a phone booth getting soaked; unmoving; a slave to his appetite for sex; hooked to the pay phone like a bull with a ring through its nose, anchored to a fence; an utterly pitiful fool. Behind the man/bull was a large green pasture, lush and fertile, but the bull's nose ring held him captive and immobile, powerless to roam the pasture. He tugged and tugged, but the nose ring held firm.

The pasture was my marriage. The nose ring was my lust. I was the bull, deprived of everything God wanted for me. I could see from His perspective how pitifully foolish I was, and I felt rattled. Then a sudden peace came over me as the phone kept ringing. On what must have been the 20th ring, the receiver in my hand felt heavy. The next ring sounded distant, dimmer. The next ring sounded even farther away. A heavy weight in me broke free and seemed to float away into space. The next ring sounded barely audible. I hardly wanted her to answer now. The last ring was very faint. My hand lifted the receiver to the hook. Sensing deliverance, I hung up.

In my heart, in a very quiet place within, I felt freedom. Overwhelming freedom and forgiveness. Also the knowledge that I would never be hooked again. I *was* delivered. I would no longer have to play the fool, the captive bull, the hapless coyote.

Answered prayers.

I rushed straight home and took Susan's hands, just like I'd done at the Marriage Encounter when she'd brought up divorce. Peering into her startled eyes, I told her every detail about Rita. Being tempted at the party. The secret phone calls. The prayers for help. The rain-soaked phone booth. The supernatural vision. The freedom and deliverance.

She grimaced at my blunt honesty, but rejoiced at the sincere disclosure of secret-keeping habits and behaviors—which I vowed were behind me. We hugged and cried together, two rookie believers bonding.

"God is healing us!" she exclaimed.

"Yes! Something unbelievable is happening!" I echoed.

Our first steps to wholeness bore fruit that afternoon, and one thing remained certain: the dismantling of my secret life had begun.

**"God speaks to us in two ways—
in commands and in promises."**

*Ray Fenton
Author's friend*

~~~ *Chapter Twelve*

Marching to a New Drummer

Rita turned out to be another rejection, another reason to feel depressed. Because we never connected, I felt betrayed by her and the hurt was very real—and hidden except from Susan. Once more, I added another secret to the long list of stolen hours: a six-week amorous adventure that happened entirely in my mind, except for Scene 1 at Jack's party. But this time there was a new and exciting twist, one other person knew about it, lessening the hurtful impact.

Hardly a week afterwards, during my daily Bible browsing, I came upon a description in Proverbs 7 of a woman who approaches unsuspecting men "decked out like a prostitute, wily of heart."[1] This woman "seizes him and kisses him, and with impudent face she says to him: . . . 'Come, let us take our fill of love until morning; let us delight ourselves with love.' . . . With much seductive speech she persuades him; with her smooth talk she compels him."[2]

Rather like Rita at Jack's party!

Then Proverbs 7 records my response: "Right away he follows her, and goes like an ox to the slaughter, or bounds like a stag toward the trap."[3] Then came this warning: "Do not let your heart turn aside to her ways; do not stray into her paths, for many are those she has laid low, and numerous are her victims. Her house is the way to Sheol [hell], going down to the chambers of death."[4]

Slaughter? Trap? Hell? Death?

I had surely been trapped like a bull ready for slaughter and had escaped hell and death in that rain-pelted phone booth. The Lord protected me there and spared me from my own desires. Again the grand mystery, something written thousands of years ago mirrored in my life's reality today. My heart pounded with gratitude and awe.

I was hearing a new drumbeat.

But in other compulsive areas, addiction still waged its all-out fight for supremacy. Fourteen years of guzzling alcohol and nine years of smoking marijuana/hashish were givens in my life and proved highly resistant to change. In the Hollywood film circles where I moved, not to savor either was odd, questionable, even suspicious. By my mid-30s I'd also experimented with cocaine, LSD, and various illicit chemicals as they became available, all condoned by the company I kept. With a new Authority to answer to, however, the battle lines were drawn—I felt tension inside me whenever I indulged and absence of tension whenever I didn't. Another new drumbeat from the new Drummer.

Dilemma: whom to please, my friends or my Friend?

As passionately invested as I was in my Hollywood career, I started picking and choosing the parties I attended and the friends I spent time with based on the probability of drug use. I made these selections voluntarily, in a spirit of freedom of choice. I started counting drinks. I rolled one less joint a day. I began skipping invitations from others to drink or smoke at wrap-time. These efforts to adjust my lifestyle irked some of my associates and generated hostile remarks: "Oh, we're not good enough now?" or "Holier than thou, John?" These pained me because my choices apparently inflicted pain on others, although my intentions never aimed to.

Fortunately, the believers who frequented Hollywood Presbyterian Church, where Susan and I now worshipped each Sunday, understood the using lifestyle and made no big deal about it. They knew such habits would change as my heart changed. Their loving attitude moved me. Neither condoning the behavior nor condemning the individual, they patiently encouraged choices that pleased God.

Susan, too, was all for our cutting back. When I mentioned the pointed barbs I was hearing from film friends and colleagues, she sympathized. "I know how it is, Johnny, and it's not going to change. Like Ralph Osborne said, 'Christians are *in* the world but not *of* the world.'"

"Yeah, that's what I'm finding out. Well, it sure feels different, all right. It's kinda petty, but it still hurts."

"It's the price the world makes those of us pay for 'finding religion.' Except I get to stay here at home comfy and cozy with Emily while you're out there getting flak. It feels uncomfortable, huh?"

"Yep. I guess it proves that we're becoming different people. But inside I feel so much joy it doesn't matter."

"Oh, yes!" She glanced at me with sparkling eyes and a Spirit-inspired smile. "I'm feeling so much more joy these days too. In fact, I've been thinking of changing my name to *Susie*. It's brighter-sounding than *Susan*. What d'ya think?"

"Susie," I repeated, listening to its sound. I'd called her *Susie* occasionally and already liked it.

"I think I'd like to be called *Susie* from now on," she said.

"Gladly. No problem for me. Then *Susie* it is."

In my private moments, addiction's all-out fight for supremacy continued. I wanted to quit or abstain from each enslavement but did not—could not—at first. I still needed alcohol and pot. Going without them felt like punishment. And I still needed to steal hours to feel better. Yet when I heard biblical promises such as, "He who comes to me shall not hunger, and he who believes in me shall never thirst,"[5] or "No temptation is irresistible. You can trust God to keep the temptation from becoming so strong that you can't stand up against it."[6] I tried to make sense of the bind I was in. Once again, I saw I was acting one way while thinking another and walking a tightrope between two opposing worlds.

Over time I discovered that the new, exciting, spiritual feelings springing up within me matched, even rivaled, the familiar highs I routinely sought outside myself. The substance-induced highs had become weaker than those first few times when I had started using and now required more booze or dope to attain the desired level, which in turn put more strain on my body and mind: nausea, hangovers, blackouts, cotton-mouth, and nagging remorse.

The fun of using early on had, over the years, turned to tiresome familiarity. With increasing spiritual awareness, I found that seeking anything outside myself to escape or numb pain was the problem. But my present inner reality never felt right or amounted to what it should have been, so the need to change that reality—improve it, escape it, medicate it—continually agitated me. Thus, the recurring need to steal hours.

Soon I realized the change would have to come from inside, not outside.

The spring months of 1978 saw numerous overhauls in my relationships and career, spurred on by spiritual motivations. The new drumbeat again. The first occurred one morning when I wrapped up all my *Playboys* and similar magazines that had been piled in the closet and put them in three brown paper grocery bags. I carried them outside to the trash and right then and there, severed the "affair" with those ladies in my photographic harem. Since my deliverance from chasing Rita, this decision had been building, and I made it entirely my own without pressure or urging from Susie—solely from divine whisperings. I fully understood that the naked models were substitutes for the real thing and, biblically, were idols. How could the real thing with Susie emerge when I allowed any competition to thrive? For the fundamental promise of our marriage to blossom, I had to remove any and all barriers under my control.

That day I stood at the window watching the garbage man at the curb throw the brown grocery bags routinely into the truck, saying farewell in my heart to my harem. It hurt. It hurt enough that I cried real tears. But as the wet drops silently slid down my cheeks, I knew that what I'd done was in my own best interest and the best interest of our marriage.

Another overhaul took place late in April while I was prayerfully walking on the hillside below the huge white H-O-L-L-Y-W-O-O-D sign. On a secluded footpath just below the concrete foundations of those 16-foot-high letters, in the intense heat from the bright sunlight, I felt a supernatural nudge, *Forgive your mother.* I stopped, wondering if I was hearing things. The inner nudge came again, *Forgive your mother.* I couldn't fathom such a thing and walked ahead a few more feet. The nudge came again, *Forgive your mother.*

I stopped, sat down in the dirt, and surmised that God's drumbeat was beckoning. *But what an impossibly absurd thing! Forgive my mother??* In the same mircosecond, I grasped the essence of a recent devotional reading, one of the first admonitions in my new journey with Jesus: "If anyone has a complaint against another, forgive each other; just as the Lord has forgiven you, so you also must forgive."[7]

"NO!" I screamed aloud. "NO, NO, *NO!*"

Silence. Then, very quietly, the nudge came again, *Forgive your mother.*

For the next couple of weeks, I held a running debate with God. Feeling the pressure to obey, I brought up every argument I could think of: that Mom did not deserve forgiveness, that she hadn't apologized or admitted her faults, that she'd made Dad so miserable that he'd died young, that if she begged then I would perhaps consider it. Memories of her tormenting us as teenagers sickened me. After days of realizing the many things I'd been forgiven for, I returned to the spot near the sign, knelt, and stammered aloud: "Mom, I . . . I . . . forgive . . . you."

Instantly sobs welled up from within me and tears exploded from my eyes. "I . . . I do forgive you, Mom. From my heart, truly." Huge waves of sorrow and grief dislodged and floated away from me. My entire body shook and trembled. I felt like a victim tortured in the holocaust who was forgiving Hitler. Oppressive, ugly, murderous grudges that I'd harbored for years departed from me in waves. My soul groaned from the release of these hurtful feelings. "Yes, I forgive you, Mom, I forgive you, forgive you . . ."

Standing up, I felt freer than I had ever felt as an adult. Mom no longer seemed the focus of my pain, no longer the villain, but I thought of her more like the mother who'd raised me before Chippewa Hills. I no longer imagined her scowling, but caring.

In the weeks and months ahead, the same gentle nudge repeated itself over and over, triggering specific memories. Like Dave's and my 14th birthday when we hauled those heavy paving stones in the 100-degree heat. Like our laying tiles on the basement floor without instruction, proper tools, or words of encouragement. Like the day we dug up those dozens of birch trees and my hatred of Mom raged in my gut.

Each time I struggled to let go of these and presented my arguments against forgiveness to God in prayer. But each time His love trumped my resistance, and I managed to obey His nudge with less resistance. Each time, as I continued forgiving Mom, another old hurt faded and lost its power. And the urge to kill her lessened until it finally disappeared. God knew what He was doing after all, and I became grateful. Grateful for my upbringing for the first time in 22 years.

The new Drummer was drumming louder.

The third overhaul took place in May 1978 as my life purpose came under question. In quiet moments I found myself doubting my motives for staying in Hollywood. I'd registered for a Christian writers' conference weeks earlier and was packing to attend the five-day national event in the San Bernardino mountains 100 miles east of Los Angeles. I pondered, then determined, that a significant factor in my coming to California was to follow my "divine calling" to become a filmmaker. But with my new perspective as a believer and the many failures through the years, I questioned if it had been really nothing more than my wanting to make a name for myself.

In other words, though my desire to make films may have started soundly, had it become—over time—more important that I get the credit and the recognition that my ego demanded? Self-will versus God's will? Lately I'd begun seeing this drive as arrogance or impertinence—little thought of God getting the glory—which left me thinking about giving up movies (dream job) and film-crew work (day job) to pursue a new course: following God's will.

But doing what? Where? How?

My ego tenaciously would not give up without a fight. Soon it became clear one more screenplay was crying out to be created, my ticket to fame. For six months, I labored: first draft, revisions, second draft, rewrites. All in the hope of creating that magical mix of marketable elements, all during spare hours when I wasn't working on a film set. The old double life.

As the script neared completion, I strove to make it everything 'they' wanted to see, those gatekeepers who grant or block access to studios. It portrayed a commercial version of my window-peeping days as a fictional character study, depicting a charming young professional man by day whose nocturnal double life of peeping in windows got him arrested and in devastating trouble with a lovely young lady. I submitted it to 'them' and it bombed. It went nowhere.

But when I read it over again, I grimaced. Even though it fit many of the Hollywood formulas, I realized that it was about as true to my perception of reality as one's fuzzy image in a fun-house mirror. Every page seemed false, contrived, overworked.

I had failed again.

Ah, but with Christ nothing is ever wasted, nothing entirely fails. Rather than the collapse of defeat, I felt the surge of release. Release from Hollywood's distorted world view, which I'd lowered my standards to mimic. Although I felt bitter due to the thumbs-down reception the script got, I did not lash out violently at Fate. Not this time. Instead, I felt twinges of peace that generated a calm I'd never known. Slowly I came to see that my forte might be another kind of writing than screenplays. Perhaps book-writing, writing for readers rather than viewers, might be the drumbeat God wanted me to march to.

Such was my reasoning for registering for the Christian writers' conference. I'd enjoyed making heartfelt entries in my journal, a spiral notebook I'd started to write in after the Marriage Encounter and an extension of my "Dailies" diary. I relished the freedom of writing about my emotions and my impressions anywhere and anytime I wanted. As I wrote down my innermost feelings, I realized to my delight that I seldom paused to correct or rewrite or polish. Words tumbled out, unhampered, and the joy of writing returned.

From these journal pages emerged my "inner landscape," the true me. In time the decision to write books took shape. Writing allowed for digressions and background data, whereas screenplays emphasized action and dialogue. I favored the subjective inner workings of book characters rather than the objective external behavior of screen characters. My reading of novels like *Les Miserables* and *The Robe,* which had achieved these goals magnificently, encouraged me. Combined with my newfound faith, these inklings led me to the conviction that my new choice of writing might somehow fulfill God's original calling. My goal became to present the Gospel in dramatic and far-reaching ways to then-20th-century secular readers.

When I arrived at the mountain retreat hosting the conference, I spoke to everyone about these ideas. While a good number approved in theory, most reacted as though reaching secular readers was "idealistic and not quite right for our readers." The impression I got was, "What we publish helps believers lead more Christ-like lives and encourages their faith." My response, "But what about reaching the millions who are hurting and don't know about Christ's love and salvation?" met with polite smiles and genial pats on the shoulder.

During free time at the conference one evening, I phoned Dave in Houston to get his thoughts. He was now reaping success in his corporate sales career and, frankly, I envied my twin. "Sounds like your fortunes are soaring," I said, "and mine are just bumping along."

Though he usually spoke insightfully, this time Dave was uncertain what to tell me. He expressed consternation about the "God angle" of my dilemma and confided, "I'm mixed up about your spiritual change, Johnny. Have you jumped off the deep end again?" He'd never quite made sense of my high-risk choice of a career in entertainment either and said, "To be honest, I can't put the two together." All he could suggest was "Follow your gut . . . and good luck."

The setting of the conference was a splendid mountain resort nestled among tall evergreens high above LA's smoggy basin. I shared a cabin with three conference participants, and each night after supper we discussed the input from publishers and editors we'd heard throughout the day. One evening I reached for a marijuana joint secretly tucked in my suitcase and casually mentioned my need for exercise rather than discussion. The others stayed and talked.

Danger was far from my thoughts as I stepped out of the cabin and stole minutes to stroll among the majestic trees after twilight in search of an isolated place to toke up. I stopped at a rugged precipice, hidden from the lights of the resort. I rationalized that it would take just a few minutes and nobody would be the wiser. Of course, I was a walking contradiction. Outwardly, I was a radiant believer. Inwardly, I was a slave to stealing hours and smoking dope. A total hypocrite, I knew it was sinful and that I was in bondage to decades-long habits.

Unable to say no to either, I put the "devil's toothpick" to my lips. But something told me to walk a few steps further, to ensure not being seen. I could hear a creek gurgling below. Disregarding the risks involved, I inched forward on the steep rocks and suddenly started losing my footing . . . falling . . . sliding further into the devil's shadow. Miraculously, my downward motion stopped—only inches from a sheer drop-off to jagged wet rocks far below.

I looked up. "You saved me, Lord! Months ago, and now again!" My heart jumped. I shook my head. *Wouldn't the enemy have scored a victory?*

I pulled myself to safety and chided myself. To hide from fellow mortals was one thing. To try to hide from God was laughable. Refusing to light up the joint, I yelled audibly, "Get out of my life, Satan! I have Jesus! You have no power over me!"

The next day in broad daylight, I stood where I'd stopped sliding the night before and saw a fatal drop to the creek 100 feet below. I envisioned the headline: "Christian Writer Dies from Fall—Found Clutching Marijuana Cigarette."

My battle to quit getting high began from that day forward. "Anyone who believes that something he wants to do is wrong shouldn't do it. He sins if he does, for he thinks it is wrong, and so for him it is wrong."[8] This passage confirmed my intentions and helped me see that smoking grass was really just a smoke screen: a stubborn, besetting sin that compromised my daily walk, a counterfeit euphoria that replaced divine intimacy with my Lord.

First, I stopped the illegal practice of buying grass. Then I stopped growing it, and later stopped keeping it in the house. These were important first steps, but they were not enough to eliminate the remorse I felt each time I toked up. *Remorse* is defined as "a gnawing distress arising from a sense of guilt for past wrongs." Remorsefully, I prayed. Remorsefully, I read Scripture. Remorsefully, I tried to stop by my own power until I had asked for forgiveness countless numbers of times. I realized I could not feel closer to Jesus unless I stopped depending on my own feeble strength. "Give me Your will to stop, Lord," I prayed. "Please take away the desire to smoke and my fear of finding Your power inadequate."

I devised an experiment: since grass gave me such a pleasant high, could my depending on Christ (not smoking) equal, or even top, the high from pot? Hadn't I managed just fine without the stupid stuff for years before trying it?

I kept from smoking for a week. It wasn't easy, but the glimpse of freedom from remorse and guilt exhilarated me. Although I wasn't in an altered state, I was in a right relationship that heightened my emotions—getting high could be topped. I abstained another week, but it got harder each day. The cunning Addict in me actively fought for his familiar fix and demanded obedience, until I contemplated one of God's keenest commands: "To set the mind on the flesh is death, but to set the mind on the Spirit is life and peace. For if you live according to the flesh you will die; but if by the Spirit you put to death the deeds of the body, you will live."[9] I wanted to live, not die! Obeying Christ and depending on His power was my out.

Then this encouragement came in prayer: *Every minute you're stoned, John, is a minute we could be sharing together.* Again, the reminder, I risked excluding Him. To make up for this error, I plowed through the Word, seeking guidance. The promises and commands I found turned me in a new direction. My new faith required that I refrain from anything I thought was sin. My Savior wanted me to have His own true character, holy and pure, even though I existed in a mixed-up, sin-ridden world.

For months I felt cravings, but each time I sent up prayers for strength and each time strength came and I resisted successfully, until the cravings became weaker and farther apart. I measured success by the amount of brown gunk I coughed up from my lungs, the same as when I'd stopped cigarettes, until all the coughing stopped and no more gunk remained. I was more alive than dead now—tangible evidence!

After a year-long process of abstaining from dope-smoking, with no relapses despite nagging cravings, I experienced a breakthrough: obedience to God's way, not my way, is its own pleasurable reward. In my spirit I felt waves of soothing chills course through my body from God's Spirit, affirming my new behavior and mindset.

The truth was setting me free.

During this same year, from 1978 through much of 1979, I began going to career-transition counseling and investigating new options. The Christian writers' conference had left a lukewarm aftertaste about pursing career goals in that field, including the dismal news that payment standards were far below secular standards. The career counselors I sought out started me on a battery of tests, interviews, and assignments. These amounted to a wholesale reassessment of my values, interests, skills, and opportunities. I focused first on an inner phase of self-examination, then an outer phase of career exploration and job change. For the first time, I was learning what it meant to live from the inside out.

The process of inner work included determining and prioritizing my dreams, interests, and preferences. It emphasized what I came to learn was my desire to work with *people* and *ideas* more than with *numbers* or *things*. In the outer phase, I gained the insight that I'd succeeded in many more ways than I'd given myself credit for and that returning home to Minnesota suited my new career goals.

With confidence in myself reestablished, I ventured out on a round of "field informational interviews." These involved my asking questions of people who actually worked in positions that I, the job seeker, was investigating. They helped me immensely because I learned inside knowledge regarding professionals' satisfaction levels, compatibility, and formal training in the areas of public health, pastoral ministry, art and design, and corporate communications.

A full year later, many months longer than I'd expected the process to take, I felt prepared to transfer my skills and talents to a more mainstream job/career outside of entertainment—*Hollywood, take a hike!* After saying for years that I would never leave California, I now learned the veracity of the axiom "Never say never."

Leaving Tinseltown was no easy thing, however. My sky-high expectations had gone unmet. I had to face the gnawing reality that I'd failed to meet the challenges, that people would say I'd overestimated myself, that I hadn't proven that I had what it took. I could pat myself on the back for trying, certainly, and for striving to live an adventurous life and career, but the results . . . *the results!* I couldn't point to anything spectacular outwardly, only to a quiet and humble change happening inwardly, unknown to the world's applause, yet affirmed privately by Susie and spiritually by the Lord.

The new Drummer was drumming louder.

The deathblows to my Oscar aspirations came during 1980 from three things—a seminar I attended, a book I read, and my own fatigue. The seminar featured eight weeks at UCLA with 400 other movie wannabes listening to high-profile producer Tony Bill, known for hits such as *The Sting* and *Taxi Driver*. Tony spoke from direct experience about his extreme discomfort working with studio execs; the crooked and cutthroat practices of distributors and marketers; and other bleak, hopeless, spurious aspects of show business. "Only money and greed, not art or enlightenment," Tony concluded, "await the one or two of you who will make it after the other 399 of you quit show biz and do something sensible instead."

The book was a slim volume by William Bayer titled *Breaking Through, Selling Out, Dropping Dead and Other Notes on Filmmaking*, containing perceptions that I'd observed firsthand but had resisted acknowledging. Mr. Bayer pointed out:

Perhaps the saddest comment one can make about the situation of the would-be filmmaker in America is that he must learn to be ruthless. It is a cruel paradox that those with qualities of sensitivity and humanity and integrity that are so necessary to the artistic success of a film may never be exercised unless the filmmaker has the ability to be ruthless. The pushiest, most ruthless, most arrogant and insensitive director may find himself at the top, while the most sensitive, honest, and humane director may never make a feature film.[10]

The fatigue came from the weariness of working long, exhausting hours on camera crews where *things—things* like set dressings—mattered most, the very kind of work I had identified as my least favorite activity compared to working with *people* and *ideas*. One more toilet bowl cleaner or B movie hardly mattered to God's scheme of things, I figured, and now I wanted my efforts to serve the significant, the meaningful, the eternal. Relentless rejections of my scripts added to my fatigue and sense of futility.

A new drumbeat had begun sounding in my inner core, and marching in step to the new Drummer became essential to the next phase of my professional, personal, and moral growth. Success no longer meant what *I* could accomplish—wealth, prestige, fame, power, even an Oscar—but what I allowed *God* to do *through* me. His provision for me and my family, His plan for our lives, would bring success if I sought His kingdom and obeyed His promises and commands. I foresaw glimpses of becoming a whole man. A man of one mind, not two. A Gospel-Keeper, instead of a Secret-Keeper.

By 1980 I'd read the Bible cover to cover—each book, chapter and verse. My questions about Jesus' divinity, His being God, had been answered. By now I had experienced three years of spiritual renewal and had marched with growing confidence to His tune. The minute I let faith have its way, I no longer remained trapped as a creature of two minds, but became "a new creation" [11] of one mind. With exuberance, I set my feet to the Drummer's new beat. Happily free of illicit drugs and with alcohol my only remaining vice, I marched on a new career path that led me away from Hollywood and back home.

MetaViews to Muse #6

To help you recognize and confront secret-keeping tendencies and habits, these reflections on what you've read in the past couple of chapters are meant to encourage you to consider your own life's challenges and choices.

✳ Secret Keepers face three ultimate choices: insanity, suicide, recovery. The first two hounded me until my recovery started when I pleaded for help in the wheat field. My recovery continued as I opened up to Susie, found a worship community where I belonged, replaced erroneous assumptions about life with new beliefs, and applied my new thinking to old behavior and attitudes.

What ultimate choice(s) are you facing? If you are currently keeping secrets, are you willing to take steps toward recovery? If so, what first step are you willing to take?

✳ Secret Keepers who commit to whole-mindedness experience tangible benefits within days, weeks, and months. My life improved as my insomnia melted away, my ulcer healed, and my harem of naked magazine models hit the trash. Improvements also occurred when I forgave Mom, quit marijuana, and averted a threatened divorce.

Are you committed to whole-mindedness, or do you struggle with double-mindedness? What tangible benefits would motivate you?

✳ Confessing one's secret life to a loved one defeats isolation, lessens hurt, and opens up avenues of trust. Shared secrets enhance intimacy, as did my confession to Susie about womanizing. When we disclose such information about our secret activities, it becomes easier to avoid caving in to their "pull" in the future because the shared knowledge helps us stay accountable.

Do you know someone to whom you can disclose some or all of your secrets? Consider what rewards your disclosure(s) might bring.

✳ Initial positive changes arouse heightened warfare from one's Addict. But a powerful tool is at your command. Remorse, a gnawing distress arising from a sense of guilt for past wrongs, can provide the Self with powerful motivation to change. If you have feelings of remorse, use the energy to combat the Addict inside you.

Are you experiencing a battle between your Self and an Addict inside you? Do you experience feelings of remorse? If so, how can you use that energy?

✳ Secret Keepers must do more than abstain from secret-keeping. They must make tough new lifestyle choices such as living from the inside out. Staying faithful to Susie—a new thought for me that became a guiding belief as I remained steadily committed to it—vastly improved the atmosphere in our home. Similar lifestyle choices can open up new avenues of communication and trust. Obedience is its own pleasurable reward!

In what area of your life are you feeling prompted to make fresh commitments? If you have already made such a commitment, what rewards have you experienced as a result?

✳ Even after some old habits have fallen away, it becomes clear that deeper emotional issues remain. Emotional lessons can occur in the areas of impatience, resentment, blame, disappointment, and self-pity—practicing acceptance and forgiveness are effective tools.

Are there emotional lessons you could be learning at this time in your life? If so, are you willing to practice acceptance and forgiveness as tools toward wholeness?

> "Most people, if they really looked into their own hearts,
> would know that they want, and want acutely,
> something that cannot be had in this world."

C. S. Lewis
The Joyful Christian

∞ *Chapter Thirteen*

Minneapolis Revisited

In a waiting area at Los Angles International Airport, Susie, Emily, and I sat patiently before boarding our flight to Minneapolis/St. Paul. We were headed home in mid-December 1980 for a Christmas reunion of the entire Prin clan—Dave's family from Texas, mine from California, and Tommy's family with Mom in Minneapolis. Susie sat beside me, busy at a crossword puzzle, and Emily head lay in Susie's lap, dozing. I closed my eyes to catch a catnap, envisioning the six grandkids, the oldest of fourteen to the youngest of five, playing wildly and screeching with glee. But I wasn't so sure we adults would be as gleeful.

Even after my victories toward whole-mindedness had taken root and some old habits had fallen away, it became clear that more emotional lessons remained. Secret-keeping had made me feel like my whole life was a performance, that the mask was always on. In many situations, I felt as though I had to prove myself again. Returning home, especially to spend open-ended time with Mom, which I hadn't done for 15 years since almost smashing her head in with the chair, triggered old tapes.

As I pondered past events, I felt resentment for what was *missing* from my growing-up years more than for the blistering setbacks and abuses. In the last few months, I'd gradually shifted from grieving my misgivings about Mom to lamenting my memories about Dad. With one exception, the time I'd stopped the flurry of shots as a goalie and Dad cheered from the bleachers, no recall of his ever having approved of me surfaced. Rather, I remembered the times when he'd disregarded me, such as the

Little League tryouts. Or the innumerable times he'd said nothing at all, like when I "made things" or got A's for school art projects. I could only conclude that I'd failed his expectations outright.

Whenever someone remains silent, you can only guess what he or she is thinking. Right? Surely if the person had thoughts to convey, he or she would say something. Recalling scant input from Dad, my mind conjured up the worst possible scenarios: he never loved me, he never noticed me, he never cared.

So, as I felt again this uncomfortable feeling of having to perform and prove myself, my reflections of Dad centered on his unyielding silence. Whereas Mom's influence had centered chiefly on her demands and intrusive dramas, Dad's influence had centered chiefly on his silence and evasive absences. My survival after age ten generally meant fending off Mom, but Dad's part during those years drew a blank because it was hazy and obscure. In Mom I'd faced active combat; in Dad I'd faced passive inattention. Mom meddled, Dad looked the other way. Until lately, when I could sit back and weigh each of their legacies, it hit me between the eyes that *Dad had as much to do with my wounds as Mom!* He was a bystander, she a perpetrator. His legacy? Neglect. Hers? Abuse.

Months earlier I'd written a soul-felt letter to the "man of silence and absences." Now, here in the airport, I flipped open my journal where I'd taped a copy of the letter and began to read it over:

Dear Dad,

It's been fourteen and a half years since you left us, and lately I've thought of those Chippewa Hills years and your declining health that led to your death. I've always equated Mom's relentless dream as the cause of, rather than merely coinciding with, your too-early departure.

But this is no longer necessarily true and I have stopped blaming only Mom. Now I'm inclined to blame you too and am writing this letter to purge myself of the hurt and rage I've been feeling all these years and to release you from the hidden hold this anger has on you. I want your soul and my soul to be free of it once and for all.

I am mad because you let Mom walk all over you, for your constant giving in to her and not standing up for yourself.

I am mad because you didn't assert yourself as a husband or father. I can count on one hand the number of times you were anything more than a provider. Your coming to my hockey games meant a lot, but there were few other times.

I am mad because you were always overweight and thus slowly killing yourself before your time. You ate poorly, smoked cigars, and never slept enough.

I am mad because you never came right out and said, "I love you, Johnny. I'm proud of you. You're a fine young man." Why did you hold back? Why were you silent? Was I unworthy? When you and I were finally old enough to talk like adults, about adult things, you died. Your death robbed me of knowing you. Sometimes I wonder if you ever cared at all.

I am mad because today at 35 I am still encumbered by the restless anger I feel. When irritations, delays, or disappointments come my way, I overreact. My response is really an indication of the huge weight I carry around, not truly in direct proportion to the stimulus itself.

Your soul must ache as mine does, knowing this pain I carry with me. And so I forgive you now as totally as I am able, hoping this forgiveness reaches you somehow in your world and that it sets you free and me free. I love you, Dad. I have always loved you, will always love you. I wish I could have heard you say the same to me.

I eagerly await the day when we will meet on your side of eternity, so I can throw my arms around you and begin anew. With this letter the hurt is out and away from me. It is over. You and I are now free of it. I hope and trust you're rejoicing like I am and that your freedom is complete.

Your loving son,
Johnny

The letter had indeed started the ball rolling on letting my feelings out. My hands holding the journal shook. My skin felt shivers. I realized my message to Dad attempted to see old events with new eyes, to perceive history from a 180-degree perspective. Writing the letter helped free my grief and brought a great deal of balance to an unbalanced, unhealthy era in my upbringing.

Like any letter, it needed to be delivered, so I thought of ways to get the job done. Weeks earlier I'd worked on a camera crew at the windy shores of Palos Verdes, the rugged peninsula southwest of LA, a wildly barren outcropping of ocean-soaked rocks stretching for miles. The pounding surf and raw energy of the waves seemed to me an ideal place to "deliver" the letter. I found a sturdy bottle, placed the letter carefully inside it, sealed the lid with canning wax, and drove to Palos Verdes.

I climbed down the steep path to the shoreline, walked out on the water-soaked blackened boulders as far as I dared, and waited for the right moment. In those few seconds of waiting for a large wave to roll in from the wide ocean beyond, I lifted the bottle high to the sky and asked God, "Please make sure Dad gets this."

Something surprising, much greater than I could have ever expected, happened next. Like the *Forgive your mother* message I'd heard when walking below the H-O-L-L-Y-W-O-O-D sign, a new message came to me at that instant: *I will be your Father.*

These words I heard God saying to me. They were His answer to the heartfelt plea I'd sobbed at Dad's graveside ten years before when I had asked, *Who will help me make the decisions a man needs to make?* and *What model of manhood do I have to go by?*

The same words came again, *I will be your Father,* and I sensed that God was telling me that *He* would provide what was missing, that despite my past and the failures of my earthly father, *He* would be my new Father. God then said something I'd yearned for: *You are my son, with whom I am well pleased. I love you, John. I'm proud of you.*

I thrilled to these words and immediately felt years of pain melt away.

Just then a large wave splashed at my feet and the moment to deliver the letter had arrived. My awareness returned and I reached back, bent low, and prepared to hurl the bottle as far as possible. With all my might, I Hail-Mary'd it just as a roaring ocean wave sucked itself back into the ocean. The bottle landed with a plop. I watched to see if the next wave would carry it in and smash it against the rocks or whether it would float away from the shore. It floated farther out to sea, then farther out again. Fortunately, each wave carried it out still farther until it became a speck on the wide expanse of seawater.

"Dad," I shouted, "you have my blessing! Be at peace!"

In my heart came a warm feeling that circulated all through me. The precious bond between a father and a son, the assurance of belonging that every child needs, felt present and alive—no longer missing as it had been on that sunny October day when I stood sobbing at Dad's grave. I felt confident Dad had "received" the letter and its reconciling message.

"Father!" I exclaimed to God. "I am yours now. With *You,* I am well pleased too!"

In the margin of the journal where I'd taped the letter, I'd scribbled:

Forgiveness is setting a prisoner free and realizing the prisoner is you.

I looked up from the journal and saw the clock in the LAX waiting area showing 20 minutes before boarding would begin. I felt more shivers, shivers of reassurance that affirmed my decision to write Dad at all and waves of gratitude from God's promise to take over as my Father. Keenly aware of having to sit on the plane for hours, I felt the need to stretch my legs, so I whispered to Susie, "I'm going to get some coffee. D'you want a Coke or something when I come back?"

She shook her head no and I got up to roam. At a stand-up café counter, I bought coffee in a paper cup and strolled down the concourse, pausing at a magazine stand to browse. My eyes went from *Time* to *Harper's* to *Fortune* past the women's magazines to the top row where *Playboy* and *Penthouse* beckoned.

No! my inner voice shouted. *Don't do it! Don't even think of opening those magazines!*

But the urge! After so many months since throwing my harem of centerfolds in the trash, the urge tugged at me. Powerfully surprised, I felt shocked that the impulse seemed as strong as ever. What lovely busts and butts awaited my appreciative gaze? I turned away and browsed among the paperback books instead. Doing so kept my eyes-off vow intact. No way was I going to plunge into that downward spiral again, I decided. But the mere impulse from thinking about the new photo spreads—naked women showing themselves with unabashed abandon for all eyes to appreciate—had me reeling.

Minutes later we three settled into our seats on the airplane and hunkered down for four hours of flight. Emily, now six, played with her favorite cutout dolls and Susie stayed absorbed in her crossword puzzle. I felt glad—and proud—I'd resisted temptation, *a secret victory rather than a typical secret defeat!* Encouraged that my loyalty to a new Drummer had passed a critical test, I relaxed to the hum of the engines. Yes, hearing the Drummer's drumbeat while I stood at the magazine rack had pulled me through.

As we lifted off the runway and went airborne, things remained quiet, but not inside me. Once again, disquieted, I took out my journal—the tool for self-reflection I'd come to depend on since my wheat-field experience—and jotted down my emotional tensions:

> *If I may protest a little, what kind of cruel joke is being played on us mortals? Us male mortals? When we see beautiful young women walking by or in photos—which are Your exquisite handiwork, Lord—we are then forbidden to desire or fantasize about them. You will not allow the worship of other gods any more than You will allow us to act on our desires for more than one woman—a wife and life mate. Yet these other women are put before us to see and admire. What torment!*
>
> *To obey, to center my desire on Susie and never find desirable the other appealing women You have made seems impossible. Something unobtainable*

in this world. Oh, how the flesh loves to lust! My appetite for these women, their beauty and vulnerability, and the fire they ignite in this natural man, persists. But the natural man in me is dead. I am now a spiritual man. What warfare is going on inside me! I'm instructed to obey and know that I must and will do so, but what about the remorse for the natural soul I'm putting to death within me?

As ever, heartfelt complexities like these added to the conundrum of Susie's and my weak love life. Something that could *not* be had in this world, an eerie echo of C. S. Lewis's wisdom, was being faithful to one woman and having freedom to romp with many. Since early 1979, a prolonged period of celibacy had crept into our relationship—unilateral celibacy by default, not as a negotiated agreement. Starting that spring, Susie had started taking a six-month prescription for birth-control pills. Although she and I had done nothing to prevent having more children, a second child had not come along in five years. Perhaps being on birth control, I hoped, would usher in a fresh period of lovemaking rather than the old unfulfilling truce.

Susie told me she wanted a satisfying sex life, yet nothing ever changed. We'd made promises to each other to "date" once a week and even heard a timely sermon about Lazarus being raised from the dead, then lightheartedly compared his resurrection from the tomb to our love life that needed resurrection. But months had gone by and lovemaking remained defunct. She renewed the birth control prescription for another six months, but the intimacy we'd hoped for had not "arisen from the tomb."

In my mind it seemed a sin against the sacrament of marriage itself—where *else* had God ordained lasting and loving intimacy between two people? The experimentation we'd agreed to hadn't materialized. I observed her often being too busy and too tired, and felt churned up about it. Avoidance by exhaustion. And no amount of sharing chores or running errands on my part lessened her busyness or changed her ever-longer to-do list. The prospect of 40 or 50 years of the same seemed too long to endure, a cruel joke.

I reflected on the "fear factor" I'd sensed in her earlier. Was Susie's being terrified of her father when she was a child so adverse that she felt paralyzed to respond to another man 35 years later? A man who was safe and loving, whom she'd vowed at the altar to love and cherish?

I recalled two or three times since becoming Christians when we'd coupled happily, sweetly, naturally—without conflicting expectations, awkward pressures, or cross purposes. Another three or four times, we'd made love functionally, out of duty. I found myself asking, was an average of twice or three times a year frequent enough? Like any active American male in his mid-30s prime, I operated under the assumption that weekly sex in marriage is the minimum and anything less signals dysfunction. On the basis that love is more about *giving* than *getting,* was I being challenged to alter this once-a-week-minimum expectation? To be content about making love a handful of times a year? Was this some kind of test?

During the rare times when Susie and I sat down to talk about this dilemma, she brought up the past. My two-timing dating of Maggie. My fantasy affair with Simone. My womanizing in Hollywood with Rita. She claimed my waywardness had shut her down, had made her clam up in self-defense. She resented my freewheeling passions in general and felt threatened by my boundless out-of-control spirit, whether for women, screenwriting, getting high, taking risks, or pushing limits.

"John, you're so-o-o-o-o dramatic," she'd chide, sometimes playfully. I conceded that her view about my philandering had substance prior to my coming to Christ, but asked her to weigh the massive turnaround in attitude since then: my track record of renouncing Rita and hurrying home to tell her, throwing out the *Playboys* and other magazines, never flirting or making passes at any woman since then. In short, I believed I'd demonstrated genuine chastity in mind and deed and pointed out my sincere willingness to be faithful to her, to grow stronger as a loving husband and father, to become the man she and God wanted me to be. I told her that my credo nowadays was "to treat an older woman like she's an aunt, a woman my age like a sister, and a younger woman like a daughter."

"I agree with everything you've said," she acknowledged, "and I'm feeling a new trust and confidence in you."

But nothing has changed, I felt like shouting. Objectively, no matter how we tried to lay the groundwork for a lasting, loving, satisfying sexual relationship, the months of loneliness and disconnection (in my view) had piled up higher than our heads. Something had to give.

Here, on the airplane, our elbows touched, and I found it humorous that only those body parts were the extent of our physical interaction! I had run out of guesses as to why. What was lacking? Fortunately, I had also heard nothing more from her about divorce since three years earlier. So I resolved to take the one option within my control, to turn down the sexual heat and wait until Susie turned up the heat—a kind of holding pattern. I adopted the compromised position of accepting *what was,* meager though it was, rather than demanding *what should be,* healthier though it could be.

Meantime, I flipped back several pages in my journal and read over the following words jotted down from a sermon:

*Deliverance is not freedom **from** temptation. We are constantly being tempted by the world, the flesh, and the devil. But real deliverance is the power given us through the Spirit to **refuse** temptation. Every temptation is an opportunity to manifest the power of God as I choose to let the Spirit respond **through** me.*

As a double-minded Secret Keeper, I was going through a character transition. I'd succeeded at eliminating my furtive behavior regarding porn, womanizing, and pot-smoking (or any illegal street drug), and whenever tempted lately, had chosen God's deliverance power. With the exception of one holdout: I still drank alcohol. It remained my only acceptable mood-altering substance. That it was legal and easily available made it seem less harmful. I still drank daily, sometimes a pint or more of liquor at a sitting, a liter of wine, or six to eight beers.

While certain outward behaviors had dropped away—and I was grateful for the benefits of selective abstinence (to be beholden to one drug only)—my unresolved emotional drives still begged for addictive thrills. I still believed subconsciously in the Lie of Addiction, that something outside me could fix what was wrong or missing inside me. I took a moment to pray that this part of me would one day be redeemed.

I looked over at Emily sitting in the window seat. Seeing her playing innocently, my mind switched gears. Her make-believe conversation with her paper dolls made me smile. I looked on proudly. "You know," I whispered to Susie, "I've enjoyed every minute of being a father." Susie glanced over and observed Emily, then nodded her silent understanding.

Without effort or letup, Emily and I had kept doing many dad/kid things together. Of course, I respected her boundaries—she was now six—never using profanities within her earshot. And I never confused my fantasies about female adult models in magazines with the reality of her being a female child needing nurturing and protection. I had never touched her inappropriately, nor would I ever.

Our favorite activity was walking hand in hand on the sidewalk to the store or kindergarten while she tiptoed along retaining walls like a gymnast on a balance beam. She'd beg, "Big jump, Daddy!" Then, as I stood back about four feet on the sidewalk, she'd jump into my outstretched arms, shrieking with glee. In playful, rough-and-tumble ways like this, we bonded, and she learned to trust and rely on a man. In Daddy's arms, she was always safe. Often I declared, "What's the best job description I've ever had? Being a dad."

The plane's engines hummed. I sighed, yawned deeply, then dozed off and fell asleep. The next thing I knew, we were landing in the Twin Cities. We deboarded the plane and Tommy met us at the gate. "Mom's all excited to see you," he said, "and has a special dinner cooking on the stove." I steeled myself for what might be a tense few hours. We headed off to Mom's house in his car. Except for occasional phone calls or birthday and Christmas cards, little communication had occurred between Mom and me in years. As I looked out the window, my gaze met the snow-covered landscape—instead of smog and brown California scenery, everything looked frozen cold and sparkly white, just like Christmastime was supposed to be.

Tommy dropped us at her door and backed out of the driveway. "See you tomorrow for Christmas Eve," we shouted, waving good-bye. We knocked on the same door I'd slammed behind me the day I'd almost murdered Mom with the chair. It opened. Mom's face smiled and she greeted us with her best manners.

"There's my little darling," she chimed, lifting Emily up. "Merry Christmas, sweetheart!"

Then she turned to Susie. "Hi, Sue, come on in. It's so good to see you!"

Then me. But before another word passed her lips, she stared in my face and cried out, "Johnny, you've changed! You look so happy! What is it?"

I smiled. The only words that crossed my lips were, "Yes, Mom, I've changed. I love you."

Abruptly, her hands flew up to her face and she gasped. "You're the first of my sons to tell me that in twenty-five years!" Letting her hands down to look again, she reached for me and I could see tears wetting her cheeks. "You love me? Really?"

I nodded. "Yes, Mom. I've forgiven you."

She was awestruck and replied, "Really? Forgiven me for what?"

Right then and there, with ham baking in the oven and potatoes simmering on the stove, we hugged, then walked together to the den where we sat privately. Susie, bless her heart, encouraged us. "Go ahead, Johnny," she whispered, making it clear in her gentle manner that she would take over cooking in the kitchen.

For the next 45 minutes, I told Mom how I felt about the horrible Chippewa Hills years and the many times I'd felt hurt and abused. She listened and muttered, "I'm sorry" or "I had no idea." In her mind, "Those years were devastating and a grand mess too," she said, "but I never gave much thought to how difficult it must've been for you boys." I explained the ways my heart had changed since accepting Christ into my life, and for the first time since being a boy I sensed she *heard* me and wanted to *understand* me without arguing or defending herself. After 15 years apart, something good was taking place.

"Do Tommy and David feel the same way? Could this be why they've been so distant for so long?"

"Mom, I can't speak for them, but I'd say so, yes."

She looked down at the floor. "Then I'll need to call them and tell them I'm sorry. I can't let any more time go by." She looked up at me, straight into my eyes. Reaching for my hands, she squeezed them and exclaimed, "I can't tell you what this means to me! It's the best Christmas present ever!" She wrapped her arms around me and sobbed. Tears flowed down her cheeks.

Something I'd thought impossible in this life had miraculously happened. We hugged and kissed, then stood up and returned to the kitchen.

A similar kind of healing rippled throughout the family that holiday, including Mom's verbal apologies to Tommy and Dave. Each expressed mixed responses and weren't entirely ready to accept her contrition, believing that it could be just an act. Still, they saw it as a good first step and hoped it would lead to real change. We all sensed a thawing in the otherwise frozen feelings we'd felt since our teen years.

The remainder of the ten-day visit witnessed the grandkids playing by the Christmas tree and screeching with glee as they opened brightly wrapped presents. Everybody feasted and the adults drank too much, but quietly in Susie's and my heart Jesus was reborn, alive and well. Nobody quite accepted or felt comfortable with our new level of faith and hinted that we shouldn't go overboard about the joy we felt—"no proselytizing, thank you." But with the softening in us toward Mom and her openness toward us, the Christmas presents that year for the Prin clan included more than just those under the tree.

During the final few days of our trip, I made efforts to find fulltime work. Another reason for our trip home involved my scouting out new work opportunities, especially in the corporate communications field. With Dave's career at Quality Tec a success, and with the company's headquarters located in Minneapolis, my hopes ran high that he could open doors for interviews there that I couldn't arrange otherwise.

After a decade of aspiring as a professional movie wannabe, I now reluctantly admitted defeat and recognized the time had come to move on. I'd squarely faced the disappointment of my faltering screenwriting dream—although rageful and blaming at times—and could now bask in the real-life experiences of having enjoyed working with celebrities like Vincent Price, Carol Burnett, Bing Crosby, Steve Allen, and Joanne Woodward. I even recalled Vincent Price bouncing Emily on his knee and cooing in baby talk during a break in the shooting of a television horror movie. But the long hours and strenuous labor had burned me out. Finally, I'd conceded that the grandiosity of a splashy Hollywood career was not God's will for me. Something else must be right instead. My task was to discover it.

I made no secret about needing help from family members and vowed to myself not to spend even one stolen hour doing anything sneaky. Dave attempted to arrange some interviews for me at Quality Tec headquarters, but nobody was available until after the new year. Tommy and Carolyn offered their house as a place for me to stay for a few weeks, and I made plans to return soon, better prepared, in hopes of succeeding at a serious, all-out job hunt. Mom got excited and promised the use of her car. Susie and I agreed that a fulltime job with benefits back in my hometown was the right goal and that all the support needed was available.

On the brink of 1981, my New Year's resolution became: I *can* go home again and *will* trust the Lord to guide me to paying work that serves His kingdom and fulfills His calling for me.

**"Life shrinks or expands
in proportion to one's courage."**

Anaïs Nin

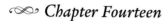 *Chapter Fourteen*

Homecoming

It took another eight months of dealing with messy loose ends in California before I landed in Minneapolis again to launch my all-out job hunt. It was the week before Labor Day, and I'd just turned 37. I was confident of God's promise that He was with me and that His plans were "for good and not evil, to give me a future and a hope."[1] But, honestly, what was in my head and in my gut felt much less secure—I wanted to believe (to have faith in) this promise of His, but it contradicted entirely what I'd experienced in real life (painful events that drained faith).

Those eight chaotic and brutal months tested Susie and me to the breaking point, often driving us to fights and arguments. The aggravations we contended with included:

- Nine crimes against our property, mainly break-ins into our van and thefts of household tools and Emily's bicycle.
- Gunshots ringing out at odd times on the street outside our windows that threatened our safety, once forcing us to duck for cover on the floor.
- LA Police helicopters disturbing our sleep at 3:00 A.M. during SWAT-team drug busts of our next-door neighbors.
- Emily's itchy scalp due to head lice contracted at school, which spread to Susie and me and led to a month-long ordeal of doctors visits and incessant scratching.
- Our landlord's rental of the apartment below us to gypsies

who shouted violent obscenities day and night and sold cars and drugs daily.

- Long lines of customers at gas stations furious about paying sky-high prices due to the nationwide oil shortage.
- Our one-bedroom apartment-turned-hotel used by a parade of out-of-town visitors and relatives who stayed from three days to three weeks or more.

In half a year, the entire tone of our lifestyle and surroundings had changed from peaceful and nurturing to hostile and annoying. It felt as if we were being driven out of California. I struggled to cope with these aggravations and one day I scribbled in my journal:

Three lessons of life . . .
Pain is INEVITABLE
Suffering is PROBABLE
Misery is OPTIONAL.

It seemed to me that the first two, pain and suffering, were unavoidable and had to be tolerated, accepted. But the third, misery, not so. I concluded that humans can choose to stay miserable or not. I told Susie about these thoughts one scorching hot July afternoon in our apartment: "Let's move back to Minnesota as soon as possible. We've suffered here long enough, Susie, and now we're miserable every day."

She acted far more hesitant. "John, what's the hurry? You're making good money right now, and we shouldn't do anything to upset the hot streak of work you're getting." She was referring to a steady string of profitable work calls and to my having raised my film-crew rate to $250 a day plus $40 an hour overtime. "The producers who've hired you are thrilled with your art directing and it shows in our bank balance."

"Yes, but we agreed last Christmas to move back to Minnesota," I countered.

"There's time, John. You're always in a hurry."

"Hurry? My birthday is coming up next month. The clock's ticking. We're more miserable here every day, but we don't have to be. We can choose to leave, Susie. Why did I go through a year and a half of career counseling and tell people back home I'm gung ho for a job hunt if we aren't going to do everything possible, *as soon as possible,* to change careers?"

Susie sulked, clearly wanting to stay put. "We may be suffering, yes, but misery, I'm not so sure. What I'm saying is 'let's make hay while the sun shines.' We don't know how long it will take to find a job or when or how much salary you'd be making if you went back home right now."

I rattled off the list of aggravations we'd put up with and repeated the list of resources and support awaiting us in Minnesota.

Susie's demeanor changed. She went to the kitchen and started washing dishes. In an almost confessional tone, she said softly, "Maybe you're right. I had to punish Emily today because she left her new bike in the front yard unattended."

"What? You punished her for that?" I exclaimed.

"Yes. It could've been stolen. And I told her she couldn't ride it until this weekend and that it always has to stay locked up."

"Geez, talk about harsh. She's an innocent child paying for another crime that she shouldn't have to worry about. It would never be that way back home."

"John!" Susie shouted. "What else was I supposed to do? Her bike got stolen two months ago and we can't let her *new* bike get stolen!"

"No, of course not. But it's another crappy part of living here. Talk about being victimized. And miserable! You've just made my point!"

I paused.

Silence. Susie fumed.

I stewed over Emily's having to pay for evil-that-could-be-avoided-by-moving-to-Minnesota. "If we lived someplace safer," I snapped, "then she wouldn't have to worry about leaving her bike out at all. So there!"

"JOHN! What is, *is!* Where we are is *here!* Emily must be taught! I'm sorry about it too, but somebody has to discipline her!" Susie started smashing glassware into the sink.

I went to her and put my arms around her.

"I'm tired of it all!" she wailed. "I'm going nuts!"

Emily, who was nearby bathing in the bathtub, started crying. "Mommy, I'm scared!"

I ran to her and Susie trailed behind. Susie nudged me out of the way, knelt down, calmed Emily's fears, and apologized to her, explaining, "Mommy gets mad at times, honey. So does Daddy. Mommies and daddies are people too. We're sorry we upset you."

Months earlier, on her 35th birthday, Susie had felt overwhelmed by the gifts and cards and small favors showered on her by friends, family, and me. "I don't deserve all this," she'd complained. "The person of sweetness and light that everybody sees isn't the real me." I'd asked her to explain and she'd replied, "I haven't faced the problems in my life that I should've by now. I feel like a hypocrite—on the surface bubbly and light, but on the inside murky and confused." She told me about keeping her own secrets and living a hidden life of her own. When I asked her to elaborate, she shrugged and said no more.

I recalled a similar remark she'd made years before, about being inundated by Christmas presents from her parents, especially her father. As an only child, she felt undeserving. Somewhere in that comment was a clue to her current adult malaise, which she'd brought up on her 35th birthday. "Getting mad and letting out feelings was never allowed in my childhood," she'd told me while unwrapping birthday gifts. "I'm telling you now, John, getting better for me means letting my anger and feelings show more."

Well, she surely let her angry feelings show now! Emily's crying had subsided by now as Susie quietly comforted her, so I went to the bedroom and flopped on the bed. I felt numb. I ached. We had never been lower since we had become Christians. Anguished but refusing to allow misery, I prayed for Susie and Emily, for our marriage, for my career, for our future. Feeling an urgent impulse, I decided to take the bull by the horns from that moment on and began mobilizing my return to Minnesota to find work, a countdown process that took another week before I landed in Minneapolis.

Back home, I stayed at Tommy and Carolyn's house as planned. Every few days, I phoned Susie in California to update her on my progress. At the start, none of Dave's contacts at Quality Tec confirmed appointments for job interviews, and Dave felt at a disadvantage trying to help me because he worked at a distance from the Houston branch office. He thought he could make better connections when he returned to headquarters in Minneapolis for sales conferences in late September. Meanwhile, nothing held me back from networking and making phone calls about communication/audio-visual openings at 3M, General Mills, Northwestern National Life, Honeywell, and smaller companies.

In spare moments between sending out résumés and checking classified ads, I quietly reflected on my departure from LA. Besides ending the longest profitable run of film gigs I'd ever had, I'd also said emotional good-byes to film and church friends. Among the latter were financial benefactors who had given us money. Their anonymous cash gifts ranged from $300 and, in one case, to as much as $1,000—all meant to show their love and to encourage us to follow God's will.

The hosts of a going-away party for us the night before my flight home told us that one reason for the party was so we could thank these benefactors for their generosity. In some ways, Susie and I felt closer and more intimate with these 40 or so members of the family of God, among them Rev. Ralph Osborne who'd counseled me, than our own blood kin. So it was with sweet sorrow that the festivities took place on a warm August evening in a garden under the hazy sky dome of Los Angeles.

Several friends entertained us with skits, jokes, and mime acts. Wine and *hors d'oeuvres,* laughter and gaiety, toasts and roasts filled the hours. As midnight approached, I stood and told about the bittersweet reasons for our leaving. I read aloud a poem I'd penned weeks before titled "Rejection Dejection." In a harsh and angry tone, it complained of the relentlessly negative reception my scripts had received and the pain of opening form letters that arrived in the mail with the word *unfortunately* in their first paragraph.

In contrast, I also showed my first published magazine article for all to see, a think-piece titled "Joe Christian and the Root Beer Commercial" printed in a four-color, popular Christian monthly. I read excerpts from it in a celebratory tone, genuinely gushing with gratitude for the triple whammy of, (1) being paid for my writing, (2) seeing my name in print, and (3) serving God's people through the article.

Then came the most memorable moment. I explained about the exciting opportunity and upcoming challenges awaiting me in Minnesota. On a table beside me sat a stack of scripts and stories that I'd spent 14 years developing and marketing unsuccessfully. My published article, the only published work, felt like a feather compared to the foot-high pile of unpublished work. In simple, direct language, I confessed the bitter frustration that the stack of scripts represented and how the struggle had defined me as a frustrated failure. I also spoke of how the Holy Spirit had so far helped free me of ulcers, dope-smoking, lying, stealing, fits of rage, and philandering.

I then read aloud a freshly written poem I'd dashed off in a burst of inspiration the night before titled "Good-bye Hollywood." It ended:

. . . ravished, i leave now
ravished by an industry founded on self-interest
conquered by my own participation in its myth
conquered, i return 2,000 mile to my roots

friends, i weep at leaving you
i cry over the loss of you, and my dream
where i will end up is uncertain

what i shall dream is unclear
but i am certain that He knows
and i cannot serve this Mistress Show Business
and serve One Master as well

the years of wreckage He will resurrect
my tears and His tears will sprinkle the ashes
and in the end He will be with me, as always
"behold, I make all things new"

Silence. The guests sat stone still. Susie's face reflected a mix of awe and anguish. Quietly, Rev. Ralph Osborne stood and stepped over to me. He put his hands firmly on my shoulders and said in a loud, clear voice, "John, it's time for you to have a new name! It's time for you to go forward from this place blessed and clothed in new power!"

He turned toward the guests and declared in an even louder voice, "By the authority vested in me, I declare your old name, Frustrated Failure, invalid!" Turning back to me and looking squarely into my eyes, he declared, "In the name of Him who forgives and transforms all, I now name you Beloved of God! This is your new name—Beloved of God—and with it you will go forth to do great things!"

Everyone applauded. I shuddered and felt a tidal wave of tears well up inside me but held them back. Several folks crowded around and soon were hugging me or patting my shoulders. Susie stood up, came over, and hugged me. "Yes, John, you *are* Beloved of God. Start believing it."

At the airport the next morning, Susie saw me off. "Remember last night's blessing," she said. "Keep reminding yourself: 'I am Beloved of God.'"

I nodded, then saw her frown.

"Johnny, the way you read those poems last night was . . . well, almost violent."

I looked away. "Maybe so, but it was honest."

"More than honest. Harsh and hurtful. Look, I know none of this has been easy for you. But you've got to get at that root of bitterness of yours and extinguish it. Don't let it fester. Don't let it show when you interview. Try not to snap at every little thing. Remember, you . . . are . . . Beloved of God."

This pierced deep. I had snapped often and certainly I still felt bitter. I tried not to let it show, but it was there in spades. The root of bitterness she referred to was something we'd come across in our Bible studies:

"Watch out that no bitterness takes root among you, for as it springs up it causes deep trouble, hurting many."[2] This very real root of bitterness in me ate away at my well-being, but how could it not? Decades old, it was woven into the very fabric of my life. It had stymied and warped me since I was eleven years old. I cringed at the thought of injuries inflicted during my teen years and college/army years when Dad died, as well the years of addiction and suicidal despair in my 20s, and nowadays the decade of failure and frustration in Hollywood. Approaching 40 years old, I was still groping for meaningful work and adequate rewards.

"Everything you've said is true," I said to Susie, hoping to encourage her. "But something *is* changing. I *am* stepping out in faith. I *am* giving over control. I *am* letting go of insisting on my own way. It gets ugly at times, I know, but if I can't show my feelings honestly and openly, especially to you, then how will I ever get rid of the garbage?"

She looked at me and sighed. "Okay, vent if you have to. God knows about it anyway. But only with Him, and only alone, okay? Or once in a great while with me. It just hurts me to see you so hurt. Others see it too and recoil at your intensity, John. You are *so intense*. And the more you let it show, the more it'll hurt your chances of finding new work, a new life. So let it go."

I placed my finger on her lips, preventing her from saying more. I wanted her to see in my eyes that I understood and appreciated her, then we kissed good-bye.

Hours later my plane landed and I launched the job hunt. Tommy and Carolyn's house worked fine as a base of operations. Mom lent me her car as promised. From jeans and tie-dyed T-shirts, I now switched to three-piece pin-striped suits and wingtip shoes. My list of possible future employers grew daily. I used the field interview format I'd practiced to get access to people in their offices, and slowly, job leads developed. Using my career transition training, I recorded each interview and listed promising follow-up details.

When I wasn't hustling job leads, I threw the Frisbee or played touch football in the front yard with Tommy's sons—Stephen, 11, and Toby, 9. This recreational play led to our laughing ourselves silly, a tonic for my stresses and strains as well as a way of bonding between us. Tommy's daughter Tracy, 6, watched frequently and laughed along, and I could foresee the benefit to Emily, now 7, of growing up with her cousins nearby, once a new job allowed us to move back home. Carolyn, bless her heart, brought out cookies and Kool-Aid for us to snack on, and she would often sit on the front steps watching with Tracy and chuckling.

Early the next morning the phone rang and Carolyn called to me, "It's Susie. She has bad news." I picked up the phone and heard Susie on the other end.

"Dad just phoned out of the blue informing me that Mom fell down the front steps yesterday during a cigarette break. She's unconscious and he's rushed her to the hospital. He's with her now."

"Oh, my God. What's her condition?"

She continued, urgently. "He says the doctors aren't sure how long she'll stay unconscious or whether she'll ever come out of it. She's had a massive stroke, Johnny. I think I should fly back to New Jersey with Emily on the next plane."

I concurred with her decision. Thus began her day-by-day vigil at Martha's bedside in intensive care. We decided later that I should stay the course job-hunting in Minnesota until I heard more about what was needed back East. Susie's aunts and uncles on both Bill's and Martha's sides of the family stood close by to care for Emily, give rides, and provide meals.

Five days later Susie's call came notifying me of her mother's death. "She slipped away minutes after I laid hands on her and prayed for her late last night," Susie told me. I offered my sympathy, then booked the next flight to New Jersey. While packing for Martha's funeral, I dug through my journal notebooks and found the entry from Christmas Day 1978 when we'd visited Susie's parents in New Jersey:

I pity Martha so much. What a sad, miserable person she is. So nervous and uptight constantly. Always being told she is stupid and can't do anything right—and she goes along with it. This morning, while opening her Christmas gift from Bill, she was so nervous that she dropped it on the floor. He scolded her like a child. Last night she fussed for hours over the turkey and gravy, getting flustered about every little thing. She is such a victim of her own fears. What a "condition" she's in! It angers me that she allows her life to be ruined like this. What a sad case. She simply does not have the courage to stand up for herself. Her only defense against Bill seems to be her chain-smoking, which he detests . . . and she knows it.

Lord, I pray for her soul. That she may know peace, someday in heaven if not here on earth. She does turn the other cheek, which is biblical, but is it biblical to be a doormat? It seems to me that she could assert herself, but Bill is indeed a formidable adversary. Bless her, Lord, here and now and in her afterlife. Amen.

How poignant these thoughts seemed to me right now. I reflected on them as I sat in my seat on the flight to Newark International the next day. While packing, I'd also come across a copy of a letter taped into one of my journals—a letter of Susie's written to her dad that she'd let me copy. It, too, spelled out her poignant thoughts and, like my letter to Dad months earlier, it attempted to make sense of a confusing, disruptive upbringing and home life.

Dear Dad,

It's hard to know how to begin. I sensed a tension, a negative charge in the air when you and Mom were with us this Christmas. I am aware that you, as a parent, have certain dreams and hopes of what my life should look like as an adult. I know that your dreams for my life aren't being realized and there are many things I don't have; our neighborhood isn't where I'd like to spend my next forty years, we have a certain lack of financial consistency, and so on.

But we are striving. We do have hopes and plans. We are in the Lord's hands and claim His promises to never let us down and to turn us into the people He wants. I say we, Dad, because John and I are working on these things together. He's a fine man, highly skilled and capable at his work, well loved and respected in our church community, a good provider and loving to Emily and me.

It's very painful to know how much you dislike my husband and how little you respect him. It makes me feel defensive and unwilling to share with you our concerns, our hopes, our goals, even our joys, for fear there might be something that's wrong, some obvious question we haven't asked, some other direction we should be exploring. It seems like nothing's ever quite good enough, and frankly, after a while it simply hurts too much to expose myself— or ourselves—to more disapproval and correction, so we don't.

This isn't the way I want our relationship to be. I want to be able to talk things over and feel comfortable about asking advice from you. You're so knowledgeable in so many areas like finances and taxes and investments. And your generosity is an example to others. But my wish for you is that someday you'll be able to identify and rid yourself of whatever it is that makes you afraid to reveal yourself to people. In spite of your ironclad efforts otherwise, you seem all blocked up behind a mask of fear that someone will find out who you really are and will see your imperfect and vulnerable parts, the parts that freely allow tears of sorrow and joy.

I'll probably never know what happened years ago to make you duck into your protective shell. But God does, and with His help and your will-ingness, you can be healed of that and live your life in a freedom and joy and release that'll set you singing.

We all have masks we hide behind, defenses for areas we don't want anybody to see. I know all about them because I have several myself, and I use them more often than I care to admit. My goal, though, is to drop as many of them as I can, so someday I can claim, "Who you see is who I am."

That's a major reason for my writing you. I've taken a risk that scares me in doing this. As for John and me, what I would ask is for you to take a new look at us as a couple and accept who each of us is based on the special talents we have that may be different from your own. As for you and me, I do love you, Dad. I don't want to see this pattern of hiding and bitter-ness and tension and non-communication continue. John loves you too and wants an end to the hostilities and inherent disapproval that overshadows yours and his relationship.

We are praying for a strong and clear healing of this family and the ties that bind you and Mom and John and me together.

Love, Susan

The "strong and clear healing" Susie had written about in her letter never occurred in any manner that anyone could tell, but the funeral was neither the time nor place to probe for reasons why or why not. To our knowledge, Bill had never received the letter. He certainly didn't behave as though he had. Susie and I speculated that Martha, always at home to get the mail first, had intercepted the letter and never shown it to Bill. This seemed feasible to us and confirmed the ever-growing idea to me that secret-keeping was commonplace in Susie's family, that both Martha and Bill, individually and collectively, wore masks that hid many secrets.

Secrets of many kinds, I suspected.

Martha's funeral took place in a beautiful setting, a traditional up-scale funeral parlor with classical pillars and walnut paneling, decked out with bright bouquets of flowers and decorated with elegant rugs, lamps, and accessories. About 50 guests filled the place and listened to the elderly Rev. Donald Rivers, the same minister who'd married Susie and me 12 years earlier in his Revolutionary War church, led the service. Martha looked peaceful, at last, in the open casket. I reflected on her earthly misery and hoped for her heavenly bliss. Unfortunately, it wasn't clear to Susie or me that she'd known Jesus in the personal way that assures one's salvation.

I felt gratitude for the generous gifts that she and Bill had bestowed on us through the years, big-ticket items like a new refrigerator, living room furniture, a color television, and $1,000 savings bonds, but in the final analysis it seemed that she'd led a cowardly life.

I remembered talking to her once while she ironed Bill's shirts in the basement, questioning her about putting up with Bill's constant put-downs. I tried to offer ideas and solutions, but she defended her doormat behavior and shut down the conversation by declaring, "I married Bill for better or worse, in sickness and in health, till death do us part, and that's that." Later when I told Susie about our talk, she said that Martha's father, a domineering German immigrant, had sternly rebuked her and his two other daughters for wanting to attend school or to work outside the home. "From domineering father to domineering husband," Susie concluded.

The plain fact was, I supported Susie as best as I could through the funeral, through the reception and the burial and the selection of a cemetery plot and headstone—details that Bill seemed immobilized to deal with. When it came time to return to my job hunt in Minnesota, Susie decided to spend another week in New Jersey sorting through her mother's closets and drawers in order to spare her father the painful task.

You might imagine how I felt once back in Minnesota: *Will I ever get momentum going? Am I doomed to constant searching? Will the elusive job offer ever emerge?*

My determination doubled, tripled. I engineered a whirlwind of interviews to large and small companies' audio-visual departments. I met with David when he came up for one of his headquarters sales sessions and pleaded with him to try harder about generating appointments. The next day he called me with three interview appointments he'd arranged with Quality Tec managers, which I followed up on immediately.

By the first week of October, only one interview remained, and I'd resigned myself to returning to California and trying again another time. As I did regularly during or after a particularly stressful day of interviews, I strolled on foot from Tommy and Carolyn's house to a park brimming with green trees and grassy lawns. Minnehaha Creek flowed through it, a quiet babbling freshwater brook straight out of a nature calendar. By its banks, I spent solitary time, either ambling along the creek shore or just sitting on a rock and contemplating. It occurred to me on the calm autumn day before my last interview that only a year or two before, this private time would have meant stolen hours sneaking a joint or indulging in some sneaky secret-keeping habit. But no longer. Now private time meant what the psalmist had written,

"[The Lord] makes me lie down in green pastures.
He leads me beside the still waters;
he restores my soul."[3]

Indeed, I felt the miracle of the Lord restoring my soul in that place and His real presence, comfort, and assurance. This was not an addictive substitute, but the real thing. For a long moment, the peace-that-passes-understanding lasted, until the root of bitterness gripping my soul sprang up again into conscious awareness. The emotional tensions I was facing as a partially reformed addict/active alcoholic reasserted themselves—impatience, resentment, disappointment, blame, self-pity.

I was impatient for results.

I resented the continual struggles.

I felt disappointed about my writing and job interview results.

I blamed the Hollywood vipers who refused to recognize good writing.

I wallowed in self-pity.

These intertwined emotions often generated strong negative feelings that created a victim mentality that was still present, strong, and immediate. Unless I called on the Lord's strength and presence for me at any given moment, these feelings would weigh heavily on me and could have driven me deeper into secret-keeping behaviors. But now I was dealing more effectively with them, not by getting high, but by praying. So, in an audible voice, the same as when I'd appealed to God in the Nebraska wheat field, I clenched my fists and cried out:

"Be real, Lord. Now. I need you *now*. Unplug my ears if I can't hear, but say something. Do something. Send some unmistakable sign. You know my predicament. I can't believe I'm living the abundant life that You promised. You must want something better than this constant frustration. You are my shepherd. Show me the way. I depend on You. Do as You promised. I am Your child. I want Your advice. Give it. I know You're here. I know You hear. I know You care. You said, 'You will receive whatever you ask for in prayer, *if you believe*.'[4] I believe! Amen."

The quiet gurgling water and the soft breeze through the trees combined with the chirping birds around me, and I heard the still small voice of God in it all. The connection in my soul with His Spirit calmed my emotions and helped me let go. I reminded myself that He was with me, that I was Beloved of God, and that His plan was for good and not for evil. In this way, the familiar secret-keeping triad of *excitement/pleasure/delight* transformed into a new dynamic:

→ the *excitement* of seeking God,
→ the *pleasure* of sharing His presence,
→ the *delight* of being loved and comforted.

At 8:59 the next morning, I shook hands with Quality Tec's Manager of Promotional Writing Services, Sandra Herns. A dynamo with an enthusiastic laugh and dressed in a trendy suit, Sandra questioned me for an hour about my background and credentials, then leaned forward across her desk and whispered, "John, I think there might be a fit here. Let's go meet some of my staff members and have some lunch."

For the next six hours, including lunch, I met with nine of her ten departmental staffers. Thrilled that I was seriously being considered for a salaried writing position, I waxed eloquent about grammar, syntax, white space, and every other related topic the staffers mentioned or asked about.

By the end of the day, Sandra shook my hand vigorously and said, "I'm sorry I can't end the suspense any sooner, but HR says they have other candidates who qualify that I need to see. This job opening needs to be filled in two weeks. So, please be patient. And tell your brother, 'Thanks for the referral.' I think he sent along a candidate who'll fit in here quite nicely."

I took great encouragement from her upbeat remarks and phoned David to thank him for the fabulous connection. Flying back to California, I spent the next several days waiting and hoping, waiting and hoping, waiting and hoping. Susie listened to me tell every detail, and we prayed together for the phone to ring with good news. I repeated Sandra's final words to me over and over, rejecting the fear that another candidate might edge me out.

The phone did ring once, and it was David saying he'd checked with Sandra, who'd explained that "a delay of another week was necessary because Human Resources wants more minority candidates to apply." He went on to say, "Apparently she's interviewed one such person already who didn't have your credentials. But HR has quotas, and they want at least one more minority candidate to be interviewed."

More suspense. More prayer. More questioning. More letting go.

The phone rang the following week and a lady from HR in Minneapolis said, "We mailed you an offer letter last Friday, John, requesting that you accept the fulltime position of promotional writer at the annual salary of $26,000. Are you still interested in the position?"

"You better believe it!" I hollered.

Susie and I celebrated, dancing around the room and praising God with our arms lifted high. The letter arrived as the lady said it would, and we packed up our worldly goods, departed from California, and purchased a suburban home in Minnesota, all in the span of four weeks.

On the anniversary of the day I pleaded with Jesus to save my life in the Nebraska wheat field four years earlier—November 2, 1981—the successful beginning of my new career as a journalist at a major computer corporation began.

**"It is not the strongest of the species that survive,
nor the most intelligent,
but the ones most responsive to change."**

Charles Darwin

୭ *Chapter Fifteen*

Sanity on Trial

Although it felt weird getting dressed each morning in a suit and tie, especially a narrow tie that constricted my neck, the blessings of a steady paycheck with health benefits brought new hope and security to our lives. Under Sandra's tutelage, my first assignment focused on one of Quality Tec's major customer's good fortune using our Prime Computers for educational and training purposes.

It delighted me to find out that promotional writing meant learning and using journalism skills—albeit in a self-congratulatory public relations manner for the company. I'd half-feared they might require some writing of technical manuals. I occupied my first-ever office with a door, a desk, and a phone.

To launch my success-story assignment, I called the customer's designated representative in Ohio and interviewed him for 90 minutes, a fact-finding conversation recorded on three legal-pad pages. I then drafted a ten-page article and circulated it for review. To celebrate my debut into "real" writing, I joined fellow staff members for their weekly three-hour lunch off-site, a fancy steak and salad affair with cocktails. The jokes and laughter made me feel the very opposite of my awkward induction into Gorden Film Lab's editing staff 14 years earlier. Ecstatic, I came home to Susie gushing with glad tidings.

The emotional and financial assurance we experienced from my first weeks on the new job—including paid holidays and generous health benefits—made the numerous struggles to land the new job fade into oblivion. In quiet moments, I indeed felt "Beloved of God."

Our new home, a three-bedroom rambler with a walkout basement and two-car garage, proved to be another rejuvenating source of prosperity as well. The advantages of owning a free-standing household made the ten years of annoyances from renting a one-bedroom apartment recede. We thrilled as each monthly mortgage payment added to our personal net worth and we enjoyed watching our equity grow. We cleaned and scrubbed the floors and shelves, removing the previous owners' 30 years of cigarette smoke and dirt. We brushed and rolled gallons of paint, refreshing the living and storage spaces until they became "ours." In all, we worked smoothly as a team and rejoiced openly about our blessings.

Our location was just five miles from Tommy's and Mom's houses and in the same community, which meant Emily attended the same school as her cousins and one day would graduate from Grayton High as I had. As we'd hoped and prayed, Emily made a robust adjustment to her new school, Brookhaven Elementary. She loved her third-grade teacher and spent lots of time after school playing with her cousin Tracy, one year younger. That winter, she made the radical adjustment to Minnesota's icy climate, romping in snowdrifts and skating on ice ponds, bundled up in her new hooded jacket, stocking cap, knee-high boots, mittens, and scarf. She and her grandmother even hit it off. They spent hours together at crafts and games, and I came to see a new-and-improved side of Mom—despite her acid tongue and narcissistic "zingers," which at times she still detonated in adult company.

At night whenever Susie and Emily went to bed early, especially on Fridays or Saturdays, I stayed up and indulged in solitary drinking, a secret-keeping habit I came to perfect. Within months, I couldn't kick the habit. Sipping a double scotch or triple bourbon on the rocks, I sat in the easy chair in our cozy den and got plastered. In the summer I'd down vodka or gin coolers for variety, and I never turned down cold beers on hot afternoons or glasses of wine for dinner. I reveled in the abundance of our new life, cheered that positive emotions could fuel my desire to drink the same as negative ones did.

At times the drunken hazes meant blackouts and complete losses of memory. The more this kind of self-sabotage took its toll night after night, the more guilt hounded me the following mornings. The imbalance of time and money I'd spent intoxicated versus praying or being in closer touch with God bothered me.

Back on the job, my writing made favorable impressions and my star at Quality Tec began rising fast. My reputation as a "wordsmith" among internal clients—who were wise about computers and electronics but unskilled as communicators—gained ground. One particular article, about the innovative process of electronic publishing, made a special hit. What I didn't see brewing was how the string of kudos that clients and coworkers made about my writing efforts masked a malevolent undercurrent smoldering secretly inside a fellow staff editor.

The honeymoon came to an end six months after my new job started in May when Sandra announced her promotion to the company president's personal communications staff. Her new job meant she would move to the top floors of the green-glass headquarters tower next door, leaving our department behind in the smaller support building called Module A in the tower's shadow. It also meant that a cantankerous editor on staff became the new manager for the department, a mean-spirited divorcée, the staff editor just mentioned. This news came as a blow to me.

Dorothy Barr had apparently awaited this crowning moment—eagerly. An overweight woman in her 40s with a pudgy, circular face, Dorothy smiled at our first one-on-one meeting after Sandra's departure. Her smile turned to a bitter scowl, however, and the hidden, two-faced Dorothy became visible. She closed her office door and sat behind her new desk, then announced point-blank: "You are useless to my new department, John. You can't write. I despise and disrespect both you and Sandra. So I am hereby putting you on notice that you can expect to be fired within 30 days, 60 days at the most."

I sat stunned. Dorothy's pudgy face flamed red with fury. "I can't write?" I stammered.

For good measure, she issued a string of threats. "Oh yes, you will be excluded from our weekly staff lunches, and you are to remain silent throughout staff meetings."

"What's that supposed to mean, Dorothy? A few days ago in our staff meeting you said my electronic publishing article was 'a collector's piece,' that 'it should be reprinted by the thousands.'"

"I was lying! Strictly to fool Sandra." She leaned forward, relishing the moment. "Now she's gone and you're all mine."

Is this a bad movie? Some wicked, make-believe melodrama? I reeled at the absurdity, disarmed. "You're out of line, Dorothy. I *can* write and everybody knows it."

"No you can't!"

"What hair-brained ideas. There's no way you can fire me."

"Try me!"

I left her office and reflected on the feedback that had accumulated about my writing. Weeks earlier, Sandra had shown me a memo from a mainframe client that commended "John's writing ability and contributions to the substance of our product brochure." Smiling, she'd added with a thumbs-up, "Top notch stuff, John. I'll put it in your personnel file." A costaff editor of Dorothy's, Joann, stated that my article about Prime Computers assisting disabled persons who worked offsite "will make a dandy cover story. It's one of the best I've seen lately, John, right on target." Then a veteran staff writer, Andrea, told me she'd overheard comments from a subject matter expert who noted, "John took my long-winded run-on sentences and made them sound like I knew what I was talking about. Really a first-rate job. Very professional." And there was my male wordsmith-friend, Jerry, who copyedited one of my stories and offered his opinion: "I especially liked how human and individualized you made a dry topic, John."

The next day I sat facing Dorothy and referred to these comments.

She cackled, a carbon copy of the Wicked Witch's diabolical laugh in *Snow White*. "Not a chance. You're on the way out the door, John. As we speak!"

I sat staring, incredulous. Alarmed, I asked for her reasons, her logic.

She leaned forward, getting redder. "Start packing your bags, John."

I regretted having to launch a counterattack. "I asked for your reasons, Dorothy. Nothing you've said makes sense. And it certainly doesn't jibe with reality. So I'm reporting this to Personnel."

"Go ahead and try it!" she thundered.

"I'm not going to stand for this. Not for a minute."

"Oh? We'll see about that. I've already contacted them. For now, this meeting is over! Get out!"

For reasons that remained murky, a tedious power struggle erupted and I learned one very important new fact that day: a ferocious enemy meant me harm. Another absurd duality in my life to fend off and struggle with, on the same order as my tumultuous teen years with Mom—but more insidious.

Just what I needed, more drama.

My tactics to avoid Dorothy's wrath took the form of daily feats of acting one way and thinking another. I developed defensive moves in the name of survival. My first strategy was to phone Personnel and speak to the supervisor in charge of our division. Her name was Helen Lunde and we met in a spare, cramped conference room two days later to discuss my complaints. A wiry woman in her 50s who smelled of cigarette smoke, Helen rattled off official-ese: "Company policy protects you from recriminations by your manager for bringing this matter to my attention . . ." and so on. She then invited me to start.

I recited Dorothy's startling statements and summarized the past months' favorable reviews of my work. Helen nodded as I enumerated the emotional challenges confronting me, not the least being "the ludicrous accusations as well as my fears about losing a good-paying job and the dire effects such a calamity would have on my family."

Helen scowled, silently lit a match and blew the smoke from a Kool cigarette in my face. Yes, blew the smoke in my face! She leaned forward, exactly as Dorothy had done and stated point-blank: "Mr. Prin, Dorothy and I have discussed your performance and I personally have reviewed your file. Frankly, I share her concerns. Perhaps you don't realize it, but not everybody is as enamored with you or your so-called writing ability as you think. Effective next Monday, you are being placed on a 30-day performance improvement plan. You have until then to consider your options."

I sat stunned. Shocked. Incredulous. "Options? What options?"

"There's EAP, the Employee Assistance Program, for one."

I knew of the then-innovative program, mandated to help employees apart from management's involvement or influence. "But isn't the issue that Dorothy's view is diametrically opposed to the view of many of our clients as well as Sandra?"

Helen shrugged. "EAP is an option available to all employees."

"You mean you don't even want to hear relevant facts?"

"Send me a memo. For now, it appears management has an issue, and it's my job to verify your efforts to meet management's expectations."

I stammered, "What's . . . what's going on?! A performance improvement plan? Management's expectations? What the . . ." I sighed. "Just exactly who else doesn't like me or my writing? Do I get to know, or is that some big secret?"

"Sarcasm? I'll have to note that in your file." She handed me an imposing stapled form of several pages with the heading *Performance Improvement Timetable* (PIT) and explained the requirements. As an employee I had to "successfully meet the performance criteria set by your manager for the next 30 days: in your case editorial standards, deadlines, and departmental rules."

"And . . . and if I don't meet them?"

"Then, Mr. Prin, you can seek a transfer—*if* you qualify for another opening—or you'll be fired."

Steaming, I shot back a bitter scowl and demanded, "And if I *do* meet them?"

"We'll see. We'll just have to wait and see."

Thus ended my first encounter with Personnel's Helen Lunde. Three days later, on a Friday, my first encounter with the Employee Assistance Program's Don Monsen occurred. A soft-spoken counselor in his late 20s with a deliberately low voice, Don made it clear that "everything you say will be kept strictly confidential and nothing can or will be used against you by management."

"Gee, sounds like I'm being read my Miranda rights."

He did not appreciate the attempt at humor. Clearing his throat, Don asked me to describe the "presenting problem."

I spilled my side of the story. He frowned whenever I quoted Dorothy's B-movie dialogue or described Helen's antics such as blowing cigarette smoke in my face—far-fetched impressions that got us off on the wrong foot, I think, because it made him question my credibility from the start. I detected this and assured him, "I'm not exaggerating, not a bit." But, it turned out, he never quite believed me.

From that point forward, everything seemed tainted. Don asked me later to write out my goals and objectives for succeeding at the PIT, but he never became the advocate I'd hoped for and never confronted head-on the flimsy basis for the PIT. He resisted challenging Dorothy's or Helen's authority or rationale, and I doubted whether his personality was the sort to ever advocate for me (or any employee)—regardless of how justified the cause—despite the EAP's mandate to do so. In this manner, my hopes for moral support and tactical help from EAP dead-ended from the get-go.

From there on I battled the PIT alone.

My defensive moves in the name of job preservation included notifying Sandra and consulting with my birth mate, David. Sandra proved unreachable the first two weeks after Dorothy's broadside because she'd gone to Hawaii on vacation, then remained distracted for another week by her demanding high-profile new job duties. It was weeks into the PIT by the time she absorbed the sour news and responded.

"You have my complete sympathy," replied Sandra. "The main reason I left that department, aside from this plum promotion, was because of Dorothy. She's the meanest, stubbornest, least competent employee I've ever managed, John, and I can tell you now that I did everything possible to protect you from her insanity while I was there. As for Helen, she's another piece of work. Fortunately, I'm close to her boss here in the tower, and if need be, I can pull strings to make her toe the line."

The gist of Sandra's and my clandestine phone discussions, as well as my long laments to David who concurred with Sandra's strategy, boiled down to this: "Prove 'em wrong, John; get past the PIT; then kick the dust off your sandals and move on." Their thinking included the notion that employee harassment could be proven once the basis for the PIT proved worthless. Meanwhile, my role had to be to stick it out and write doubly well, at the same time not allowing a hint of my rage to be discernable in the office.

And so, home became a haven. The person I poured my heart out to daily was Susie. She listened patiently to each day's shenanigans over cocktails before dinner. Dumbfounded, she shook her head repeatedly about company politics.

"All the crap that's getting thrown at you is tough to swallow, Johnny. But it's not you or your work. It's not even Dorothy or Helen. These kinds of battles aren't against flesh and blood, but are spiritual warfare fought against the forces of evil in the heavens." She was referring to the passage of Scripture from Ephesians, where believers are urged to "be strong in the Lord and in the strength of his might" and to "put on the whole armor of God, that you may be able to stand against the wiles of the devil."[1] She'd often hug and assure me, "Johnny, I'm with you all the way."

"I hear you, Susie, but it's just that the enemy is playing dirty and I have to stand and take it. Playing fair hurts!"

More late-night drinking sessions followed these conversations. As my emotions peaked and plunged, frequently minutes apart, I began feeling unglued. The excess alcohol numbed the seesaw, roller-coaster-like highs and lows, but only for a blissful hour or two. It medicated my dour moods and allowed me periods of escape, but in the mornings I came to realize just the reverse was happening: that the excess alcohol actually magnified, not medicated, the continual upheaval of feelings.

Captive to a common mistake of addictive thinking, I now realized on a different level that things outside me couldn't remedy what was wrong or missing inside me, that happiness did not depend on what others did or said or on what happened around me. I was starting to realize that happiness was a result of being at peace with myself from *within*. Basically, I was still believing the Lie of Addiction and didn't yet understand the principle that "it is what comes out of a person that defiles. For it is from within, from the human heart, that evil intentions come."[2] "First clean the inside of the cup, so that the outside also may become clean."[3]

These feelings of being torn and pulled apart, of being divided and walking a tightrope between two opposing worlds, were based, I learned later, on the self-talk I let swirl in my mind. Self-talk such as:

I'm really a failure and nothing can change it.
Sex with Susie will never be an adventure.
Those ten years in Hollywood were a total bust.
I'll never make up for lost time.
Mom hasn't changed since I forgave her last Christmas.
Drinking in secret makes me a hypocrite.
Am I running life or is life running me?
My life is saved, but saved for what?
I'm doomed to a double life and will never find happiness.

An acquaintance from the writers' conference in California I attended in 1978—when I'd snuck out after dark to smoke pot—had recently mailed me a list of 20 questions titled "Are You an Alcoholic?" I'd confided to him in a letter days before about my battle to quit marijuana and hinted that I was drinking too much. He wrote back saying in a note attached to the list that he'd overcome the same addiction years ago and that, perhaps, my answers to the questions would help guide my thinking.

I read the 20 questions and checked off five YES responses:

1. Have you ever felt remorse after drinking?
2. Do you crave a drink at a definite time daily?
3. Do you drink to escape worries or trouble?
4. Have you ever had a complete loss of memory as a result of drinking?
5. Do you drink alone?

Doing the scoring, I checked the ratings, which mercilessly shocked me:

(A) If you have answered YES to one of the questions, there is a definite warning that **you are an alcoholic.**
(B) If you have answered YES to two of the questions, the chances are that **you are an alcoholic.**
(C) If you have answered YES to three or more, **you are definitely an alcoholic.**

Me? Definitely an alcoholic? No! Impossible! There has to be some mistake. I could not and would not accept this verdict. The test was flawed.

Unfair. And so the debate began that would run in my head for the next 15 years: was I, or wasn't I?

I groaned and sighed, convinced that my behavior—and character—was not acceptable to God, a very uncomfortable feeling. Mixing another drink, I sat down with my Bible and flipped through verses and passages until certain ones jumped out at me:

> Everything is permissible for me . . . but I will not be mastered by anything . . . Do you not know that your body is a temple of the Holy Spirit . . . ? You are not your own; you were bought at a price. Therefore honor God with your body.[4]

I'm mastered by booze. My drinking dishonors God.

> The mind of sinful man is death, but the mind controlled by the Spirit is life and peace; the sinful mind is hostile to God. It does not submit to God's law, nor can it do so. Those controlled by the sinful nature cannot please God.[5]

My mind is hostile to God. My sinful nature controls me.

> Whose heart is filled with anguish and sorrow? . . . Who is the man with bloodshot eyes and many wounds? It is the one who spends long hours in the taverns, trying out new mixtures. Don't let the sparkle and the smooth taste of strong wine deceive you. For in the end it bites like a poisonous serpent; it stings like an adder . . . You will stagger like a sailor tossed at sea, clinging to a swaying mast.[6]

Sounds like you-know-who on many a morning after.

> When I want to do good, I don't; and when I try not to do wrong, I do it anyway. It seems to be a fact of life that when I want to do what is right, I inevitably do what is wrong. I love to do God's will so far as my new nature is concerned; but there is something else deep within me, in my lower nature, that is at war with my mind and wins the fight and makes me a slave to the sin that is still within me . . . Oh, what a wretched man I am![7]

Oh, I am wretched indeed!

My character was in question. I felt I was on the losing end and knew clearly that I was not measuring up. It felt like my inner Self was a battlefield, a place where constant struggles raged on opposing fronts. Between wisdom and stupidity. Honesty and deception. Health and addiction. Whole-mindedness and secret-keeping. God and the devil. Everywhere I turned, the biblical evidence piled up. The painful inescapable duality just as the Bible described.

There was even a song by Bob Dylan on the radio at the time that echoed this theme of duality, pertaining to my life or anyone's. The lyrics of "Gotta Serve Somebody" described the many ways human lives are divided and pulled in opposing directions. The refrain stated that we all have to serve either the Lord or the devil, but that nobody was exempt or free of this dilemma.

Back at work, the crux of Dorothy's "you can't write" complaint never could be proven because my published articles required only modest editing and appeared at times as cover stories. Dorothy's strategy concentrated on tripping me up on current assignments and pressuring Joann and Andrea to edit my drafts heavily. They complied. She also managed to distance Jerry, the only other male on staff, from me by preventing our chatting together. She convinced her boss, a director named Bruce Wilman, to schedule weekly hour-long "hot-seat meetings to review your work for errors."

Privately, she assured me, "Bruce's involvement will lead to your termination, John." When I challenged her for presuming the outcome, she fired back, "You can bet I'll do more than those meetings to get you off the payroll!"

And more she did. She made nasty calls to subject matter experts asking them for criticisms and blew up at me when she discovered that I'd already devised a simple satisfaction form that registered their written feedback. These forms I showed to Bruce at our hot-seat meetings, which irked Dorothy particularly because none of them contained damaging information. She also went behind my back in various ways, and in time I learned from Jerry, who spoke off the record, that her three-hour, off-site lunches had become alcohol-infused "bitch sessions" wherein she ordered drinks for everyone and pontificated on her prejudices (especially against me) while getting sloshed on the company's expense account.

I felt isolated, enraged, and threatened. That the other writers had caved in to her demands and resisted associating or collaborating with me lowered my opinion of them and felt very disheartening. That Don

Monsen in EAP shrugged and did nothing to uphold written company policy when informed of Dorothy's drinking splurges on the company's expense account lowered my already-poor estimate of him as well.

At weekly "hot seat" sessions with Bruce, Dorothy bad-mouthed my writing. Never did she miss an opportunity to list her reasons why I alienated her and should be fired. I claimed, "Her reasons rest on personality conflicts of her own making." Glancing at Bruce, a bookwormish administrator in his mid-50s with hunched shoulders and wire-rimmed spectacles, I sometimes shrugged and murmured, "Does this sound like a bad B movie to you?" Once or twice he actually nodded.

The Byzantine gyrations required to defeat Dorothy at her own game worked like this: I enrolled in a journalism class at the University of Minnesota per my own admission that I'd never majored in journalism. Bruce confided that he looked suspiciously upon literature majors and approved the idea: "Then we won't have to spend time on things like Inverted Pyramid Structure and the 'Five Ws of a lead paragraph,'" he concluded.

The good news/bad news by-product of this decision meant that Bruce extended my PIT another sixty days—good news because it meant two additional months of guaranteed employment, bad news because it kept me under Dorothy's thumb a full three months. Based on the skills I picked up in journalism class, however, each writing assignment that I submitted over the next few weeks met more favorably with Bruce's critical eye. He often found little to correct, which made Dorothy fume.

Immediately after these meetings, I wrote a "meeting memo" addressed to Bruce, Dorothy, and Helen in Personnel, documenting my "progress" and quoting Bruce's favorable verbatim comments. Privately Dorothy harangued me, furiously spewing verbal abuse for my doing so.

"But it's perfectly legitimate, Dorothy," I responded matter-of-factly, "and even Bruce himself said it's my right to document what we all know took place." Without corresponding evidence of complaints from anybody, the air went out of Dorothy's balloon and her claims lost credence.

⁂

In icy cold December, 1983, Bill Troeller paid a visit to the Prin household for Christmas. Accompanying Susie's father from New Jersey was Ramona Conlan, a neighbor widow who lived across the street and had chummed for 50 years with Martha and Bill while her husband was alive. It soon became apparent that Bill and Ramona behaved more like sweethearts than companions. Susie and I speculated privately whether they were having an affair—in fact, whether they'd carried on secretly for decades.

Now retired, my father-in-law drank more than ever and was a sloppy drunk. He embarrassed himself in front of Emily by talking too loud and held Susie captive on the couch near the Christmas tree with saccharin stories and sentimental tears. Most evenings he gushed on about being a "bad father and poor example during your childhood." Susie consoled him, doing all she could to squirm away from his clutches. With the PIT still dragging on, we carefully avoided saying anything in his presence for fear he'd think I wasn't putting my all into the job.

In fairness to Bill Troeller, I recalled his astounding $40,000 down payment that he gifted us for our house, a sign of his whopping generosity—but not without a price. For two long months, I'd tolerated his nasty phone calls prior to the house's closing, frequently made during one of his drunken binges. He demanded to know trifling details about the prospective home's construction/condition and its legal/financing terms. Mixed with my deep appreciation for his funding help came the animosity spurred by the blatant duality of his abusive personality I had to endure.

In my spare hours, the insanity of Dorothy's vendetta also ate away at me. I racked my brain, "Was she jealous of me for some reason? Could it be envy from a woman five years older who perceived unfair advantage afforded to a male rival? Could it be her way of getting revenge on Sandra? Or misplaced rage against some abusive male relative in her past? Was it advanced alcoholism?"

In my journal I safely poured out pages of impressions. Feeling battered, I took stock of my emotions: hate, impatience, self-pity, humiliation. Urges to strike back, to get even, to harm. Seeking God's help, I asked, "Am I still 'Beloved of You,' Lord? It sure doesn't feel like it!"

I turned to the Bible and found considerable solace and insight: Joseph had suffered from false accusations and years in prison before being gloriously vindicated; Esther had rescued her people from the false accusations of her tormentor Haman and had seen him hanged on the gallows of his own making; Nehemiah had endured vicious and wicked plots while following God's call to rebuild the damaged walls of Jerusalem.

In my lucid moments, I realized the powerful similarities of Dorothy's craziness to Mom's erratic nonsense in Chippewa Hills—both women acted obsessed by a thwarted dream lurking in their dark shadow lives, made worse by distorted, drugged behaviors resulting from alcohol or prescription pills. I came to see Dorothy as a sick person whose sickness spilled over on me. I prayed for her, literally asking God to "ease her sickness and heal her wounds." As an oppressed soul, I viewed her oppression toward me as a misguided means to relieve her own torment. In time, with the Spirit's help, I "prayed for my enemy" and pitied, rather than villainized, her.

"But I'm also human," I lamented to Susie. My response to the strain over time led to stolen hours of continued heavy drinking, which she vaguely suspected. As a way of calming my nerves and as a sedative to help me sleep, I fell prey occasionally to this addictive pattern. Ironically, I looked down my nose on Dorothy's alcohol-laden lunches and spoke out against them, all the while consuming large amounts of alcohol myself alone at home. I nursed grudges and felt sorry for myself at night, yet drove to work the next day—often with a not-so-slight hangover—and performed high-functioning tasks under duress. As usual, my insides didn't match my outsides. I wore a mask every day.

It all came down to a showdown.

Bruce Wilman at last grew openly tired of our three-way meetings and Dorothy's screechy tone. While room for improvement in my writing remained, which I acknowledged quietly to him, the need for the dire improvement demanded by Dorothy's inflated claims never met with Bruce's full agreement. In time Bruce shook my hand and, at our last meeting with Dorothy present, said, "Good job, John. You've come a long way."

The PIT threat died that afternoon.

Although I will never know exactly how it happened, the manager of another communications division approached me just hours later and offered me a writing position that included video scripting, producing, and directing. The next morning I started reporting to him and rapidly became his right-hand man, helping his department shoot videos for the worldwide sales force.

Dorothy watched my career flourish. After her vendetta backfired, she went on to hang herself months later on the gallows of her own making—alcoholism and irresponsible behavior unbefitting a manager.

Meanwhile, I survived and proved to be the "species most responsive to change." Only the imbedded secret of my drinking alone at home remained a stubborn habit that I carefully concealed from everybody. My star at Quality Tec was again on the rise.

MetaViews to Muse   #7

To help you recognize and confront secret-keeping tendencies and habits, these reflections on what you've read in the past few chapters are meant to encourage you to consider your own life's challenges and choices.

* No matter how lofty one's motives for renouncing secret-keeping, what's been done in secret still has shame attached to it. Despite my early efforts to eliminate furtive behaviors regarding porn, womanizing, and street drugs, the character transition that followed was hindered by unresolved emotions like shame that still begged for addictive thrills to medicate or numb them.

   Is shame a recurring factor in shaping your behavior?

* The journey to wholeness means accepting that: pain is inevitable, suffering is probable, misery is optional. Until I wrote the letter to my dead father, I couldn't let go of the misery of what went missing in my childhood. Until I saw those old events with new eyes, I couldn't understand the principle that pain and suffering may accompany many of life's situations, but that misery is an attitude we choose or can un-choose.

   If you feel miserable, what other options could you choose?

* Secrets, being fear-based, serve to protect one's reputation or to project a more acceptable image of ourselves. If one's whole life is a performance, then the mask is always on. But ridding ourselves of secret-keeping involves proving that we can keep promises to ourselves when nobody is looking: when I felt tempted in the airport to look at naked women in magazines but refused to do so, a secret *victory* occurred rather than another secret *defeat*. My reputation with myself and self-image sky-rocketed.

   Do you keep promises to yourself when nobody is looking?

* If you are a Secret Keeper, realize that you have conditioned yourself to feel normal by balancing two incompatible worlds. These habits require changing one's self-talk (what we say to ourselves, our thoughts and beliefs) and take considerable time to break. My name change from Frustrated Failure to Beloved of God exposed my root of bitterness and, once my self-talk repeated it, eventually lessened my intensity by showing me the downsides of insisting on my own way. My misery from the dysfunction in marriage improved once I started saying to myself, "Love is about *giving* more than *getting*," thereby allowing my self-talk to help change my two-timing attitudes.

Does something in your self-talk need to be challenged or changed? What is your current self-talk? What changes does it need in order for you to move forward?

✳ Answers to emotional dilemmas can come in creative or supernatural ways—stay alert. After I cried out in need of a father, God heard and said, *You are My son; I will be your Father*. During my job search back home, I discovered in a personal way the truth of Scripture, "He leads me beside the still waters and restores my soul," when I sought His company by the still waters of Minnehaha Creek.

Are you benefiting from the countless ways holy messages can help soothe and smooth the trials in your life?

✳ The three principles of whole-mindedness, below, free up one's emotions:
> ✦ the *excitement* of seeking God,
> ✦ the *pleasure* of sharing divine presence,
> ✦ the *delight* of being loved and comforted.

In contemplating these principles, what do they mean to you personally? Are you experiencing intimacy with God?

Part 4

> "Happy is he, even though he suffers, whom God has endowed with a spirit worthy of both love and misfortune."
>
> *Victor Hugo*
> *Les Miserables*

꧁ *Chapter Sixteen*

Quantum Leaps, Forward and Back

I stood in the elevator speeding up to the top floor of Quality Tec's headquarters tower where my duties as a speechwriter for the top echelon of executives awaited me. I got off on the spacious 15th floor and walked past the posh executive suites to Hank Rice's office, the head of Human Resources. His secretary smiled when she saw me approaching. "Mr. Rice is expecting you, John, but he won't be out of his meeting for a few minutes. Can I get you some coffee?"

I asked for ice water instead and sat down in one of the plush chairs in his personal lobby.

It was 1985, two years later, and the turnaround in my career had proven astounding. I was now part of the world headquarters communications staff and privy to the comings and goings of the president and his cadre of company officers. Unfortunately, the daily media headlines proclaimed gloom and doom for Quality Tec Inc. (QTI). From a nearby floor-to-ceiling window, I could see the company's shipping docks where disk drives—the size of refrigerators and washing machines—sat unpaid for. Meanwhile, the newly introduced personal computer (PC) by competitor IBM had enticed consumers into a buying frenzy. With 30,000 of our firm's 62,000 employees getting laid off that year, I questioned the precariousness of my future in the ailing company. Lately, I'd tossed and turned at night, stressing over the risks of staying on a sinking ship or starting my own video production company.

Actually, my secret life dominated my daytime hours, as it did that day by distracting me with persistent thoughts of drinking—what I later learned was called *preoccupation* in addiction terminology. I recalled one morning earlier that week when a paste-up artist in Quality Tec's graphics department—whom I worked with regularly—Sally Bowman, noticed my hungover appearance and asked, "Are you feeling all right today, John? You don't look so hot."

I mumbled something vaguely about "one too many last night."

Sally perked up, looked me squarely in the eye, pointed to an AA saying printed on a poster hanging in her cubicle, and whispered, "'When alcohol becomes a reward, it's time to stop.' I know. Take my word for it."

With this kind of awareness by others, I felt prodded to impose on myself a 30-day non-drinking fast in order to prove I didn't need alcohol to feel better or to improve my gloomy moods. For 30 days I succeeded and verified that I "could quit anytime I felt like it." The next day I celebrated by carefully limiting myself to two single-strength Manhattans in order to convince myself that I could imbibe moderately.

This lean pattern lasted a few weeks until gradually my old excessive fall-asleep-while-reading-after-too-many or find-myself-passed-out-on-the-floor-the-next-morning patterns returned. No matter how hard I'd tried not to steal hours this way, I couldn't shake the secret-keeping power of this self-destructive behavior.

While waiting in Mr. Rice's lobby, the case for staying with Quality Tec struck me as weak. Like any corporation, its glaring "We versus They" hierarchical inequalities epitomized the mercenary principles displayed throughout the corporate world. The leaders at the top of the hierarchy granted themselves privilege after privilege, then flaunted those privileges before the lower echelons of men and women who did the real work. I'd heard a company executive lament: "Why aren't our people motivated to boost productivity and cut costs?" He seemed to have no clue about something so obvious.

At times Mr. Rice and I strategized over the wording of his speeches, trying to answer that question for employees in failing divisions. I diplomatically brought up my own daily experience of walking by offices on lower floors where deadwood executives, who were paid salaries of $75,000 to $100,000 (comparable to $350,000 to $500,000 in post-2000 times), sat looking bored doing nothing. And I cringed whenever I recalled the hundreds of thousands of dollars management spent on glitzy incentive programs and rah-rah sales events in far-off places like Las Vegas or Hawaii to motivate employees—employees who were put down by that same hierarchy rather than being recognized with better wages and fairer treatment based on merit. It was like the management/labor aristocracy that ruled in the factories of old, only modernized with white shirts, personalized workstations, and clean bathrooms.

Coupled with the world market's jitters and panic over the failures of QTI's computer designs and disastrous sales, there appeared to be little hope for support staffers like me. I was neither an engineer nor a computer programmer and therefore expendable. Fortunately, my acquired writing/video skills and corporate experience would fit in just about any industry, thereby advancing my career anywhere.

Ironically, Bruce Wilman and I had developed an ongoing liking and respect for each other in the months since Dorothy's fizzled vendetta, and he had gently encouraged my writing endeavors apart from corporate journalism/PR in the areas of fiction, children's books, and movie scripts. Sandra Herns had moved on to juicy assignments in California.

After my speech-drafting meeting with Mr. Rice that day, I stayed late into the evening hours drafting my novel-in-progress. The old fiction bug had bitten again, this time for writing books. Once more I was stealing hours—sort of. This time I was stealing hours away from being with Susie and Emily at home to indulge in the fantasy wish of becoming a respected novelist.

Broken Blessings, based on the real-life account of a man from a large family who had survived the Depression, fit the nostalgic saga mold of *The Waltons* or *Little House on the Prairie* from television. In truth, writing novels was a spin-off of my old Hollywood, Oscar-winning filmmaker/screenwriter dream. Thanks to the efficiencies of computer word processing available at the office, I'd spent dozens of weeks writing this novel and various articles and essays. A new form of quasi-secret-keeping had sprung up and taken root, but one that Susie knew about and tolerated.

"You have every right to gripe," I told her one evening. "But this novel also acts as a counterforce to my leaving Quality Tec. I need to keep earning a steady paycheck there because of the free word processing."

"It's the Little Place all over again," Susie replied. "Plain and simple, it's who you are." She saw me start to protest and repeated, "It's who you *are*, John."

"Agreed." I told myself it was a way of being good to myself while also proving that Dorothy's accusations were groundless and Bruce's instincts sound. As current failed expectations increased, my sense of incompleteness and lingering resentment about 15 years of failure as a dramatist in Hollywood had rekindled. Struggles with editors' rejections and delays led to disappointments and tenacious rewriting.

I squabbled with God—"Why do You allow so many difficulties to interfere with *Your* calling for me?" God either permitted or prevented everything, I believed, and I felt acutely the duality of the long-term, penniless investment of becoming a published author versus the biweekly predictability of paychecks for my writing QTI propaganda. It seemed I was now back on that same track of rejections, often bemoaning the lack of rewards and paltry results from writing fiction/articles/essays and bemoaning so much time, effort, and passion in doing so.

Susie told me one day, "The pain I see you going through from writing rejections makes me ache, Johnny."

"I feel like Cain," I replied. "Now I understand the pain he went through when his sacrifice was rejected and God found it unacceptable and banished him."

"Hurt pride," she added. "Rejections always injure one's pride."

"More than that, I think. His brother Abel's *was* accepted. Both *he* and *his sacrifice* found favor, but not Cain or his sacrifice. That added envy on top of both the person and the offering being rejected. Ouch! That had to hurt."

The muddying influences of envy had crept into my psyche from seeing others' literary success happening ahead of mine, and I found it difficult to believe I was still "Beloved of God." Despite my gratitude about my current career as a well-paid flourishing speechwriter and video director at Quality Tec, in my private moments whenever I opened popular magazines and saw other writers' work in print, I felt cheated. Doubt and bewilderment forced me to ask:

Do I really know my true calling?
Am I really sure about my true self?
Is this ordeal the standard paying-your-dues development period
   most new writers go through?
Or am I overreacting?
Or is God testing me?

Very subtly over time, this pursuit of stealing more hours in fiction-land became an idol, an avenue for delusional thinking that seemed innocent at the time.

Envy also resulted from comparing myself with Dave and Tommy. Dave's income, job security, and long-established business reputation far surpassed mine; his salary scored in the six digits. Tommy played piano professionally like Dad used to and, compared to me, had more applause and acclaim going in his career, including people who funded his recordings and concerts. Clearly I viewed them both as being ahead of me—one more hardworking and competent at managing his affairs than I, while the other's charisma and talent drew people to him like flies to honey.

The antidotes to these struggles came from scriptural affirmations I either memorized or recorded in my journal, such as "trust in God," "wait for His timing," "He is with me always," "humble thyself," and "I am loved no matter what." I repeated these phrases to myself, replacing negative thoughts in my self-talk with these kinds of promises and avowals.

Compared to ten years ago when I was suicidally self-willed, I felt relatively at peace. One proof: no ulcer. It had healed on its own and had stayed healed, thanks to the calming presence of the Holy Spirit. I felt grateful rather than cheated—most days. But I was still balancing two incompatible worlds. I was still stealing hours in clandestine ways, like at times when Susie didn't want to go to a gutsy or sexy movie, I ducked out on my own and went anyway.

These chronic painful moods sent me to the liquor bottle for pain relief. What turned out to be my second attempt to control my drinking resulted when I imposed another ban on myself in August, this time for 60 days. I white-knuckled it successfully without caving in. But the very next day, I celebrated with "just one" glass of wine at dinner. That night, however, I wrote in my journal:

Why would somebody without a drinking problem give up drinking? Maybe God wants to purify my brain from the deadening effects of alcohol. Maybe God is waiting for me to obey in this area in order to bless my writing. Maybe God intends to deliver me from double-mindedness and duplicity to single-mindedness and simplicity. Maybe God is tired of my seeking solace in an earthly substitute, a toxin really, rather than seeking comfort in His promises and heavenly Spirit, the genuine real deal.

As I reflected on these ideas, I held a running debate with God about other struggles such as whether Susie's and my sex life would ever come to life and whether the meaning and significance I was searching for would ever come at all. My moods peaked way up and plunged way down. In the midst of these conflicted sentiments, I came across a poem while searching for a fresh way to say grace prior to our upcoming Thanksgiving meal, a tradition I had started as a way of expressing gratitude to God on this national holiday. The poet, identified only as an unknown

Confederate soldier, had summed up perfectly the ironies and paradoxes that I felt profoundly in my own soul:

ANSWERED PRAYER

I asked God for strength that I might achieve,
I was made weak that I might learn humbly to obey.

I asked for health that I might do greater things,
I was given infirmity that I might do better things.

I asked for riches that I might be happy,
I was given poverty that I might be wise.

I asked for power that I might have the praise of men,
I was given weakness that I might feel the need for God.

I asked for all things that I might enjoy life,
I was given life that I might enjoy all things.

I got nothing that I asked for . . .
but everything I had hoped for.

Almost in spite of myself my unspoken prayers were answered.
I am among all men most richly blessed.[1]

Absorbing this soldier's gifted way of encapsulating earthly and divine truth, I felt waves of gratitude for all kinds of blessings, among them my health, my salvation and ongoing sanctification, my wife and daughter and twin brother, and the blessings of nonfiction writing after so much frustration trying fictional movie scripts. In all, I calculated, my earnings totaled over $250,000 from my business writing/journalism and, on that level at least, my work finally was connecting and felt fulfilling.

Beloved of God!

One of these business-writing successes came from a high-paying freelance scriptwriting project for a large life insurance company, my first half-hour video drama shot professionally and acted by paid actors. Even with positive experiences like this one, however, I tossed and turned in bed at night, stressing over the risks of staying on a sinking ship (Quality Tec) or starting my own media production company.

"I understand your resistance to the risks of my going into business on my own," I told Susie, "but something is telling me it's time, at 42, to be true to myself and to make such a move."

"John, I'd rather you stick it out awhile longer at QTI, so we can pay off more of the house and other bills."

"Okay," I conceded. "I like the security too, but it does come with a price."

One day while taking a break at home from professional tensions like these, I tuned in to the Minnesota Hockey Tournament being broadcast on TV. Ever since high school, I'd stayed a fan of the sport and, lo and behold, there on the tube were the Grayton Grizzlies, my alma mater, competing in the state championship. And there, too, was Coach Mack, the same enigmatic tight-lipped "Buzz" who'd stymied me more than 20 years earlier. As I observed the team's wild excitement at achieving the first place trophy and the stoic triumph of my nemesis, my insides churned with seething spite. Seeing him interviewed and lauded by the media triggered my memories of his denying me a varsity letter. Shaken and bewildered, I realized I still felt he owed me.

But I was no longer willing to sulk away. Now his equal as an adult and parent, I decided to hold his feet to the fire and demand an account. Agitated, I sat and prayed to God about it. As a new Christian, I didn't want to act rashly. A peace came over me as I examined my feelings before the Lord, so the next day I sat at my typewriter and drafted a letter:

```
Coach Mack ,
    You may or may not remember me: I was the second-
string goalie on Grayton's 1960-61 varsity hockey
team. Open the yearbook for that year to page 163,
and you will see me seated four shoulders to your
right. Because of my involvement with the team, I
expected an varsity letter, but never received one.
```

I then recited the facts of my playing in scrimmages and games and the specifics of the hallway incident as I remembered them, and concluded:

```
    . . . Since then 24 years have passed and I believe
you still owe me an explanation—and a belated letter.
I wish to hear from you in the near future, preferably
to have an appointment with you in person.
```

I signed the letter and mailed it to his home address, to spare him any embarrassment at school. I waited, and waited. After two long weeks, I phoned him at home. His wife answered, said he wasn't in, and took a message. I thanked her and waited all evening. Nothing. Nor did he call the next day.

A week later a brief letter of apology from Coach Mack arrived in the mail along with a seven-inch cloth "G" letter. As part of the packet, he'd signed an accompanying certificate making me an official Grizzly athlete. It seemed like a cowardly backdoor way to handle my request, but the successful result—much-anticipated—touched me greatly. I let myself feel the thrill of getting justice at last. I ordered a fine wooden frame and matted both the "G" letter and certificate together under glass. The satisfaction of seeing it hanging on the wall of my home office made up for decades of emotional damage. Feeling a surge of gratitude, I thanked the Lord for the go-ahead He had given me to assert myself.

By now, I also had to assert my views with Susie regarding her objection to my going into business on my own. "It's too risky, Johnny," she declared one early spring evening before dinner. "We've only had a stable income and health benefits for four and a half years. And Emily's just starting high school."

"I realize that," I countered. "But let's take a minute and look at the options. My communications skills are honed now—they're fully transferable and state of the art. And they're not tied to computer technology. My reputation has grown throughout the corporate community. Now just may be the time to captain my own ship."

"Back to freelancing? Depending on freelance writing to earn a steady income? No, it's too unreliable."

"Point taken. It's just something to consider is all." Writing, directing, and producing marketing videos for Quality Tec, along with those encouraging freelance projects and the extra income, had elevated my skills to a higher plane than I was able to achieve in Hollywood. Nowadays I was in charge of budget, creative concept, and hiring of camera/editing personnel. These challenges had awakened my entrepreneurial spirit and provided desirable credits and genuine qualifications. It seemed plain from the outset that my new business should offer video services to a wider array of organizations needing to promote their agendas.

"I know and understand all you're saying, John," Susie bargained, "but the idea of resigning a high-paying position with good benefits—even when the company's future is iffy—is too scary for me."

On a certain level, I couldn't argue.

The solution? We joined hands, prayed about it, and waited. The answer came unexpectedly, and—as in my teen years—via a movie. We went to see *Out of Africa* weeks later, and during the scene when Meryl Streep's character courageously pursues her dream of running a coffee bean plantation, I felt moved at the core of my spirit to follow my gut like she had.

After the movie, I held Susie's hands and told her of this message: "It was like those supernatural nonverbal 'zingers' I've heard before, those *Forgive your mother* and *I will be your Father* inner nudges." Expecting questions and objections, I watched as her eyes penetrated mine.

Slowly her gaze became mixed with acceptance and an appeal for strength. "Johnny, I can see your mind is made up."

I paused. "Yes, but it won't do any good if you feel forced to go along. It can't be that way, or I'll stay put. Really I will."

Sighing, then smiling, she gave her blessing. We hugged and kissed.

On July 15, 1986, I resigned from Quality Tec after a cake-and-balloons good-bye party put on by coworker friends. The next morning at 9:00, I sat in my first client's office, writing two training video scripts. My days as president and producer of J. P. Enterprises started off strong and steady, a sign that affirmed my quantum leap into self-employment. Five new corporate clients including major projects for manufacturing corporation Honeywell followed in the next year, as did a handful of video projects from Quality Tec, despite its continued employee layoffs.

In quiet stolen moments, I celebrated my good fortune with double and triple Manhattans.

Things clipped along in this vein until a year and a half later. With my footing firm as a freelance video professional and media consultant in November 1987 and several well-paying JPE productions "in the can," I previewed my latest corporate promotional video in a Honeywell screening room. An intercom buzzer abruptly interrupted our meeting: "John, there's an urgent phone call from your wife."

I grabbed a phone. "I just got a call saying Dad suffered a massive stroke this morning," Susie told me. "He's been rushed to the emergency room. I'm booking a flight to New Jersey as soon as possible."

I concurred with her plans and arranged to hold down the home front. We decided that I should hold off traveling to New Jersey until we knew more about Bill's unconscious condition. Meanwhile, I would care for Emily and our dog Pumpkin until further developments dictated otherwise.

The next few days witnessed the beginning of a decade-long saga, one that turned our lives up-side-down and pushed us to the breaking point—a quantum leap backwards.

"Love is my decision to make your problem my problem."

Author Unknown

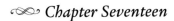 *Chapter Seventeen*

Marriage Vows on Trial

During the first month Susie was away, my old secret-keeping habits reasserted themselves. I resisted, but slipped a little. Two months later, in February 1988, Susie's father died. I flew there, realizing she was left with the funeral to manage, a tangled estate to administer, and a three-story house to empty of lifetime belongings before selling it. With no siblings, she had none to depend on, so I pitched in to help her, which mainly involved propping her up emotionally for weeks.

Her truthful feelings about her father's death? Susie felt relieved more than grieved, and I felt entirely sympathetic. We both knew his public image was diametrically opposite to his private personality, the former being glowing and the latter glowering. Her pain at hearing mourners laud him moved me, because she knew the truth about the private man, yet she gracefully acknowledged their friendships without spoiling their illusions. Privately, she mourned the decades of painful humiliation her mother, who'd died seven years earlier, endured as a victim of his raging alcoholism.

Back home alone in Minnesota, I cared for Emily—now in ninth grade—fed and walked Pumpkin, bought groceries, and cooked meals. Susie's focus shifted almost 100 percent to estate matters in New Jersey, where she spent up to two weeks at a time every month, despite her eagerness to return home to Minnesota as often as possible. For our benefit, she would prepare a weekly schedule with encouraging Bible verses in colorful ink, complete with preplanned menus and little love notes to Emily and me.

During the long nights when Susie was gone, I hit the bottle pretty hard. A dependency on alcohol inexorably assailed me. I ruminated on the connection between her dad's alcoholic, domineering, tyrannical influence on her as a child and our lackluster intimacy and love life, which I calculated to be 16 years at that point. My drinking never abused others and was totally unlike his, therefore it could not be a factor, I determined. There had to be another connection, I believed.

That summer, Susie reached me by phone from a dance conference she attended in San Francisco. Experiencing flashbacks from past abuse, she confided about remembering at a tender age "my father's advances. He'd creep into my room and molest me when I was very little, and I don't remember Mom making any attempt to confront him or protect me." I listened closely and tried comforting her long distance, believing him entirely capable of such ignoble actions. *Incest* entered our discussions and became an often-used term in our vocabulary.

Seeing Susie struggle sapped my energy. Her trips to New Jersey continued and long-distance phone calls late at night wore me down as I heard about her hurtful memories and ugly stories. Not having her around doubled my domestic chores and feelings of loneliness and powerlessness to help her. My home-based business, already invaded by household interruptions, groaned under the added stress. With my extra drinking factored in, I was in lousy shape to tackle the innumerable challenges facing me each morning.

Curiously, eight of my freelance-written articles and essays saw print that year. The published stories paid modest fees, boosted my confidence, and encouraged my screenwriting and fiction efforts. In my "spare" time—what I came to call "my second 9-to-5 job," that is 9:00 P.M. at night to 5:00 A.M. in the morning—I kept working on major projects: my novel about the large family surviving the Depression, now titled *Dust and the Devil;* a screenplay drama about three young children dealing with the fallout from their parents' divorce, titled *Between Planes and Parents;* and a musical play about my dad's career in live TV and radio, titled *Toby!*

But time and energy spent creating them still fell outside the realm of my main occupational, income-earning focus. Although I was getting paid small fees to teach classes in writing and video directing, which I loved doing at local colleges and nonprofit arts organizations, these efforts still didn't bring in enough income to merit my continued involvement. Never one to shirk a day's work, I put my shoulder into aggressively promoting my video business and broadening my marketing focus to include print-based communication projects such as brochures.

In this wave of activity, I came to experience a very unfortunate setback. For a client's brochure that I had been hired to write and project-manage,

I directed a photo shoot at a still photographer's studio in downtown Minneapolis. During a break one day, I saw a *Playboy* in the men's room and felt an irresistible temptation to thumb through it. For ten years, since dumping my harem of centerfolds into the trash in California, I'd avoided any "lust of the eyes." Other than being caught off guard by occasional magazine covers of sexy women or seductive movie ads, I'd voluntarily kept chaste and avoided backsliding.

That day I risked picking up the *Playboy*. Like a skydiver free-falling from 25,000 feet, I hurled headlong into the vortex I'd protected myself from and got sucked down in the swirl of blind lust for female nudity.

Late that night with Susie 1,500 miles away, I mixed a triple scotch-on-the-rocks and opened my Bible for help. I reviewed in 2 Samuel the story of King David's lust for Bathsheba, the same David God referred to as "a man after my own heart." This same David succumbed to his lust for the naked beauty of a neighbor's wife and even had Bathsheba's husband killed, so he could claim her for his own.

In Genesis, I read of Shechem's lust for Dinah, which led to rape and family warfare ending in a massacre, then of Jacob's trickery to outwit the birthright from his twin brother Esau.

In the book of Judges, I read how Samson had fallen head over heels in love with Delilah's beauty and lost his renowned strength (by telling a secret!) as well as his eyesight and his very life. All kinds of men like me and predicaments like mine, but knowledge of God's justice and forgiveness in these situations did little to help me wiggle out of the guilt that plagued me over my own plunge off my obedient perch.

I felt myself in an impossible bind that might vex me all my life. Whether God forgave me or not, I felt bombarded with memories from my closet harem of centerfolds in California as well as my former reading about literary whores and the scintillating images from my excursions to nude beaches and porn movies. My relapse, as real as when a recovering drunk binges after a decade of sobriety, reminded me of the old flesh versus spirit struggle that the Apostle Paul wrote about in Romans and the "lust versus love" dilemma.

Of course, this renewed insurgency remained a secret struggle, which I kept from anybody's awareness and disclosed only in my prayers and journal.

In the face of Susie's absences because of her tasks in New Jersey and our sterile love life at home, things eventually took a positive turn. I made brief trips back to New Jersey where Susie and I worked well as a team. So much work confronted us that we spared no time for anything else. By June 1989, we'd managed to sell her girlhood home, transport and absorb a large U-haul of furnishings into our Minnesota home, and become an intact family again. Emily, now a sophomore in high school, expressed her strong feelings about having greatly missed her mother. "Mom, you're home! Stay and don't leave this time!"

"Yes, honey!" exclaimed Susie. "Home to stay!"

Susie and I also entered counseling to deal with her worsening mood swings. Our appointments with the first therapist skipped over incest issues, so we sought out another therapist who helped us to better understand dysfunctional family dynamics. But neither of us ended up coping better. My small-business health plan did not cover mental health conditions, so payments came out of our own pockets at full rates, which added additional stress. Combined with the snail's-pace progress in dealing with the incest issues, my hopes and motivation deflated.

In time Susie and I grew at odds with each other. Tension. Accusations. Misunderstandings. Fits of temper. Bouts of depression. One day she accused me of being like her father, persecuting her and being unfair.

"Susie, that's outrageous!"

"Well, it's true! You're just as demanding and self-centered and controlling!"

"No I'm not, and you know it! What you see as controlling is only my way of trying to help us get closer and deal better. Get a grip, okay?"

She insisted I was acting like her dad and "imploded" within herself.

Insulted, flabbergasted, I withdrew. Sex became totally out of the question, even talking about it. The estate, a convoluted mess with the Internal Revenue Service, dragged on and showed no signs of closure. The only sure thing we knew about it was that the dollar value would one day total a sizeable sum, *when* it ever settled. Day by day Susie shut down and inwardly collapsed. I became overfunctional; she underfunctional. I did more, she did less. I felt persecuted, having to hold everything together while she tuned out—including no longer doing routine chores. She also ate little, cooked less, and stopped buying groceries.

"What a travesty," I complained to God in private. "Do You ever mean for us to be happy again? She deserves my loving support and I am giving it, but at what price? Can this be Your will for our lives, or is it some kind of test? Show Your love and please come rescue us."

In terms of a secret life, as I'd done when Mom was wacky in Chippewa Hills, I subconsciously "got lost" and hid my pain from anyone outside the home, presenting a happy face, a mask. Once again, the hypocrisy of acting one way while feeling another, of my insides not matching my outsides, of appearances first and reality second. Again, the dejected, lonely, hurt Self inside. Again, the Addict knocking on the door of my heart and will in order coax me to steal hours and somehow fix the mess. Unable to refuse or maintain limits, I sank further into the alcoholic/addict/now-enabler pit. Messed up again, I isolated and became a wanderer drowning his sorrows in rivers of booze, a lonely seeker of God searching for solace and wandering like Moses in the desert, aching like Jeremiah in sackcloth, and running from God like Jonah.

Over the next couple of years, I toughed it out in my marriage and observed Susie lose two dozen pounds, swallow several prescriptions a day, visit still another doctor for new mysterious symptoms, and experience frequent flashback attacks. Watching her in the fetal position shaking uncontrollably from fear while sucking her thumb and writhing on the floor, I protected her from harming herself and questioned the justice of her inheriting large amounts of money from the man who had traumatized her. Other than to hold her in my arms during these fits of psychic trauma, I felt powerless and incidental.

In time, Emily resented these episodes, and I could not console her. By 1992, when she graduated from high school, Emily got mad because her graduation party at home fizzled due to Susie's forgetfulness and my frazzledness. Emily hurried off to college, 250 miles south to Drake University in Iowa, verbally upset about her mom and dad coming apart. She was visibly hardened from the deteriorating condition of our home life, her mother's daily lapses of memory, and the disorganized housekeeping (now my duty). Sadly, I watched these damaging effects on her and regretted the harm done, but felt grateful that she would no longer have to witness our relentless breakdown.

It felt like life was on hold, and it became daily drudgery. Scriptures such as, "If you suffer for doing good and you endure it, this is commendable before God"[1] and "Rejoice that you participate in the sufferings of Christ"[2] provided some level of meaning and comfort. But I hardly felt very "Beloved of God."

Every month or so, I ate breakfast with Tommy and Dave at our favorite café called the Original Pancake House, a popular hangout in the community that served as a meeting place for hundreds of steady customers like us. We indulged in eggs, pancakes, waffles, syrup, butter, and the best coffee for miles around—while bantering and belly-laughing like we had done as boys after the Chippewa Hills years. One Saturday morning the tone shifted and David lamented about his marriage getting worse, then Tommy confided that his marriage was already hitting bottom. Tom announced that the counselor they were seeing had challenged him to quit alcohol and that for the past month he had done so.

"Wow, Tommy, quite the news." I'd suspected his marriage might be suffering and waited to hear more, but all he added was that they were at opposite corners in their marriage and trying to work things out. The closet alcoholic in me perked up about his nondrinking experiment and I peppered him with questions. Mainly I wanted to know, "How difficult has it been for you?"

He answered, "Not very, once it was clear that either the drinking or the marriage had to go."

Like my quitting cigarettes, Tommy had quit on willpower alone. I quietly kept to myself my own misgivings about drinking and took his example as a sign that the time was coming when I'd need to do the same. I made a mental note to monitor whether his drinking was really the root of their problems or not. If his quitting didn't resolve issues, then it seemed they were on their way to the divorce lawyers. Would they come through this and, regardless of the outcome, would he stick to his nondrinking vow in the weeks and months ahead?

David then talked about the difficulties in his marriage. "We just don't see things eye-to-eye anymore," he muttered. "It looks as though we're headed for a separation." About the time Dave's family returned to the Twin Cities five years earlier, after his conversion to Christ when we'd knelt at his request and prayed together, he'd admitted to me his concerns. He took another sip of coffee and sighed deeply. Seeing the pain in his eyes, I felt similar twinges of my own, yet still marveled that I'd never seen him do anything crazy or addictive to numb his suffering.

I pondered the state of my own marriage. Nothing pointed to improved intimacy or one-flesh, one-mind, one-spirit unity. Everything pointed to the same kinds of destructive stresses and strains as Dave and Tommy were experiencing. Were we three peas in a pod?

On spring break during Emily's sophomore year at Drake University in March 1994, we drove home in the car from Des Moines without Susie. She was home sick in bed. As we headed north, the chain-link fence bordering Interstate 35 and the flat monotonous cornfields beyond rolled silently by the windows of my Honda Accord. My mind brooded on Susie's ever-worsening depression and how it was overwhelming our home life and causing monstrous discord.

Emily asked me, "How are things going for you and Mom?"

I decided to be honest. "Not so hot." I paused, then filled the silence, trying to sound upbeat. "Mom and I are neck-deep in counseling with our fourth therapist. And we've just finished attending a 20-week seminar together on Tuesday nights called *Breaking the Silence*."

"About incest?" Emily replied.

I nodded. Outwardly we were going through the motions, I thought to myself, acting like a happy family, while inwardly we were withering away.

"Is the therapy ever going to end?"

I shrugged, then told her about our plans to spend an additional two weeks at a treatment center in Southern California, hoping to sort out ways to deal with her mom's dissociative episodes. Frequent memory losses had become common, I explained, "as minor as her putting the mustard jar in the medicine cabinet or the Band-Aid tin in the refrigerator; as severe as her driving to pick up the dry cleaning and ending up fifty miles away hours later without remembering how she got lost."

"Geez. Do these episodes have to do with her childhood memories?"

"Yes, honey."

"Have they gotten worse?"

I hesitated, wishing not to have to answer. "Yes."

Emily shrugged and stared out the window.

Three weeks later as inpatients in San Pedro, California, Susie and I participated 12 hours daily in New Life Treatment Center's group and individual sessions with other dysfunctionally damaged clients. All of us were dealing with ongoing depression in some way. Susie and I were paying full rates for services, hundreds of dollars a day plus airfare and expenses, no thanks to my small business insurance policy that covered nothing. But, fortunately, we also were spending some of Susie's "blood money" from the just-completed inheritance, money from the man who had molested her that was now being used to unravel the damage he caused.

During scheduled hour-long counseling sessions, we discussed the numerous times in the past three years when Susie had suffered from spells of memory loss and devastating flashback attacks. We explained how, as we had gone from counselor to counselor, her diagnosis had gone from "incest survivor" to "clinical depression" to "PTSD" (post-traumatic stress disorder) to "Dissociative Identity Disorder," or what was formerly called Multiple Personality Disorder. Commonly, she might wake up as one person and flip into another personality sometime during the day, only to find herself hours later having lived as a totally separate person.

Terrifying for her, dumbfounding for me.

These unpredictable and difficult-to-manage episodes frustrated both of us, especially her. But I, too, expressed frustration, the flashback attacks being the most frightening aspect for me. "The first of several happened when she collapsed on the kitchen floor," I told Susie's empathic female counselor and the ponytailed male counselor assigned to me. "She writhed in agony, shrieked at the top of her lungs for forty-five minutes, then sucked her thumb in a curled-up fetal position for three hours. All this time I prevented her from harming herself, wiped her sobbing tears, and rocked her in my lap until the attack subsided."

They took careful written notes and turned to Susie.

"Afterwards I slept for 20 hours," Susie added. "It was the worst thing I've ever gone through. It took days to function again and feel normal. It was like I left my body, shattered into dozens of pieces, and was left to hang out and dry. Awful, just awful."

"No matter how much I love her and want her not to suffer," I said, "at times I've reached the point of exasperation and intolerance." Feeling the burnout, I held my tongue and didn't say what was on my mind, that I'd been thinking about divorce.

The lessons we took away from New Life boiled down to:

(A) Susie's depression and dissociations from her repressed, abusive childhood would not get better soon and her healing process had only started.
(B) Incest survivor support groups back home and Twelve Step meetings would provide a forum for Susie to voice her ongoing needs and concerns.
(C) My role of keeping everything from falling apart was called *codependency* and my new role—if I chose to accept it—would require "detaching, letting go, and doing less micro-managing." And I'd need to go to Twelve Step meetings for my own sake.

Within days after we returned to Minnesota, Susie got worse, not better. She tried one or two survivor support groups and Twelve Step meetings, but didn't continue going. Basically she became a walking stick figure with an impaired immune system and suffered more flashbacks. She came down with double pneumonia and dropped to 100 pounds, from 120. Besides her daily prescriptions, she took new meds to fend off pneumonia. Combined with total bed rest, these complications deepened her depression.

For my part, I went batty running a home-based business, caring for her sickbed needs, resenting having to micromanage every household detail, *and* being told I was a codependent for doing so. Hadn't I vowed "for better or worse, in sickness and in health?" Weren't loyal spouses supposed to stand by their mates in the worst of times? How could I be doing something wrong by doing what was right?

Following advice from New Life, I attended my first Twelve Step meeting in July 1994 and left the Codependents Anonymous session astounded. In the course of 90 minutes, I heard a dozen ordinary folks like me express similar accounts of struggle and mayhem—I was not alone. No matter whether they talked about a husband, wife, mom, dad, daughter, son, boss, or neighbor, each person appeared embroiled in an impossible, unfair relationship. But they were coping. Somehow they weren't going crazy. Hopeful, I returned the next week, and the next.

Besides applying the Twelve Steps as a way to cope, the Scriptures and the Holy Spirit once again provided some help and comfort. I discovered counterparts to my predicament in the biblical book of Hosea where the author wrote of suffering on account of his dysfunctional wife. I read about Jacob, who served seven extra years of unjust labor for his second wife, and Jesus Himself, who suffered condemnation without ever having committed any wrongdoing. At times during prayer, I felt the presence of the Lord lift my sunken spirits. Strengthened, encouraged, I plodded on, occasionally even smiling or cracking jokes.

Books and other sources of reading also helped. In the span of four years since 1990, I'd read authors Robert Bly, Carl Jung, C. S. Lewis, and Melody Beattie (see Appendix-Reading List), whose books I now reviewed to glean insights. It was my good fortune also to tune into the PBS series featuring Joseph Campbell, a brilliant but funny scholar who synthesized the myths of diverse cultures and made them relevant to today's world. I saw how my struggles with others—Susie, Mom, and even Dorothy—had mythical counterparts in history and literature, and how my double life—anybody's and everybody's double life—also had common roots with other cultures'.

I also found help in literature classics by authors such as Robert Louis Stevenson, who dramatized mankind's duality in the deformed, hellish Mr. Hyde, and James Thurber, whose timid Walter Mitty lived fantasy adventures through his alter ego. Jung named our lower nature the *Shadow*, Freud called it the *Id*, Goethe the *Wurm*, and Saint Paul *the flesh*. Still other writers and teachers—such as Cherie Carter-Scott, Robert Hardy, John Bradshaw, Richard Leider, Anthony deMello—supplied further valuable perceptions to my collection of knowledge.

In time I came to thank God once more for the continued blessings of being born an identical twin. Dave and I attended Bible studies together in a weekly men's group, and in many ways we'd grown closer and supported each other in our individual predicaments. Often after these meetings, he would pour his guts out about struggles in his career and home life. I'd listen, put my arm around him, offer affirming words, and we'd end in prayer. Many times he'd promised himself that he would initiate divorce proceedings, but now, August 1994, with our 50th birthday just days away, it became my turn to pour out my guts to him about my unsatisfying marriage.

"Essentially I'm at the lowest point since my wheat-field experience 17 years ago," I told him. "I wonder if, like you, divorce is inevitable." By now our brother Tom was entwined in divorce proceedings, and I added, "It looks as though I'll unavoidably be next in line after you guys." In the next breath, I described my torn feelings about the ways Susie was holding up strong from the damages of incest and showing enormous courage and stamina. She'd organized a bus trip to Chicago for Emily's concert band, she was keeping active as a sacred dancer, she'd helped Emily move from her college dorm room to an apartment, and she patiently endured my crabby moods and efforts to micro-manage.

Dave commiserated with me, especially about Susie's dissociative episodes and the costs of counseling and other efforts that had brought no discernable improvements. Susie's daily functioning, her emotional welfare, and the quality of our intimacy showed few hopeful signs. As before, we put our arms around each other and prayed.

The day of our birthday arrived. To Susie's credit, she hosted a blow-out party at our home for "you twinsters" despite her weeks of fever from pneumonia and a hacking cough. Both she and Emily went all out with creative, colorful touches, and Dave and I felt honored. Several of our close friends and high-school buddies like Bobby Harris and Jay Wilson celebrated with us.

Yet a pall hovered over the festivities: Dave's wife and kids were absent, Tom's wife and kids were absent, and Susie stayed bedridden behind the bedroom door, exhausted from the above-and-beyond preparations. I felt grateful to her, but it also felt terrible to have her miss the fun and payoff from compliments about her superb efforts. After the last person departed, Dave and I did two hours of cleanup.

When he stood at the door about to leave, we looked knowingly at each other, aware once again—like in Chippewa Hills days—that acting one way while thinking another had been the order of the day. We vowed to live more authentically and went our own ways. The next week he phoned and said, "I've initiated divorce proceedings."

Returning to college that September for her junior year, Emily rode in our Dodge minivan packed for the semester as I drove and Susie remained at home bedridden. Emily ignited in anger over her mother's and my deteriorating relationship. "I'm fed up seeing you both so defeated and overcome every minute." She also demanded answers: "Is Mom ever going to get well? Is God ever going to stop watching and start helping? When is it going to be different?"

I reached over and patted her shoulder, pained by the price she was paying.

Teary-eyed, she squeezed my hand and whispered, "I'm standing by you, Dad, no matter what. We're a team. Always have been. Always will be. And we'll see this through together, no matter what. I love Mom too and only want to see the best for you both."

Secretly, I realized my "well was going dry" and something had to change. Home was no longer the place to run a business that involved as many as 35 people on a four- or five-month project, such as the preproduction, shooting, and editing of *Between Planes and Parents*. It was my company's most massive undertaking, which finished production two years before and was now in active distribution nationwide. I'd also been serving as president on the board of directors for the Twin Cities chapter of the International Television Association (ITVA), a role demanding many volunteer hours.

Outwardly, I made sure things looked better than they actually were (typical!), but I found it impossible to bring my best to work most days. Nonetheless a list of award-winning productions resulted from high-paying clients like Honeywell, Best Buy, Johnson Institute, and the State of Minnesota Human Services Department. Something nagged at me that life was incomplete, however, and that meaning from the outside-in could not equal or replace meaning from the inside-out.

Despite my earlier victories over marijuana, tobacco, gambling, porn, and womanizing, my drinking still dragged me down and made my already bad feelings worse. I knew deep in my soul that I had to do something to curb or stop my intake of alcohol. I felt sick and tired of living in two worlds—my public, normal outside; and my private, abnormal inside.

By late October, Susie started functioning again and was back on her feet. But her weight had dropped so terribly that she could be mistaken for a concentration camp survivor. While physical improvements came gradually, the emotional and psychological struggles between us mounted. When we went out in public, it felt to me like we were playing the "Happy Couple Game," putting on appearances to cover up what was missing in private—a show of solidarity in public when all was spiraling downward in reality.

A little voice inside me whispered, *Take off the mask. It's time to leave.*

I packed a suitcase, said that I'd be gone for a couple of weeks in a note that I taped to the door, hopped in my Honda, and drove off. Without a hint of where I was headed, I left the Twin Cities driving randomly. At a liquor store, I purchased a quart of bourbon, some mix, and ice. Before leaving the store's parking lot, I created a makeshift wet bar in the trunk and mixed a stiff one for the road. By dusk, when I stopped at a tiny Wisconsin town's mom-and-pop motel for the night, I'd downed half the bottle. I drank the remainder of it until midnight with a lit candle burning as I journaled my heart out. For the next two weeks, I roamed rural counties, drinking heavily, sleeping late, hiking for hours, journaling, praying at night, and often weeping.

When I arrived home, I gave Susie a one-page letter that I'd mulled over and recopied. It stated my intentions to move immediately to an apartment.

"Don't do that!" she exclaimed. "Why? Why are you punishing me like this?"

"I'm not punishing you. The time has come for something to change, that's all. I think you need the space to get well on your own, and I definitely need to 'detach and let go.' It'll be healthier for both of us."

"No!" she protested. "This is a huge mistake!"

Knowing her fears that I might never return, I told her, "I love you and do not want a divorce. But it has to be this way for now, or I'll have a severe meltdown."

"NO! NO! NO!"

Seventy-two hours later, I moved into a one-bedroom apartment two miles away and tried to practice living in the present rather than fretting about the past or worrying about the future. As I struggled for a unified marriage, a whole mind, and a fulfilling career in the days ahead, my secret life became a ferocious beast. I battled for a closer walk with Christ as well as professional survival and sanity itself, made worse by my dependence on my chief ally—alcohol—which in reality was my chief adversary hiding in sheep's clothing.

MetaViews to Muse #8

To help you recognize and confront secret-keeping tendencies and habits, these reflections on what you've read in the past couple of chapters are meant to encourage you to consider your own life's challenges and choices.

✳ A key sign of secret-keeping is an ongoing, unending internal debate within yourself. The day my coworker noticed my "morning-after" hangdog appearance and warned, "When alcohol becomes a reward, it's time to stop," my decade-long internal debate began. All my attempts to control or moderate my drinking failed, yet the debate raged on. Eventually I realized that as long as I had to debate my actions and motives, I had a serious problem.

Sound anything familiar to what you're experiencing?

✳ Secret Keepers relapse when they steal hours to medicate their emotional pain, then strive to shine as high performers the next day. This describes the pattern I fell into during my PIT battle, that of performing well during work hours but medicating my stress at home alone with alcohol and nursing grudges while feeling sorry for myself. It also happened whenever Susie spent weeks away from home settling her father's estate.

Consider how you or a loved one's insides may not match your/his-her outsides by medicating/performing.

✳ Finding nonchemical, nonaddicting ways of coping with shame and pain can effectively relieve unhealthy tensions. Attending Twelve Step meetings, reading personal growth books, taking time for a solo retreat, hiking and journaling, praying and claiming scripture verses, all made a major difference in my ability to cope and discover fresh ideas and energy.

List your nonchemical coping strategies.

✳ Gratitude is a sure sign of recovery. The many times I felt grateful—the farewell party in Los Angeles, "big jumps" with Emily, the gifts of a new refrigerator and living room furniture, the writing job in Minneapolis that allowed us to move, the realization that my happiness did not depend on anything outside myself but resulted from being at peace with myself from within, the poem written by an unknown Confederate soldier—these and similar such occurrences counter-balanced the victim mindset that often fed my secret-keeping. If you focus on what you *have* instead of what you *don't have*, gratitude comes easily and will lift your spirits.

Are you constantly aware of what you don't have? Are you grateful for your everything you do have? Consider writing down those things for which you feel thankful.

✳ The Bible contains stories of secret deeds and sly behavior, but shows ways to rid oneself of guilt, shame, and self-defeating behaviors. Lessons from Cain and Abel, Shechem and Dinah, Jacob and Esau, Samson and Delilah, and David and Bathsheba can assist the individual who is seeking help and understanding. They also assure Secret Keepers that others have preceded them with the same kinds of duality, that they are not alone, and that God can provide solutions and forgiveness in these situations.

Are you open to the lessons God's Word can teach you?

✳ Self-imposed guidelines and limits are vital during early attempts to reach wholeness. Combined with past successes in mastering secret-keeping, a track record of success can help prevent new episodes of secret-keeping. My 30-day and 60-day attempts to remain sober demonstrated beyond a doubt the severity of my drinking and the powerlessness over my stealing hours to do it. Without these and similar failed attempts to expose my secret-keeping, it would have taken longer to hit "bottom."

Are you willing to impose guidelines, limits, and risk failure in order to learn more about yourself?

> "Nature doesn't move in a straight line,
> and as part of nature, neither do we."
>
> *Gloria Steinem*
> *Revolution from Within*

∞ *Chapter Eighteen*

Bachelor on the Rocks

I crawled out of the sleeping bag on the floor of my new apartment, sensing the excitement of a new beginning. For the first time in years, I'd awakened refreshed. Starting then and with each new day ahead, the months of sleep disturbances began tapering off and I discovered the joys of taking care of myself, cooking, shopping, and picking up after myself—all done with ease. As I practiced detachment, I experienced new levels of calm and became my own best company.

While doing chores and setting up housekeeping, I reminded myself of the self-imposed rules of my move here:

(1) I will not prevent communication with Susie; if the phone rings or she knocks on my door, I will respond civilly at all times and remain open to talking.

(2) I will allow her to succeed or fail, to heal or get worse, on her own; no longer will I micromanage, cover up, observe, or disapprove of Susie's behavior.

(3) I will not seek a divorce for one year, if ever; this time apart is meant to evaluate not threaten, to give us both a chance to sort and sift our options.

(4) I will not have affairs, flirt with, or date other women; this separation is meant to strengthen our bond, not weaken it.

To improve professional operations, I set about establishing my video company's office in the limited living space. Technically my new home, I realized that I had to define mental boundaries in this new space: if the phone rang during the day, it was business; if during the evening, I would treat it as personal. I revised the company name to JP Mediaworks, Inc., reprinted stationery, upgraded the computer/fax and telephone systems, and negotiated with my part-time secretary/production assistant, Carrie Almaer, to increase her hours and pay. Carrie's professional competence and compassionate listening had helped me cope in the past months and her proven skills again boosted my time and energy, enabling me to assertively market JP Mediaworks' services.

The more I concentrated on business, the more I saw how greatly it had suffered. Still gainfully self-employed, I was focusing now on making videos on social topics such as teen parenting, child adoption, and domestic violence. In short succession, I landed a series of excellent projects. With the first months so busy, the bank account balance reversed its downward trend.

Psychologically, the geographical distance from Susie allowed me a measure of peace I hadn't known in years, and both my energy and creativity surpassed old levels. I continued going to Twelve Step meetings, including a new one, Emotions Anonymous, modeled after AA where participants seek fellowship for unmanageable emotions.

Ah, the emotions! This was the area where my secret life most controlled me. Hardly a day passed when the old rage, the old intensity, the old root of bitterness didn't wag me. Like the proverbial "tail wagging the dog," my extreme emotions wagged me—I (the dog) didn't wag them (the tail). My feelings went up, then down, then up again, then down again. "Peaks and Plunges," I came to call it, peaks and plunges all day long.

On a scale of zero to 100 percent, I might start the day okay (50 percent) then hit a snag and plunge into despair (zero), peak to elation when a client phoned notifying me of their enthusiastic approval of a video script (100), plunge again to disappointment when I learned of a crucial-but-delayed payment (near zero), peak again to optimism when Susie gave hints of her improved health (up near 100), and so on like a yo-yo a dozen more times before bedtime.

Exhausted, seeking escape, I went to weekly Emotions Anonymous meetings and became friends with other strugglers like me—mostly normal, high-functioning folks on the "outside" who admitted to painful and disabling extremes of emotions on the "inside": corporate managers, housewives, insurance adjusters, single working moms, and construction workers. Some were volatile and overreactive as I was; some were the opposite, disengaged and underreactive—yet each of us sought aid and solace from the fellowship of others who admitted they, too, suffered from the same afflictions.

EA sayings like "We can't change anybody but ourselves" and "My happiness does not depend on what happens outside me; it results from being at peace with myself" reflected my inner landscape and boosted my sense of belonging. When I told EA co-members about the impasse in my marriage, often my main topic, I staunchly described my unmet expectations as being reasonable, but in the same breath I admitted (with futility), "I know instinctively that I can't demand changes from Susie as a prerequisite, but need to examine my own attitudes first and make changes there, first."

In time I found myself confiding, for the first time to anyone, some of my secrets:

> "I drank too much last night and woke up passed out on the floor."
> "My inflated expectations about fiction-writing drive me crazy."
> "My hatred of my mother so overwhelmed me that I had urges to murder her."
> "I was caught for shoplifting once because my mind was so screwy."
> "Not long ago I kept a wet bar in the trunk of my car and drank alone a lot, but nobody had a clue I was getting wasted."

With disclosures like these, the concept of secret-keeping first came to the fore. The beginning of recognition! In the process, I learned the benefits of disclosing nasty bits of information about myself, of freely informing others of my clandestine habits and behaviors, and thereby unloaded the heavy, guilty feelings that burdened me—all without making listeners run screaming from the room. In essence, I learned that I was not alone and that the ancient proverb "Confession cleanses the soul" was indeed true.

Gradually the view of secrets as a protective device, a strategy to protect myself from fear of exposure, gave way to the process of disclosure (or confession), a strategy based on my security as a Christian believer who experienced God's love. "Perfect love casts out fear."[1] Rather than needing protection, I needed transparency. With less to hide, there was less to fear.

As a child of God ("Beloved of God") whose ultimate home was in heaven, I began trusting the truth of "resting in the everlasting arms." Rather than cringing from earthly fears stemming from my sinful behavior, I rested in the assurance that I was already forgiven by Christ's redeeming sacrifice on the cross. As long as I didn't anchor my beliefs in material existence rather than depending on spiritual truth—"So we fix our eyes not on what is seen, but on what is unseen. For what is seen is temporary, but what is unseen is eternal"[2]—I grew openly confident and less isolated or sly.

This process, I came to discover, worked for others in EA as well. Many co-members shared my symptoms, and they, too, strove to rid themselves of the traps their secrets had locked them into. We strove together and it was very freeing.

Another place I searched for answers was among the shelves of bookstores and libraries. As before, psychology and self-help books like M. Scott Peck's *The Road Less Traveled,* Melody Beattie's *Codependent No More,* and Gershen Kaufman's *Shame* offered insightful ways to adjust my perceptions and helped me shift from feelings of powerlessness to those of determination. I had the power to choose, *if* I chose to.

But while searching the bookshelves one day, I stumbled upon an erotic book that had once sabotaged me in California and, caving into sexual temptation once again, I opened its pages. Then came the headlong plunge again, the same as when I'd opened the *Playboy* in the photographer's men's room. On the same shelf was a sex fantasy series by a celebrity author, which I also sampled. Again, I experienced the disturbing downward plunge.

From lapses like these, now I had *real* secrets to keep again, but living on my own meant nobody knew (who was human, that is). At EA meetings, I couldn't bring myself to disclose these fantasy sexual transgressions due to the intense shame they generated—too fresh, too X-rated, too taboo. More secret-keeping!

For each two steps forward in the secret-keeping battle, another step backward, it seemed.

Professionally, I also reverted to drafting new movie scripts. The Hollywood Bug had bitten again. These I envisioned for full-scale Hollywood-level production and distribution, and I spent evening and weekend hours writing new, and rewriting old, fictional scripts. I devised an innovative strategy, however, and sought to create collaborative partnerships with fellow video directors and veteran professionals to make funding proposals to locally based retail firms with nationwide customer bases such as General Mills and Target. The deal-making swirled excitedly for two of these projects and the synergy of working with collaborators enthused me. But no matter how hard we tried, these deals eventually fell through, leaving gaping deficits financially and stinging disappointments emotionally. Once again the old pattern of failure and rejection. One day I shouted at the ceiling, "Get away from me, Movie Monster! I'm sick of you!"

Other factors also boded ill for my business. The IRS started cracking down on dozens of Minnesota's media employers because of problems collecting taxes from freelancers. They required firms like mine to submit new detailed record-keeping documents about freelancers we hired with stiff legal penalties for noncompliance, shifting the burden of payment from delinquent freelancers to stable employers like me. *Foul! Unfair!*

The digital revolution also was transforming existing analog video resulting in tripling my—and every firm's—production costs in the face of client pressure to keep costs low. By late 1995, it became apparent that even my visibility on the ITVA board of directors as the local chapter president and annual awards festival chairman had failed to help stimulate new business contacts or opportunities.

My doubts piled up higher than my head. Would I ever write saleable stories? Would I ever run a successful business? Would I ever fulfill my calling or even really know what my calling was? With each failure, my drinking increased—"Poor me, poor me, pour me a drink." Once more I was losing a grip on my hard-earned self-respect, although a small part of me clung to the fact that I was still a faithful husband, still a nonsmoker and nongambler, and still a loving dad. But as every major professional initiative failed, I doubted my future as well as the ability to control my drinking.

For solace, I disciplined myself to turn to the Bible rather than substitutes, at least at times. Late at night with a candle burning, I found encouragement from: "We are hard pressed on every side, but not crushed; perplexed, but not in despair; persecuted, but not abandoned; struck down, but not destroyed."[3] And I found hope from: "Who shall separate us from the love of Christ? Shall trouble or hardship or persecution or famine or nakedness or danger or sword? No, in all these things we are more than conquerors through him who loved us."[4] Also from the Old Testament: "Do not grieve, for the joy of the Lord is your strength."[5]

These Scriptures mirrored my life. Jesus and the prophets and apostles had suffered, so had I, though my mild sufferings paled in comparison to theirs. Nevertheless, in some ways suffering is suffering no matter what the degree.

Marriage-wise, I vacillated between blaming the incest situation for Susie's being stuck and my emotions for making it worse than it had to be. I tried not to blame at all. A key question I asked myself over and over was: "Since I can't change Susie, what can I change about *myself?*" My vague suspicions about alcohol surfaced as a major factor in my resentful feelings—negative feelings destroy one's peace of mind—and I once more viewed my drinking habits as something I should change or terminate altogether. Long ago I'd set a limit of two drinks a night, three on weekends, and vowed to never begin drinking before 5 P.M. Alone in the evenings, I drank doubles and triples, justifying them as one drink each, and at times I simply ignored the other rules and woke up passed out on the floor in the morning.

How many times could I tell my Emotions Anonymous friends the same fact and not change my behavior?

I confided in several other friends who offered their steadfast support: a single man who belonged to the same church and with whom I had discussed my readings of Scott Peck, Joseph Campbell, and the Bible; a group leader of Codependents Anonymous, with whom I often shared insights after meetings about relationships; an Emotions Anonymous group leader, with whom I met for coffee and explored tips about how to deal with my emotions; and two business associates, my insurance agent and a business advisor, both of whom saw through my secret-keeping veneer and knew me well enough to courageously but gently confront me about my addictive attitudes and behavior, always suggesting sober alternatives like AA.

As for Susie during the first six months of separation, she made little progress. She seldom contacted me or phoned.

Then came a knock on the door and a visit from her. I noticed she had gained a few pounds and that color was returning to her cheeks. I complimented her. We talked for hours, went out for a casual dinner and a walk. Moved by her efforts to heal and reconnect, I agreed to attend weekly sessions with her newest sexual abuse counselor.

Months passed and Susie regained her full weight and showed other signs of health, including getting out of the house two days a week by volunteering at a large supermarket where she collected day-old baked goods and distributed them to food shelters. Thrilled for her, hope was rekindled within me. She also resumed dancing at churches on sacred holidays. After a year, I recommitted to my promise not to initiate a divorce and felt relieved that I'd never taken such a step.

But the great sexual divide between us remained wide, in spite of our tender and consistently respectful conduct with each other when together. Susie asked one day, "Are you considering returning home?"

I paused, not wanting to hurt her. "I don't think I'm ready."

This answer, while honest, seemed doubly difficult because it reflected on the one area where she felt wounded the most—intimate love life. Injured by both her father and me, it was the one area where she and I both felt major conflicts and misunderstandings. "Is there such a thing as a celibate marriage?" I asked. "Can a marriage last without intimacy," I added, "when its very God-given design is based on mutual intimacy?"

She looked away, silent.

"Until a breakthrough occurs in this area," I told her, "I doubt whether I'll return home." Taking her hands as I had years ago in California when *she* was on the verge of divorce, I looked into her eyes and said softly, "In those days, you were the anchor in our marriage. Now I am the anchor. Basically, unless we go beyond the sterile love life we've settled for, unless we both become whole individuals capable of expressing our sexuality fully, then how can we ever come together as a whole couple? We need to heal more, and more time is needed."

She nodded an unspoken response, then reluctantly agreed to wait longer about my moving back in.

Another layer of complexity complicated things, that of my mother's eldercare. At 85 she required help with ordinary daily activities and decisions, but David was out of town too often on business making high-stakes sales calls on Fortune 100 companies, and Tommy still seemed too angry at her from the Chippewa Hills years to lift a finger—so the burden of her care fell on my shoulders. We boys fought about sharing the duties, but nothing changed.

It became another area of codependency for me, one that kept me going to Twelve Step meetings and drinking secretly. Again, I felt squeezed. Obliged to sell her house because she could no longer manage its upkeep, I arranged to move her into an apartment and took days off to load furniture and supervise the movers. No tangible help from David or Tommy. Resentments!

A year later, Mom plainly needed the 24-hour medical services of an assisted-care facility. Regardless of my appeals to my brothers for help, only lip service followed. I could not fathom such insensitivity. I'd forgiven her, why hadn't they? Only Susie came to my aid, and occasionally Tom's ex-wife, Carolyn. Emily, who was visiting home from Drake U, appeared pained at seeing the commotion of moving furniture and boxes.

"It's just one more indignity foisted on you, Dad. I'm sick of it and what it's doing to you."

"You're right, honey. I can't stand it either, but who else will step in?"

"No one, I guess. But that doesn't make it any less wrong."

"No, but somebody has to do what's right, no matter how unfair or ugly."

"Okay, but how come it's always you?" She then affirmed my strength of character and whispered, "I'm in your corner, Dad." Her spirits also brightened at seeing her mother carrying boxes and enjoying the work-out. "Sure is good to see Mom doing better. What a difference." Later, she asked, "Still no plans of divorce on the horizon?"

I shook my head and whispered back, "Nope. The jury's still out."

By early 1996 I was still facing the daunting issues of juggling outer forces like these with the inner pressures of a secret life—frequently with a double or triple bourbon- or scotch-on-the-rocks in my hand. Should I refuse helping Mom, thus forcing David and/or Tommy to? But what if they didn't cooperate? Should I quit running my business? Should I move back home? Should I stop drinking?

Should I stop drinking? What a bombshell!

The thought reverberated and ricocheted off the canyons of my cranium. *Is alcohol a complicating, destructive factor? Could it be the culprit? Am I an alcoholic?* Rather than a wife problem, did I have a drinking problem? Rather than a career problem, did I have an attitude problem made worse by drinking? Did my Higher Power approve of my quitting?

YES, OF COURSE!

Twice before I'd tried stopping, once for a month and again for two months. Each time I'd white-knuckled it, both times rewarding myself the day of the deadline with drinks. The question I asked myself now in February 1996 was:

*Instead of being a drinker who **can't** have a drink,*
*can I become a nondrinker who doesn't **want** a drink?*

The radical idea of being happy without liquor was, well, radical.

I made lists of reasons why I was not an alcoholic and why I was. Both grew long and seemed to cancel each other out. But deep down I knew the answer. Then one of the strangest invitations I've ever received came in the mail: to attend a work associate's 25th AA anniversary party. The day came and I stopped by to wish her well and stayed long enough to witness a houseful of guests laughing and whooping it up without a drop of liquor. I was amazed. Flashing like a blinking neon billboard inside me, another of those supernatural signals, came the message:

You belong here, John.
Yes, you can be happy without drinking.
In fact, drinking makes you unhappy. Get it?

My next, and last, drink occurred during Emily's spring break in March when she, Susie, and I went out to dinner. I secretly drank two stiff Manhattans beforehand at the apartment, sucked on a breath mint, then looked good by drinking only one tall beer at the restaurant. That night I experimented by sleeping at home beside Susie to encourage our intimacy and had a vivid dream, so jarring—like a flashing neon sign— that I awakened at 4:00 A.M. and announced aloud: "I'm an alcoholic! I need help! Will you still love me?"

Susie squeezed my hand and sleepily answered, "Yes, John. I know it's been a problem for you and I'm behind you. Of course I will still love you. I'm behind you no matter what."

"**Simplicity is freedom. Duplicity is bondage.
Simplicity brings joy and balance.
Duplicity brings anxiety and fear.**"

Richard Foster
Celebration of Discipline

∽ *Chapter Nineteen*

Bill W.'s Friend

On April Fool's Day, two days later, I walked into my first Alcoholics Anonymous meeting at a nearby church, thanks to directions from my 25th-AA-anniversary friend. I admitted aloud to the 40 seated men looking at me, "I'm John, an alcoholic." Then I stated the reason for my showing up: "My life is a mess, and I'm here to start sobriety as much as to stop drinking."

They welcomed me with open arms, and I felt the warmth of belonging, my first step taken on the path of substance abuse recovery. The first person to welcome me and shake my hand introduced himself as Dave, and the second person introduced himself as Tom. Immediately I felt at home among "family." With practice came weeks, then months, of *abstinence*. With abstinence, came *sobriety*. And with sobriety, came *serenity*, at least glimpses of this elusive state of mind called "the peace that passes understanding"[1] which many of us, addicted or not, rarely feel. During a member's reading from a devotional pamphlet, two of "The Promises" jumped out at me:

"We will comprehend the word serenity and we will know peace," and
"God is doing for us what we could not do for ourselves."

My first realization about abstinence was that it is *not* negative. Generally, whenever you abstain from something, it's something you want badly but can't have. In AA, however, abstinence means freedom. Freedom from hangovers, freedom from wondering how you got home the night before, freedom from agonizing over what you said the night before, freedom from guilt over spending money on booze instead of more worthwhile things, freedom from the downward spiral of self-loathing the morning after . . . Freedom!

In AA, abstinence is the floor on which sobriety is built. It isn't "going without;" it is "having more." More clear-headed time to think. More raw energy to exercise. More money in one's checking account. More self-esteem inside and more honest eye contact with anybody and everybody outside . . . More!

And for me, *more* translated into sobriety, otherwise felt as less pressure to wear the heavy, old mask.

With the shared fellowship of regular Joes like myself at AA meetings, my will/desire/need to drink left me. Seeing others succeed and hearing their stories, some happily sober for 20, 30, or 40 years, helped immensely. In time I told fellow members that my drinking had been an attempt to find solace for all that was not going well. My AA buddies and sponsors, Gene and Jeff, listened and suggested relevant books and pamphlets on surrender, acceptance, and releasing resentments/insecurities/self-pity.

Self-pity was my biggest barrier, I discovered. I had let it pollute my thinking, leading to a "victim" mindset, a free-floating sort of misery that demanded daily medicating. By adopting Twelve Step ideas and adjusting my beliefs, however, specifically my self-talk, I started healing from the inside and thereby confronted the forces behind my drinking.

Doing a 4th and 5th Step, a fearless moral self-inventory and confessing my character defects (such as impatience and self-centeredness) to God and another human being (an AA veteran of 30 years), did much to rid me of resentments and bitterness.

Bill W., the founder of AA, would have cheered me on with a bright smile.

Gradually, the intensity of my emotions also came under more control. As I focused less on myself, a habit from feeling under attack and victimized since Mom's relentless work projects, and focused rather on others, my peaks and plunges eased up. God's loving presence increased as the extremes in my life lessened and as my sobriety dismantled the foggy filter from the liquid barrier between Him and me. With His loving grace came assurance rather than apprehension. My closeness to God now felt tangible again. No longer was I courting His displeasure.

Gratitude now filled me and I knew the joyful reality of "my cup overflowing."[2] The need to hide, sneak, dodge, fib, pretend—all devices of a secret-keeping mind—gave way. The satisfaction of living according to the Twelve Steps and newly reclaimed scriptures acted together to buoy my spirits: "I will not be mastered by anything,"[3] "God provides a way out of every temptation,"[4] "Be transformed by the renewing of your mind,"[5] "Let us throw off everything that hinders and the sin that so easily entangles."[6] Let the mask fall away.

The dynamic new triad of *excitement/pleasure/delight* soothed my soul again:

→ the *excitement* of seeking God,
→ the *pleasure* of sharing His presence,
→ the *delight* of being loved and comforted.

Acceptance of reality also became easier because my internal reality, my new drug-free state, was so much clearer, cleaner, cheerful. As I'd learned in EA, forces and circumstances outside of me were beyond my control and could neither make me happy nor unhappy. Only my chosen reactions would or would not. But attending AA carried me another step farther, and my inner landscape finally came under my control—now that my emotions no longer were drugged, distorted, or magnified. As I allowed "what is" to be just that—without demanding it to be otherwise (my way, or how it *should* be, not its way)—my insides settled down and leveled off.

I rejoiced when I discovered an important passage in a story written by an early AA member. By applying its wisdom to my wounded life, I learned that *acceptance* was the answer to all my problems. Whenever I was disturbed, it was because I found some person, place, thing, or other fact of my life *unacceptable* to me, and that I could find no serenity until I *accepted* that person, place, thing, or fact as being exactly the way it was supposed to be at that moment. Unless I *accepted* life completely on life's terms, I could not be happy. I needed to concentrate not so much on what needed to be changed in the world as to what needed to be changed in me and in my attitudes.

When I practiced the wisdom of this passage regarding my marriage, I said to myself, "I accept my marriage the way it is. I accept Susie the way she is." When I practiced the wisdom of acceptance regarding my troubled career, I told myself, "I accept my video business the way it is. I accept the reality of it and will work to change my attitudes about it."

In tiny bits and spurts, acceptance along with honesty, accountability, surrender—the tools of a whole mind—reemerged in me. I experienced a familiar AA phenomenon, "progress not perfection," and each day seemed a bit less disturbing and a little more satisfying. Instinctively I started practicing the opposite of secret-keeping, a term I later called *secret-liberating* behavior.

Secret-liberating behavior meant *acceptance* of "what is" ("I am addicted"), *honesty* ("I need help"), *accountability* ("I will stay connected with others striving for sobriety"), and *surrender* ("I will choose God's will and AA principles over my own"). That meant I needed to turn from my self-centeredness (egotistical absorption, victim mindset, anxiety, insecurity) toward other-mindedness (awareness of others as equals, contributor mindset, peacefulness, security). For me, success following this new path only occurred by remaining sober, both in terms of realizing what *liberation* meant and by practicing these four principles "one day at a time." This path was to become the same I would counsel my addictive clients to take in the years ahead.

Recovery also meant certain lifestyle changes:

(1) Susie learned of my progress and cut back on her drinking, both in frequency and amounts, or chose not to drink at all when I was around, although I never asked that of her.

(2) Friends and work associates either affirmed me (the majority) or went quietly their own way (the minority). In a bar where the familiar video crowd ordered drinks, I ordered a soda or lemonade. One or two associates frowned and nudged me to imbibe; most encouraged me to stick to my guns.

(3) Family members expressed amazement when they learned of my new path, but I insisted it was because my hiding and covering up had fooled them, not because the reality of my binging in secret did not merit full-time recovery. I described times when Susie or work associates had noticed telltale signs and hinted that I needed help.

These changes made a huge difference in how I responded to daily events. Feeling less anger or hostility toward Mom, especially since the burden of her eldercare fell on my shoulders, I arranged to move her a third time from the assisted-care facility to a nursing home and took days off to load what little furniture she would need. She was also taking more prescription meds and over-the-counter painkillers, and her cranky, short-tempered, irritable behavior grated on anybody and everybody.

Once more, without tangible help from David or Tommy, came resentments. Again, the reminder from AA that resentments are the number-one offender, that they destroy more alcoholics than anything else. Caring for Mom continued as another area of codependency that motivated my going to Twelve Step meetings—but it didn't motivate me to drink. No relapses for me! By practicing acceptance, I felt more honest love for Mom, and my healed feelings for her showed in our relationship.

The month before she died, her deteriorated condition resembled Dad's from 22 years earlier. Seeing her lying in a bed enclosed by metal rails saddened me. From a hearty 140 pounds, she'd dropped to under 100. Besides collapsed veins, which impaired blood circulation to her hands and feet so that they stayed clammy, her kidneys started failing, her constant companion was a bedpan, and she could only sit up for a few minutes at a time without struggling to breathe.

I heard from staff members that she pressed her call button incessantly and ordered everybody in a commanding voice anytime they tended to her—why was I not surprised? A sigh of sympathy and a knowing look were all I could offer them. Deep within me, I felt twinges of gratitude that I'd been spared more grief. Along with Susie, who always spoke calmly about cheerful things, I spent my visits focusing Mom's attention on the flowers outside her window or telling her of little daily events at home or work. The few times I brought up my sobriety, she looked away disinterested, as though I might be shaming her with unnecessary or uncomfortable secrets that reflected badly on her.

By now Emily and the other grandkids had stopped coming to see her, perhaps as much because of the mortal miseries foisted on her frail body as her own distancing demands barked indiscriminately at anybody healthier than herself, "who is lucky enough to not be going through the hell I am!"

The day before she died, I paid her one of my every-other-day visits. Her demeanor could be described as withered-to-the-bone physically, forlorn-to-the-core emotionally, and starved-to-the-soul spiritually. She'd still never expressed any love of God and now seemed fearful of death. Short of breath, she couldn't utter more than a word or two. I'd brought my Bible and gently started reading passages from John's Gospel into her ear, especially from Chapter 3 about being reborn. I hoped to inspire her spirit, based on God's promises that He wills all "to be saved and to come to a knowledge of the truth,"[7] . . . "not wanting anyone to perish"[8] . . . so that everyone will have eternal life and one day "they will see his face."[9]

She died the next afternoon while I was working downtown. I trust she knew some peace at the end. I can't say I genuinely grieved for her so much as felt sadly relieved. Despite my residual anger toward Tommy and Dave, I deliberately practiced the Big Book axiom of "Unless I accept life completely on life's terms, I cannot be happy."

We buried Mom next to Dad on April 1, 1997.

⟨∞⟩

A year and a half after my sobriety date, I faced the demise of my video business, a choice I made on my own without urging or persuasion by others. Interviews for a new career as a corporate trainer led to my landing a well-paying position with dandy benefits at a human resources consulting firm—the same company where Dave now worked and was held in high regard. As with Quality Tec, his influence helped open doors. Although I had some frustration and despair about giving up my video dreams, I entered the new job with real enthusiasm and gratitude and worked to establish my own reputation in the Training and Instructional Design department.

Then, almost three years after living in my apartment, I returned home to live together with Susie. But it only lasted four months before fizzling. "We still aren't quite ready to nurture each other, and acting married feels dishonest," I told her.

"The days of the Happy Couple Game aren't over?" she replied.

I nodded and moved back into the apartment, but with none of the blaming and drama of my first exit. Our feelings, far more calm than agitated, made for a real change.

As a kind of Christmas present to both Susie and myself six months later, I returned home to stay. We came to realize that in the three and a half years since my moving out, she had managed to surmount many of her own struggles. We both were now stronger and wiser individuals, more capable of making a renewed commitment to love/making love.

"Let's develop a weekly intimate life and invite more friends and family over socially," I suggested.

"Agreed."

I discarded thoughts of her as being an adversary and put to rest divorce as a future option.

Six months later, in July 1998, one of my AA buddies, Ken L., asked me to go out for dinner before our Monday evening meeting. He was enthused "about a new career training opportunity" and, as I listened to this blond-haired baby boomer in his late 30s, his excitement about entering the field of chemical dependency counseling bubbled over.

"Helping other alcoholics and addicts get sober and stay sober will fulfill my professional goals," Ken explained. "And counseling also satisfies the mandate of Step 12, John—'to carry this message to other alcoholics.'"

"Sure sounds to me like it's something you've thought through. And I can see your exuberance and how it will motivate clients." I challenged Ken's thinking on small points, asked philosophical questions, and generally enjoyed exploring his decision with him. Then, as we were leaving, a little voice asked, *Is counseling right for you too?*

Immediately the answer from my spirit resounded *YES!*

A swirl of actions and decisions followed: I decided to disband my video business and enrolled in college courses. I worked part time at a chemical dependency treatment center while attending Addictionology/ Counseling classes and taking exams. I practiced new counseling skills at outpatient and inpatient treatment centers during six months of internships. And I prepared for the Minnesota State Department of Health written and oral exams to get my license—a prerequisite for full-time employment.

These steps to my current position as an addictions counselor stretched me and blessed me in new ways. Any topic I studied applied both professionally and personally, because the learning that enhanced my professional competence with addicted clients also boosted my personal ability to stay recovered from my own addictive habits.

Another bonus? As I worked with addicted clients, it became clear that *their* stories included many kinds of secrets too. It became apparent that secrets comprised a huge part of addictive thinking and behavior, mine and many others'. From this insight the concept emerged of secret-keeping itself and, over time, its many manifestations such as "stealing hours," "acting one way while feeling another," and eventually all eight traits, or splintered mindsets, of a Secret Keeper:

→ Placing appearances first, reality second.
→ Acting one way while feeling another.
→ Stealing hours doing what is required to feel better.
→ Walking a tightrope between two opposing worlds.
→ Living from the outside, in.
→ Getting your way any way possible.
→ Maximizing pleasure and minimizing pain.
→ Treating others last and oneself first.

On a personal level, I discovered more than ever that I was acting one way and feeling the *same* way—double-mindedness was finally dissolving and whole-mindedness was becoming a stronger and firmer reality. Rather than relying on the techniques of deception and protection, I chose disclosure and transparency—"What you see is what you get," as the computer nerds called it—and was beginning to feel good. With less to hide, there *was* less to fear.

And, at last, I was beginning to *feel* the truth of my real name, "Beloved of God."

> **"There is nothing worse than to be something
> on the outside that you aren't on the inside."**
>
> *Gandhi*

∽ *Chapter Twenty*

United and Whole

In the spring of 1999, the New Millennium gained frenzied media attention and Y2K fever spread. On the eve of this momentous shift in eras, Susie and I still faced more speed bumps on our newly united path. With her now as my ally, and with the numerous resources and benefits from my working the Twelve Steps as well as from companions in the recovery community who urged me on, I jumped still more hurdles in my search for a whole mind and more ways to stop stealing hours.

Once again my battle for a whole mind heated up, this time by stealing hours after midnight three or four nights a week sitting at our home computer rewriting my latest movie script. Yes, the Movie Monster had attacked *again!* Compulsive to the core! I could have been sleeping in bed next to Susie or doing Chem Dep Counseling homework or studying for my state license instead, but for the umpteenth time I was trying to resurrect the Oscar-sized dream I'd left behind in Hollywood, the long-shot of hitting the movie jackpot with my celluloid fiction.

The project, an edgy drama titled *Night Secrets,* portrayed a peeping tom in his 30s who falls in love with an attractive woman through her window and, after getting arrested, has to reveal the secrets of his past (clearly about secret-keeping). Truthfully, I felt weary of being hung up on this far-fetched dream, and my obsession to beat the odds of making it come true was making me and others who'd observed previous attempts weary.

So ingrained was my attachment to this lofty goal, so deeply imbedded and compulsive, that I scheduled private sessions with a psychotherapist who specialized in helping persons with addictive personalities. In his office, I took another secret-liberating step and confided about the nagging sense that this breakthrough project would not break through, that it would not bear fruit regardless of how hard I tried. He then listened to the reasons why I suspected my Movie Monster might be a bona fide addiction.

"After so many years," he asked, "why can't you just say no and be done with it?"

"I wish I knew. It's caused me nothing but misery, but I still feel pressured to obey it. I used to think it had to do with ego and fame, but it goes deeper than that, I think."

He and I spent hours in discussions exposing this mental and spiritual stronghold and the roots of my dogged determination to achieve success in the face of decades of rejection: Dad's public career as a media celebrity, my reliance on movies as a teenager for emotional support, my exaggerated responses to Mom's histrionic outbursts, all the ways I had used intensity and going to extremes in everyday life to express myself or get my way, the trance-inducing ritual of writing itself, my thirst for public approval, my "divine calling" to make movies, etc. In short, the longer I was sober and the more I applied recovery principles to this dilemma, the less genuine it appeared and the less power it had to wag me—*if* I chose to let go of it.

I came to understand a concept my therapist used, emotional logic, which is the inner Addict's primary weapon in seizing control from the real Self. Summed up, emotional logic amounts to "I want what I want and I want it now."[1] I saw how emotional logic had tripped me up and held power over me. Emotional logic . . .

> creates an inward focus and isolation and is sustained by the mood change produced by acting out the addictive process. On a thinking, intellectual level, the Addict knows that intimacy with an object or activity cannot bring emotional fulfillment. Intimacy, positive or negative, is an emotional experience. . . . Addiction is an emotional relationship with an object or event, through which addicts try to meet their need for intimacy. When compulsive eaters feel sad, they eat to feel better. When alcoholics start to feel out of control with anger, they have a couple of drinks to get back in control.[2]

As my awareness of emotional logic's wiles increased week by week, and whenever I practiced new methods of thinking, its power lessened. As

I'd done with drinking and codependency, I admitted my powerlessness over the Movie Monster (Step 1) and my exaggerated need for approval as a character defect (Step 6). I humbly asked God to remove this need (Step 7) and planned to make amends to the persons I'd harmed—most notably Susie—because of it (Step 8). I also continued to monitor whether the Monster returned (Step 10) and prayed for the knowledge of God's will and the power to carry out His plan rather than my own (Step 11).

Besides my therapist, I discussed these dynamics with my AA sponsor Jeff H., my single friend from church, my insurance agent friend, my brother Dave, and Susie. A consensus formed: Whether the Movie Monster was an addiction or not (let's not be too quick to label everything as addictive), it certainly had some kind of stranglehold on me. I saw eye to eye with my advisors and decided on a do-or-die solution. I vowed to rewrite *Night Secrets* one last time and to submit it to a public play reading:

(A) If the audience cheered and others' energy started moving it forward, then the dream stood a chance of being genuine and I would continue on.

(B) If they booed or didn't cheer or others' energy did not develop, then the dream had to be false and I would abstain for good from all screenwriting—exactly the same as I'd done with alcohol, marijuana, tobacco, gambling, womanizing, and erotic magazines and books.

Meanwhile, my balancing act continued: commuting 60 miles north to Hazelden Treatment Center in the countryside where I interned full-time daily; renting a room at a nearby farmhouse five nights a week to be close to the treatment center; studying for my state written and oral licensing exams; spending weekends at home with Susie and rediscovering ourselves as lovers; and attending church and journaling regularly, all while investing the final hundred or more midnight hours rewriting *Night Secrets* with the editorial help of a paid freelance editor. At Hazelden, I also filled out employment forms for a counseling position, got a pre-employment physical, and waited to hear about job openings.

As I continued working with clients, more insights about secret-keeping informed my practice, and the following continuum gradually came into being. I used it to help answer the numerous questions people asked about secret-keeping (see box on page 244).

Over the next several weeks, a composite profile of Secret Keepers

"Continuum of Secrets"

1	2	3	4
Simple Secrets	*Silent Secrets*	*Secret Keeping*	*Criminal Behavior*
everybody has	dark & nasty but passive	acting out ethical and moral wrongs but not illegal	arrestable offenses

1. *Simple* secrets are those that emerge from isolated, rare events, the kind of harmless mistakes or lapses in judgment that seldom require self-disclosure or therapy—often memories from childhood or adolescence. A young student peeks at her classmate's test answers or an underage driver takes his dad's car out for a joy ride. Indirectly secrets like these open the individual to dualistic thinking that can sneak in and take hold.

2. *Silent* secrets are those that become ingrained thoughts or attitudes, which can risk one's mental health. They remain in one's thought life. Three college fraternity brothers get drunk and go boating together. One falls overboard and the other two jump in to save him. The two drown but the first survives. He feels intense guilt and conceals any hint about their drinking at the young men's funerals, and years later he feels exhausted, dirty inside, and burdened by having caused his pals' deaths and deceiving their families. One act (getting drunk) leads to another (falling overboard while boating) that compounds into a tragedy (two drownings) that leads to a cover-up (concealing truth from the victims' parents) that leads to years of torment from silently keeping the truth secret.

3. *Secret-keeping* goes one step further and includes acting out, more specifically the habits or rituals that can lead to risking one's safety, health, or sanity and that of others; the kind of harmful patterns that make us sick and that benefit from disclosure and often therapy. Secrets in this category include behavior patterns and rituals that lead to stealing hours away from one's "normal life" to feel better. These hidden acts stretch, and eventually break, *ethical/moral standards* and *relational boundaries,* but do not cross the line into crime (breaking the law). The head pastor of a cutting-edge evangelical church engages in an ongoing extramarital affair, which breaks ethical, moral, and biblical rules, but he is not hauled off in handcuffs when caught, nor does he face court charges or serve time in jail.

4. *Criminal behavior.* Secrets in this category may include a mixture of secrets from the previous categories, but acting out violates *legal boundaries/standards* thereby making them crimes punishable by law. Sara Jane Olson fits this description. After evading arrest for attempted murder in California as a fiery member of the rebellious Symbionese Liberation Army, she lived 24 years inconspicuously as a suburban mother and housewife in St. Paul, Minnesota, until being discovered and sent to prison.

emerged. Secret Keepers live in a parallel universe based on the intentional concealment of what is shameful or discreditable beyond the limits of privacy. By their very cleverness, they elude getting caught–thus only seldom appearing in tomorrow's headlines. The people closest to them may suspect their excuses or alibis at times and think to themselves *how odd or eccentric* they are, or *they seem lost in a private world of their own.* But hard evidence almost never surfaces and telltale clues, if there are any, go unnoticed.

Secret Keepers, even when they function smoothly in their public lives, carry with them the concealed secrets about themselves that nobody knows about–not wife, not parents, not siblings, not friends, not the boss. And so they live a double life continuously, whether stealing hours to act out or not. Secret Keepers are generally too smart and too clever to overstep legal boundaries (with rare exceptions). They may skirt the law, but hardly ever get arrested or labeled as criminals. They may be alcoholics or drug addicts, but not the obvious ones who abuse openly and deceive no one. Men and women, young and old, individuals of every race and nationality, they are human beings with two opposing selves existing in one body.

Projecting a wholesome self for all to see and approve of, Secret Keepers carefully hide their secret selves for none to discover and denounce. Meanwhile, the competing selves within them wage war and, over time, wear down the person until a crisis (still another secret unknown to everybody) threatens their sanity. Unavoidably, their inner warfare then leads to a buildup of pressure to disclose intimate knowledge to somebody, wreaking daily suffering until they surrender or "do something."

In time it became clear that a solid third of my clients led a sophisticated double life such as visiting multiple liquor stores to avoid being perceived as a heavy drinker, hiding bottles in closets or behind storage shelves, carrying flasks of liquor or marijuana rolled into emptied cigarette casings to work, taking frequent "bathroom breaks" and long lunch hours, and myriad similar behaviors to conceal their addictions.

The remaining two-thirds of clients made little or no attempt to conceal their use/abuse. They started bar fights, argued with their spouses until neighbors called the police, crashed their vehicles or were arrested for DWIs, were fired from their jobs for calling in sick too many times, and otherwise made their addictions so obvious to everybody that no secrets could form or be sustained.

The main point is that at least one out of ten Americans[3] qualifies for treatment for their substance abuse or dependency (29,000,000 people per 2000 Census) and, based on my research of treatment clients, 35 percent of those are Secret Keepers (10,150,000 people). Now add the number of similar persons in other countries and you get a sense of the immensity of secret-keeping's damage in human lives.

Moreover, I found that secret-keeping plagued others besides alcohol abusers and drug addicts. Secrets were also a key factor for:

- *Bulimics,* who secretly vomit up food, but live an otherwise normal-appearing life; like a married mother of three children who has never confided her secret purging behavior to her husband of 18 years.
- *Compulsive gamblers,* who chase the high from "the action," but eventually bankrupt their life savings/retirement funds; like an elected legislator who slips away to casinos during work hours wearing clever disguises and piles up debts until news reporters reveal his destructive secret life.
- *Compulsive shoppers,* who buy items that they never open or use with money they can't afford; like a widow who hides the purchases of 160 pairs of shoes in her bedroom until the boxes pile up and fill the room, forcing her to sleep on the living room sofa.
- *Obsessive/compulsives,* who arrive late to work or important meetings because they can't manage to leave the house until checking everything numerous times; like a high-ranking community leader who has to make sure the stove and faucets are turned off dozens of times before feeling ready to leave the house.

My studies of psychological and behavioral authorities yielded a rich tapestry of useful theories and insightful practices. Cumulatively, the ideas of these pioneers and researchers provided wonderful tools to help unlock the secrets I was keeping and those of my clients. As time marched on, I also recorded the revelations about celebrities' ways of keeping secrets, including some of the world's movers and shakers:

- President Bill Clinton's cover-up about his sexual escapades with Monica Lewinsky resulted in a national scandal when Americans learned of the sordid details and numerous secrets he'd kept concealed.
- CBS journalist Charles Kuralt's 28-year secret affair with a mis-

tress became public knowledge when she arrived at his funeral and his wife discovered the "other woman" wanted her share of his estate.

- Robert Hanssen, the nice guy next door who worked for the FBI and sold countless secrets over the years to the Soviet KGB, and made headlines for his world-class secret-keeping tricks when arrested and held in custody for high treason.
- Media luminaries like Princess Diana, Michael Jackson, Rush Limbaugh, and Martha Stewart as well as professional sports figures like Kirby Puckett, Kobe Bryant, and Pete Rose all hid secret activities that made news and stirred the public's appetite for sensationalism.

No matter where I looked, Secret Keepers' deeds popped up everywhere. On the front page of the paper or evening news or radio talk shows, the secrets of millions showed up.

Elevated by the very nature of their lofty positions in society, celebrities demonstrated that no one, regardless of how high and mighty, was immune from the lowest and sleaziest acts of deception and concealment. In the New Millennium, the world would soon learn about the CEOs of Enron, WorldCom, Tyco, and Adelphia who allegedly hid multimillion dollars of falsified stock records and cheated thousands of employees out of their hard-earned retirement savings. It became clear that secret-keeping occured on institutional levels, in business and government and the military, as well as on individual levels.

⁂

The evening of the screenplay reading finally arrived in mid-December, 1999. Eight volunteer members of a Twin Cities dramatists' group gave *Night Secrets* a fair reading and nobody liked it. Nobody. The round of feedback jangled in my ears, categorically downbeat and glum. A sudden peace—a serenity, a letting go—came over me, and I felt no urge to argue, defend, persuade, or justify. My attachment to the stronghold of my Hollywood dream of winning an Oscar shattered. I thanked everybody and left quietly.

My Movie Monster stayed in the room and didn't chase after me.

The next day my boss at Hazelden called me into his office. "We have a floating counselor position," he said. "You're hired." He shook my hand, "Welcome aboard, John."

Grateful and humbled, I started earning my first full-time paycheck in my new field and two days later sat among 240 applicants at the Minnesota Department of Health taking the written exam for my license to practice as an LADC, Licensed Alcohol and Drug Counselor. When I left the testing room, I felt reasonably certain that I'd passed it. The sun was shining and I stopped at a gourmet coffee shop for a hot cup of Sumatra, my favorite brew.

When I got home, Susie asked, "How did you do?"

It would be three weeks before I could answer affirmatively, and in that time the year 2000 with all its hoopla and hype had arrived. As I opened the envelope from the State Department of Health containing the exam results, I looked back on my nearly 40 years of hard-fought victory for a whole mind. My score exceeded the cutoff of 100 by 26 points.

My answer to Susie was, "Passed with flying colors!"

MetaViews to Muse #9

These reflections on what you've read in the past few chapters are meant to encourage you to consider your own life's challenges and choices.

✳ Strangers in self-help groups can make a difference. They've gone through the same things you have, even though you've never known them, and prove that you are not alone or unique. Essential to a Secret Keeper's path to whole-mindedness is the fellowship—the direct connection with individuals just like themselves—who meet together regularly.

Are you meeting with supportive friends and allies regularly, people with whom you can be transparent? What nuggets of wisdom have you gained from their experience? Evaluate how that wisdom might apply to you.

✳ Motivation from external pressures and consequences may get us started on the path to wholeness, but internal motivation keeps us there. Sustained internal motivation comes once we summon the courage to change the things in ourselves, not others. It can be as simple (and difficult) as accepting what *is* rather than demanding what *could* or *should be,* like the time I chose to undergo another career transition from video producing to counseling.

What is your level of internal motivation? Are you open to changing things in yourself?

✳ For Secret Keepers who change their ways, the AA Promise proves true: "God is doing for us what we could not do for ourselves." A journal can be a huge help in recording these moments on your journey. It benefits you by providing tangible reminders of the stages of growth on your healing journey. Think of it more as a simple notebook that you jot things into rather than a formal hardbound diary you must lock up—the simpler, the easier. Just do it!

✳ The antidote to secret-keeping is *secret-liberating* behaviors: *surrender, acceptance, disclosure, accountability*—the tools of a whole mind. Past success in mastering secret-keeping provides a track record of success to help prevent new episodes of secret-keeping. With less to hide, there's less to fear. In my case, the first steps toward transparency came when I disclosed secrets to fellow Emotions Anonymous members. Depending on God's love also gave me a strong sense of security, allowing me to become openly confident and less isolated or sly.

Are you gaining freedom and control from adopting secret-liberating attitudes and actions?

✱ Various addictions and compulsive behaviors easily fall prey to secret-keeping: pathological gambling, eating disorders (bulimia), overspending, Internet sex, video games, obsessive/compulsive disorders such as "counting" and "checking," and so on. Also, celebrities are no less susceptible to secret-keeping and famous cases abound.

With your increased awareness of secret-keeping, are you more keenly aware of observing its signs and symptoms in everyday situations?

✱ If you are a Secret Keeper, as you battle secret-keeping, treat yourself well along the way. Find little ways to reward yourself. Become your own best companion, enjoy solitude rather than stealing hours, deal with unmet expectations, combat emotional logic, practice letting go, and detach from unhealthy entanglements. Don't just *stop* a compulsion or addiction, *start* your recovery.

In what ways can you treat yourself well as you go through your journey? Depending on God for guidance, wisdom, and power works . . . *if* you let it. If you haven't accepted the reality of the divine in your life yet, do so now and let God's presence strengthen and embrace you.

> **"The more I am able to be myself,**
> **the more it enables other people to be themselves."**
>
> *Oprah Winfrey*

∽ *Epilogue*

Liberation

In my career as an addictions counselor and educator, I've finally found my calling. I love going to my office at the treatment center and seeing the transformation occurring "one day at a time" in so many persons' lives. I enjoy being a part of unraveling their secrets and watching them apply the insights gained from secret-liberating principles.

My recovery serves their recovery.

Recovery, I've discovered, is a process unto itself, one that transforms an individual's being—physically, mentally, emotionally, and spiritually. It starts with *physical* detoxification and the abstaining person's return to natural body/brain chemistry ("repent and live!"[1]), moves to the individual's *mental* changes from distorted beliefs to healthier self-talk that makes sobriety easier ("be transformed by the renewing of your mind"[2]), then moves to his/her *emotional* changes from intensely negative feelings to more balanced and positive feelings ("Weeping may remain for a night, but rejoicing comes in the morning"[3]), then on to his/her *spiritual* connection with God, or a Higher Power, and the sense of reconnecting with others and nature ("I am with you always"[4]). Living life on life's terms becomes the creed, the pathway, to health in all four dimensions.

Of course, one of our secrets is that we *love* other people's secrets, sometimes the sicker the better. But we are terrified when *our* tiniest secrets might be made known. For many of us, our deepest fear is to be exposed, to be found out, to be discovered. We hide behind the clever masks we've invented. The pain of being "uncovered" keeps many of us from getting help. We keep secrets that make us sick until we either permit the suffering to disable and cripple us, or we admit our need to get help and undergo the painful, but health-restoring, functions that redirect our energies to heal and stay healed.

The choice is always ours. We can make it any minute, hour, or day.

Four of the essential principles of recovery are *Surrender, Acceptance, Disclosure,* and *Accountability:* surrender to abstinence, acceptance of help, disclosure of secrets, and accountability to others. These mirror the first five steps of the Twelve Steps. The latter, disclosure of secrets, is powerful because it reflects the ancient wisdom of confession, as when King David confessed his adultery with Bathsheba and pleaded for his "contrite heart" to be "washed whiter than snow."[5] Most clients fear that they will be met with judgment and condemnation, but the very opposite may happen: mercy and reconciliation (as King David experienced). These help free them from the shame and guilt of their past behavior and harmful deeds to themselves and others.

Herman was one of my clients who sought treatment for his alcoholism, but never disclosed his use of cocaine. When I learned from his probation officer of his positive urinanalysis for cocaine, I raised the issue of dishonesty and Herman broke down in tears—grateful tears. He admitted that having kept this secret felt far worse than it now felt having it be known, and he pledged to fight his addiction to cocaine and stay abstinent. I emphasized his additional need to pledge "rigorous honesty," as the Big Book urges, and he did so with such passion that his nickname became known to co-members in the group as "Honest Herman."

Another of my clients, Kurt, reluctantly attended treatment for his abusive drinking, but nothing much happened until he came clean during a private meeting about the 200 porn videos he'd hidden in the ceiling tiles of his basement. Like Herman, Kurt's addictions were multiple and, until each was admitted to and met the bright light of day, his full healing and release from bondage could not be complete.

Like Herman and Kurt, dozens of other clients' inner selves have responded appropriately to each new moment in life as they disclosed/confessed/came clean, finally living in the healthy present versus the hurtful past or repetitive addictive future. They began to realize the benefits of whole-mindedness and making clear-headed choices and became willing to live honestly.

This chart shows the transition from secret-keeping to secret-liberating mentalities that many have started to embrace. It serves as a self-checking device that helps uncover the self-defeating beliefs and behaviors each of us may be battling at any given moment.

Secret-Keeping Mindset	Secret-Liberating Remedy
Placing appearances first, reality second	Abandon the notion of manipulating others' impressions and let your newly claimed whole self shine through. RESULT: *Reality comes first, appearances become known for what they really are . . . masks.*
Acting one way while feeling another	Surrender to awareness of this double standard, have courage to remove your mask, and own each feeling. RESULT: *I can act the same way I feel.*
Stealing hours doing what is required to feel better	Accept that hiding or retreating from life's challenges or problems (isolating) is self-defeating and personality-splitting. RESULT: *Honestly engaging with others is safe and satisfying and counteracts insecurity.*
Walking a tightrope between two worlds	Admit that double-mindedness leads to loss of identity, guilt/shame, and exhaustion. RESULT: *Disclosing secrets and renouncing hidden behaviors begins a life of recovery and ultimate fulfillment.*
Living from the outside, in	Realize that things outside can't fix what's wrong inside and that trying to do so rots your center core and ends in desperation and depression. RESULT: *Living from the inside out is authentic and feels better.*
Getting your way any way possible	Accept limits and "what is;" lower expectations and admit desires cannot always be satisfied. RESULT: *Self-pity transforms to serenity.*
Maximizing pleasure and minimizing pain	Admit that life involves pain and at times suffering, but misery is optional. RESULT: *Opening up to spiritual values maximizes lasting pleasure and minimizes lasting pain.*
Treating others last and oneself first	Recognize ways one's lower nature feeds on external applause compared to one's higher nature that grows quietly via inner healthy choices. RESULT: *Others regain their rightful place in your life and self-seeking slips away.*

To some extent we are all battling self-defeating behaviors. Some of us will find ways to free ourselves from these inappropriate, crippling thoughts and fear-based behavior patterns; some of us won't. Fortunately, when we depend on the Holy Spirit ("perfect love casts out fear"[6]), when we perceive our existence as "Beloved of God" instead of "condemned in Adam,"[7] and when we seek help from intelligent professionals who care for our best interests, then numerous effective therapies become available and prove useful.

Refer to the authorities cited in the Reading List. Their ideas have provided me, and can provide anyone, wonderful tools to unlocking the secrets we keep.

Thankfully, I've found that nothing is truly wasted if we are open to doing good with what has happened to us. For example, my work as a recovery counselor incorporates, and demands, the diverse experiences that my past struggles helped develop: self-examination, disclosing, making amends, teaching, writing, speaking, managing, facilitating, and listening. Listening lets the secrets whisper their way out of our psyches.

The truth is: we want to tell the secrets, because we want to be whole.

My hope for each reader of *Stolen Hours: Breaking Free From Secret Addictions* is that you liberate your secrets and find the exciting adventure of living in the present, free of shame and guilt, with a whole mind to guide and comfort you.

John Howard Prin, BA, LADC
Licensed Alcohol & Drug Counselor

**"I believe that mortals weave in their own lives
the garment they must wear in the life to come."**
Abraham Lincoln

Endnotes

Chapter Six

1. *Kansas City,* Wilbert Harrison songwriter and vocalist, 1959, Fury label.

Chapter Ten

1. Ecclesiastes 8:6 NIV

Chapter Eleven

1. Psalm 34:18 RSV
2. Psalm 40:2-3 TLB
3. Ecclesiastes 2:17, 23 NRSV
4. Hebrews 12:15 RSV
5. Romans 8:28 NRSV
6. Psalm 37:4 NIV
7. Psalm 37:5 NRSV
8. Psalm 37:8 NRSV

Chapter Twelve

1. Proverbs 7:10 NRSV
2. Proverbs 7:13, 18, 21 NRSV
3. Proverbs 7:22 NRSV
4. Proverbs 7:25-27 NRSV
5. John 6:35 RSV
6. 1 Corinthians 10:13 TLB
7. Colossians 3:13 NRSV
8. Romans 14:23 TLB
9. Romans 8:6, 13 NRSV
10. *Breaking Through, Selling Out, Dropping Dead and Other Notes on Filmmaking,* William Mayer, Limelight Editions, ISBN 0879101237. Used by permission.
11. 2 Corinthians 5:17 RSV

Chapter Fourteen

1. Jeremiah 29:11 TLB
2. Hebrews 12:15 TLB
3. Psalm 23:2-3 RSV
4. Matthew 21:22 ISV

Chapter Fifteen

1. Ephesians 6:10-11 RSV
2. Mark 7:20-21 NRSV
3. Matthew 23:26 NRSV
4. 1 Corinthians 6:12, 19-20 NIV
5. Romans 8:6-8 NIV
6. Proverbs 23:29-32, 34 TLB
7. Romans 7:19, 21-24 TLB

Chapter Sixteen

1. Confederate Soldier's poem, author unknown.

Chapter Seventeen

1. 1 Peter 2:20 NIV
2. 1 Peter 4:13 NIV

Chapter Eighteen

1. 1 John 4:18 RSV
2. 2 Corinthians 4:18 NIV
3. 2 Corinthians 4:8-9 NIV
4. Romans 8:35, 37 NIV
5. Nehemiah 8:10 NIV

Chapter Nineteen

1. See Philippians 4:7.
2. See Psalm 23:5.
3. 1 Corinthians 6:12 NIV
4. See 1 Corinthians 10:13.
5. Romans 12:2 NIV
6. Hebrews 12:1 NIV
7. 1 Timothy 2:4 NIV
8. 2 Peter 3:9 NIV
9. Revelation 22:4 NIV

Chapter Twenty

1. *The Addictive Personality,* Craig Nakken, Hazelden Foundation, © 1988 & 1996, page 9. Used by permission.
2. Ibid, page 8, 32.
3. SAMSHA—Substance Abuse & Mental Health Services Administration, Washington DC.

Epilogue

1. Ezekiel 18:32 NIV
2. Romans 12:2 NIV
3. Psalm 30:5 NIV
4. Matthew 28:20 NIV
5. Psalm 51:17, 7 NIV
6. 1 John 4:18 RSV
7. See 1 Corinthians 15:22.

References

Reading List

Addictive Personality, The, Craig Nakken, 1988, Hazelden, ISBN 1568381298
The explanations in this informative volume will help shed understanding on the mysteries of the Self and the Addict in a split psyche.

Awareness, Anthony deMello, 1990, Doubleday, ISBN 0385249373
Warnings and encouragement from a Jesuit priest about people-pleasing and approval-seeking. The only approval you need is your own and God's.

Codependent No More, Melody Beattie, 1987, Hazelden, ISBN 0062554468
Beattie's ideas and suggestions helped save my sanity at a time when anger and depression were making me ill. Valuable for anybody living with a Secret Keeper.

Dr. Jekyll and Mr. Hyde, Robert Louis Stevenson, 1886 (first published), 1994, Bantam, ISBN 055321277X
A fictional portrayal of the duality of opposing selves in a human being. Loaded with literary insights into the split psyche that science later named and described.

Emotional Intelligence, Daniel Goleman, 1997, Bantam, ISBN 0-553-37506-7
We have two minds, says the author, one that thinks and one that feels. Moods are molded by cultural influences and this book shows how the individual can tap into the power of positive thinking by choosing actions that generate harmonious feelings.

Getting the Love You Want, Harville Hendrix, 1988, Pocket Books, ISBN 0805068953
The author offers therapy tips on how to overcome the hurtful wounds in our relationships and ways to restore the "joyful aliveness with which we came into the world." Excellent for couples.

Healing the Shame That Binds You, John Bradshaw, 1988,
Health Communications, ISBN 0932194869
The author exposes the massive destructive power of the "core demon" and how it can rule a person's identity, forcing individuals to abandon the functions of the authentic self and to cover up the false self.

Hero's Journey, The, Joseph Campbell (editor, Phil Cousineau), 1990, Harper & Row, ISBN 006250102X
Both a portrait of this scholar's life and a review of his studies of The Hero in various cultures and eras. Campbell's insights opened my eyes to the process and risks anyone undergoes who ventures into the unknown seeking answers to life's mysteries.

If Life Is a Game, These Are the Rules, Cherie Carter-Scott, 1998, Broadway Books, ISBN 0767902386
Based on the premise that there are no mistakes in life, only lessons that are repeated. The author deciphers the wisdom of ten such lessons and how we can apply what we learn to improve our lives.

Iron John, Robert Bly, 1990, Addison Wesley, ISBN 0201517205
A fanciful, often poignant view of the human condition that explores the dark and light sides of personality. Bly debunks the societal admonition that we should acknowledge only the light side and encourages more inclusion of the dark side—our denied selves.

It's Not As Bad As You Think, A. Jack Hafner, 1981, Hazelden, ISBN 0894861166
A dandy booklet that examines why people become upset. It's as simple as what we tell ourselves. The tips contained in this easy-to-read primer explain the ABCs of adjusting your self-talk.

Key, The, Cheri Huber, 1984, Zen Center, ISBN 0961475404
How we see things matters more than what we see. A Zen approach to helping us find ways to comprehend how our minds work (the internals) rather than the ways we can manipulate people, money, jobs, opinions, etc. (the externals).

Mere Christianity, C. S. Lewis, 1980, Harper, ISBN 0060652926
Lewis examines systematically the reasons for God's existence without candy-coating the difficulties and dangers of adhering to the creed followed by faithful believers.

Meeting the Shadow, Jeremiah Zweig & Connie Abrams editors, 1991, Tarcher, ISBN 087477618X
A rich assortment of writings about the dark side, or Shadow, in human beings. Examines the many possibilities of how our dark sides can both harm and heal.

People of the Lie, M. Scott Peck, 1983, Touchstone (S&S), ISBN 0684848597
These case studies describe the kind of mind-boggling behaviors one encounters in Secret Keepers. It offers hope by diagnosing the bizarre mixture of motivations that can prompt such mental dysfunctions.

Power of Myth, The, video interviews of Joseph Campbell by Bill Moyers, 1988, Apostrophe S Productions, ISBN 1561764620
These taped video sessions convey the dynamic enthusiasm Professor Campbell so passionately felt all his life for mankind's search for meaning. A great introduction to the inspiring, frequently humorous insights of a cultural genius.

Opening Up, James W. Pennebaker, 1990, Guilford, ISBN 1572302380
The experiments in this user-friendly volume demonstrate the powerful benefits of writing about one's feelings and how doing so improves a person's inner temperament and positive outlook on life.

Real Power, Janet Hagberg, 1984, Winston Press, ISBN 0866838236
Hagberg defines power in numerous ways including outer (action) and inner (reflection). A major boost to my early exploration of personal change.

Road Less Traveled, The, M. Scott Peck, 1978, Touchstone (S&S), ISBN 0671250672
A gem of a book that states flatly "life is difficult" and informs the reader of ways we can take control of our own destinies and live happier lives.

Self-Defeating Behaviors, Robert Hardy and Milton Cudney, 1991, Harper, ISBN 0062501976
Full of useful ideas and practical exercises, this book gives insightful examples of how we can master the conflicting urges and behaviors that often defeat our goals and spoil our intentions. Loaded with helpful examples.

Serenity Principle, The, Joseph Bailey, 1990, Harper SF, ISBN 0062500392
Serenity is the antidote for addiction, states Bailey. The opposite is insecurity. In a healthy state all our emotions, thoughts, and behaviors act in unison. This book describes ways to deal with insecurity and how to strive toward a spiritual awakening and changed level of consciousness.

Shame, Gershen Kaufman, 1980, Schenkman Books, ISBN 087047006X
A definitive work that describes the inner torment of shame and how it acts as a source of splitting and self-hatred, "dividing us both from ourselves and from one another." Very helpful for increasing one's awareness of why we act the ways we do.

Taking Charge, Richard Leider and James Harding, 1985, Leider/Harding Enterprises, ISBN 096075041X
A daily self-management program that counteracts "inner kill" (dying without being fully alive) by focusing on growth that involves risk-taking. Challenges you to either accept things as they are or take responsibility for changing them.

To order additional copies of *Stolen Hours:*

Web: www.amazon.com (after April 1, 2004)

Phone: 1-800-901-3480

Fax: Copy and fill out the form below with credit card information. Fax to 651-603-9263.

Mail: Copy and fill out the form below. Mail with check or credit card information to:

Syren Book Company
C/O BookMobile
2402 University Avenue West
Saint Paul, Minnesota 55114

Order Form

Copies	Title / Author	Price	Totals	
	***Stolen Hours* / Prin**	$15.95	$	
		Subtotal	$	
		7% sales tax (MN only)	$	
		Shipping and handling, first copy	$	4.00
	Shipping and handling, ___ add'l copies @$1.00 ea.		$	
		TOTAL TO REMIT	$	

Payment Information:

__ Check Enclosed __ Visa/Mastercard		
Card number: Expiration date:		
Name on card:		
Billing address:		
City:	State:	Zip:
Signature : Date:		

Shipping Information:

__ Same as billing address __ Other (enter below)		
Name:		
Address:		
City:	State:	Zip:

Look for John Prin's next book on secrets

Living Secret Lives

Coming in 2005

www.johnprin.com